Parenting Skills and Collaborative Services for Students with Disabilities

George R. Taylor

ScarecrowEducation
Lanham, Maryland • Toronto • Oxford
2004

Published in the United States of America
by ScarecrowEducation
An imprint of The Rowman & Littlefield Publishing Group, Inc.
4501 Forbes Boulevard, Suite 200, Lanham, Maryland 20706
www.scarecroweducation.com

PO Box 317
Oxford
OX2 9RU, UK

British Library Cataloguing in Publication Information Available

Library of Congress Cataloging-in-Publication Data

Taylor, George R.
  Parenting skills and collaborative services for students with disabilities / George R.
Taylor.
    p. cm.
  Includes bibliographical references and index.
  ISBN 1-57886-169-1 (pbk. : alk. paper)
  1. Children with disabilities—Education. 2. Education—Parent participation. 3.
Home and school. I. Title.
LC4019.T35 2004
371.9'04—dc22

                            2004009998

∞™ The paper used in this publication meets the minimum requirements of
American National Standard for Information Sciences—Permanence of
Paper for Printed Library Materials, ANSI/NISO Z39.48-1992.
Manufactured in the United States of America.

Contents

Appendices

List of Tables

Preface

Considerable attention has been given to parental involvement in education during the last several decades. Factors responsible for the increase include federal and state legislation, national parental groups, and organizations. The movement has empowered parents and has given them a legal and moral right to be involved as partners in collaboration with the schools and community agencies in the education of their children.

It is generally recognized how parental reactions to their children with disabilities may be crucial to their adjustment as well as to the nature and type of interventions and adjustments needed by their children to successfully adjust in school and cope in adult life. In many instances, both parents and children may need psychological intervention. Some suggested strategies have been outlined in this text.

The text provides a collaborative model which parents, teachers, and community agencies may employ to meet the needs of children with disabilities. Specific activities and intervention strategies provide an approach for parents and teachers to jointly develop programs. Each will have equal responsibilities and rights in the process.

The first chapter discusses the impact of children with disabilities on parenting and provides an overview of parental involvement in the schools. The impact of societal conditions and federal state legislation upon parental involvement is fully explored. Chapter 2 discusses the need for parenting skills and some recommended strategies to employ to aid in the adjustment of children with disabilities. The importance of parental reactions to their children with disabilities and their perceptions toward the disability are explored in chapter 3. Chapter 4 discusses the need for counseling parents of children with disabilities. Specific strategies and techniques are summarized. The importance of federal legislation on parental involvement is stressed in chapter 5. Major aspects of the law mandating parental involvement are highlighted. Chapter 6 is devoted to techniques for improving parental involvement in the total school program. Recommendations for working with families from diverse cultures and strategies for promoting diversity are summarized in chapter 7. Innovative ways of jointly sharing information and ensuring confidentiality of information are pinpointed in chapter 8. Ways of reporting information to parents are discussed in chapter 9. Chapter 10 is devoted to discussing parents as resources in the school. Strategies are discussed for promoting parental involvement. Parental perceptions on inclusion are reported in chapter 11. Recent research findings are summarized to reflect parental perceptions. Chapter 12 discusses school and community interactions. Chapter 13 discusses conclusions and recommendations.

This text was written to provide information to parents and educators that may be applied to minimize the affects of parents having children with disabilities on family members, as well as to provide strategies for educators to employ in educating children with disabilities. The major thrust was to indicate how parents, teachers, and community agencies could collaborate to provide appropriate services and strategies for children with disabilities.

Many of the materials used in this text are a direct result of in-service presentations, consultancies with public schools and private agencies, teaching in-service teachers, and research projects dealing with collaborative projects involving parents of children with disabilities.

Acknowledgments

Compiling this text was not an individual effort. It would have been impossible to complete this awesome task without the assistance of others.

A special thanks is given to my graduate students at Coppin State College for their suggestions, feedback, and encouragement during the process of compiling the information needed for developing this text. To the staff at Rosemont Elementary School for their invaluable input concerning strategies they employed when working with parents of children with disabilities. To Dr. Geraldine Waters for making suggestions and proofing the final manuscript. A special thanks is extended to Mrs. Emma "Sisie" Crosby for her sincere commitment and dedication in typing the final manuscript.

CHAPTER 1

A Systems Perspective of Human Development

The family systems perspective of human development related to disabled children does not consider a disabled child as the client, rather the family unit is seen and treated as the client (Fine and Carson, 1992). From a systems perspective of human development, the way an individual acts is a product of the interactions that occur between a person and his or her environment. This section examines recent developments in family system theory related to the interactions within families and the interactions between families and professionals.

As early as 1974, Minuchin summed up and characterized the importance of family systems. He wrote:

> The individual influences his context and is influenced by it in constantly recurring sequences of interaction. The individual who lives within a family is a member of a social system to which he must adapt. His actions are governed by the characteristics of system and these characteristics include the effects of his own past actions. The individual responds to stresses in other parts of the system to which he adapts; and may contribute significantly to stressing other members of the system. The individual can be approached as a subsystem, or part of the system, but the whole must be taken into account. (p. 9)

Minuchin's view of family systems theory provides a framework for understanding what a family is and how it functions. It also provides professionals with a model of how to collaborate with families and how to assist them in understanding and coping with problems presented by having disabled children within the family structure.

Seligman (2000) discussed the value of professionals understanding and recognizing the family dynamics when working with parents of children with disabilities. McGoldrick and Giordano (1996) supported this premise by agreeing that professionals need to understand unique family characteristics to aid families as well as appreciate the richness of family life. Turnbull and Turnbull (1996) described three assumptions that are central to family systems theory. They are: (1) the input/output configuration of the system; (2) the concept of wholeness and subsystems; and (3) the role of boundaries in defining systems (Whitechurch and Constantine as cited in Turnbull and Turnbull, 1996). The first assumption explains how the inputs (family characteristics) interact with the system to produce outputs (family function). For example, when a child with disabilities is born (family characteristics), this places a new set of stresses on the family and may change how family members interact with each other and with individuals outside of the family (family function). The second assumption is that the system must be understood as a whole and cannot be understood by examining only its component parts (Whitechurch and Constantine as cited in Turnbull and Turnbull, 1996). For example, it follows from this assumption that it is necessary to understand the family and understand the child. Finally, the third assumption is that family subsystems are separated by boundaries that are created by the interaction of family members within the family unit and with outside influences. For example, the boundaries set with professionals are likely to be different from the ones set with family members.

Much of the knowledge about the changes in the relationships between parents and professionals that have occurred during the past two decades can be attributed to the work done by Bronfenbrenner (1979). He stressed that parenting behavior is influenced by environmental factors that are both internal and external to the family. These parenting behaviors then influence the child's behavior. For example, Bronfenbrenner (1979), as cited in Dunst, Trivette, Hamby, and Pollock, 1990, stated that

> whether parents can perform effectively in their child-rearing roles within the family depends on role demands, stresses, and supports emanating from other settings. Parents' evaluations of their own capacity to

function, as well as their view of their child, are related to such external factors as flexibility of job schedules, adequacy of child care arrangements, the presence of friends and neighbors who can help out in large and small emergencies, the quality of health and social services, and neighborhood safety.

This quotation emphasizes the role that outside influences can have on families. (p. 117) Recognizing that role has been a critical factor affecting many of the changes that have occurred in the parent-professional relationship. It is important for anyone working with families to have an understanding of family systems theory because it provides a framework for understanding families in an individualized and personalized way. Professionals who possess such an understanding are more likely to be attuned to the families and their strengths, expectations, priorities, and needs. Such an understanding in turn leads to a more effective and collaborative relationship with families—and families are most able to promote students' positive educational results (Turnbull and Turnbull, 1996).

Research findings have clearly indicated that collaborative planning and partnerships between parents and professionals can solve early dispute problems and significantly reduce or eliminate costly legal court battles, mediations, and due process hearings. According to Blue-Banning, Summers, Franklin, Nelson, and Beegle (2004), the development of collaborative partnerships between parents and professionals is frequently not successful due to factors associated with interpersonal relationships and the gap between recommended practices for collaborative partnerships and the implementations of those practices, in spite of federal and state mandates to develop collaborative partnerships (Osher and Osher, 2002; Turnbull and Turnbull, 2001). (Refer to chapter 5 for specific details concerning federal legislation.)

The importance of establishing interpersonal relationships has been voiced by McWilliam, Tocci, and Harbin (1998); Park and Turnbull (2003); Summers et al. (2001); and Paretee, Brotherson, and Huer (2000). They recommended factors such as trust, respect, communication, shared vision, and cultural sensitivity as essential in developing interpersonal skills.

Concerning the gap between recommended practices and implementation, Dunst (2000) stated that the gap may be attributed to the failure to operationally define in layman's terms the meaning of partnership. Educators as well as parents need to be apprised of an operational definition of collaborative partnerships in order to know what is expected of them (Winton, 2000; Lynch and Hanson, 1998; Sileo and Prater, 1998). Training and workshops will do much to close the gap in this area.

It is evident from the above analyses that significant social changes have occurred between families and the professionals (see table 1.1). The challenges appear to be very positive in that they have promoted improved collaboration between the families and the professionals. Kelly (1995) and Cunningham and Davis (1985) assumed that child development was characterized by making sense of events accurately. They also articulated that child development is influenced by diverse factors, such as the environment of the family toward the disability. Schaffer (1984) wrote that a conducive environment is where interaction and change are reciprocal. Collectively, research reported by these authors placed parents in key roles for fostering interaction by displaying warmth, sensitivity, and responsiveness toward their disabled children. In essence, the authors attempted to make explicit assumptions, not only the stimulation of child development, but about parental and general family functioning and family interactions with professionals. Chapters 9 and 11 provide additional insights into collaborations.

IMPACT OF THE DISABILITY ON PARENTING

There is a preponderance of research on the impact of a child with a disability on parenting (see chapter 2). Studies have covered the gamut of disabilities and have indicated what adaptations and modifications parents should make to meet the needs of various types of disabilities (Alper, Schloss, and Schloss, 1994; Bradley, Knoll, and Agosta, 1992; Lian and Aolia, 1994; Stoneman and Berman, 1993; Turnbull and Turnbull, 1990; Green and Shinn, 1995; Shea and Bauer, 1991; Westling, 1996).

Data in table 1.1 reflect the many collaborative social changes between parents and professionals over the last four decades. Social changes have significantly changed to aid parents of children with disabilities.

Parental involvement should begin early, in many instances before the child enters school. Parents should learn as rapidly as possible the

Table 1.1   Social Changes: A Model for Parent-Teacher Collaboration

Factors	1950s	1990s
Family	Extended, traditional nuclear	Neolocal, nuclear
Neighborhood	Personal, cohesive	Impersonal, multicultural
Neighbors	Concerned, responsible, active passive, or indirectly active	Concerned, defensive,
Companions/friends	Close, cohesive, socially and emotionally supportive	Often distant or unavailable, nonexistent for many needing social and emotional support
School	Small, in the neighborhood, personal	Large, outside the neighborhood, impersonal
Teachers	Accepted as friends, neighbors, community leaders	Perceived as strangers, professionals, specialists
Knowledge	Limited, manageable within existing standards of behavior and application	Exploding, unmanageable within existing standards of behavior and application
Church standards/ values	Influential	Relatively less influential, relatively fragmented, emphasizing the bizarre and unacceptable.
Work	Simple, personal, available, sufficient to produce needed goods, supportive of artisans	Mechanized, impersonal, automated, specialized, unavailable to many, less supportive of artisans
Material goods	Limited, emphasizing necessities for living	Available to majority, emphasizing luxuries
Mobility	Limited for most people	Nearly unlimited
Communication/ transportation	Limited, slow, inefficient	Nearly unlimited, rapid, more efficient
National and world events	Not widely followed or understood	Extensively followed and understood

role of professional and special services offered in their communities. Early intervention should be designed, introduced, and engage parents in collaborative planning as well as apprising them of special services offered in their communities (Dunst, 2000; Park and Turnbull, 2003; Winton, 2000; Taylor, 2000).

The majority of research in this area indicated that parenting involves many complex processes from the birth of a child through adulthood. For parents of children with disabilities the process is more pronounced and prolonged. The impact of children with disabilities on the family structure is dynamic. Interactions and collaborations between the various faculty members can be adversely affected by the presence of a disabled child in the family. In many cases, the family structure will need to be adapted and modified. In the process of change, many parents will need professional advice, services, and information. (Refer to chapters 3 and 4 for additional information on the impact of a child with disabilities on the family.)

Individuals with disabilities, as well as all children, follow developmental milestones in all areas of growth. Parents will need professional information in these areas. Professional information will assist parents in working with their children where there are developmental problems and the need to pattern the learning of skills in a more predictable manner. It is commonly agreed that parents should be provided with as much information as possible concerning their disabled children. Heddel (1988) recommended the following guidelines relevant to communicating diagnostic information to parents:

- Parents should be told as soon as possible, preferably by a doctor. This information should be communicated in an appropriate place, such as in an interview room or an office.
- There should be no casual observers—this is a private matter.
- Both parents should be told at the same time. It should not be left to one parent to inform the other.
- The newborn should also be in the room, if possible.
- Parents should be given time and opportunity to ask questions, even though they may be confused and at a loss for words.
- Another interview should be scheduled, not more than a day or two later. Parents should be encouraged to bring questions that will inevitably come up in the interim and should be told that other persons having experienced the specific type of disability will be at the next meeting to help answer questions and suggest sources of help. Information is also needed on strategies that parents can employ in working with their disabled children at home.

OVERVIEW OF PARENTAL INVOLVEMENT IN THE SCHOOLS

Parents were instrumental in developing schools in the early centuries of the country. They provided the climate for the creation of public schools. They formed organizations to raise laws to build schools and petitioned legislators to pass laws to build, construct, and support public schools. Historically, parental input was sought and encouraged in the early formation of public schools. Unfortunately, the movement to create public schools did not include disabled children. Formulation of public schools was premised on the concept that they were developed for "normal children." This concept prevailed well into the present century.

During the early part of the twentieth century, society's understanding of disability increased due chiefly to advances and research in all areas of human functioning. Specialized provisions were made for educating children with disabilities. Attitudes and concepts concerning disability began to change due to increased research in all aspects or disabilities, the affects of World Wars I and II, federal and state legislation, and the rise of national parental groups (Mallory, 1996).

Parents of children with disabilities face extensive challenges. Frequently, these challenges will require the assistance of the total family. The family must be flexible, forgiving, and supportive of each other when addressing the needs of a disabled family member. If not, the family may succumb to the many stresses imposed by the disabled family member. The impact on the parents varies considerably due to their past experiences. Some take having a disabled child in stride and plan constructively for meeting the challenges imposed by their disabled offspring. The reverse is true for parents who hold negative views. These negative views will have an adverse affect upon the family (Vann Hasselt, Strain, and Hersen, 1988; Darling, 1979).

IMPACT OF RESEARCH

Research in the fields of biochemistry, medicine, psychology, sociology, education, and other allied disciplines have added immeasurably to our understanding, treatment, and reduction of many types of disabilities. Many disabled children who once died at birth or at an early age are now living due to medical breakthroughs. All types of medical interventions are being conducted. These efforts have resulted in many children with disabilities being saved.

INFLUENCES OF WORLD WARS I AND II

The impact of World Wars I and II significantly changed the public's reactions toward disability. Many recruits who went into the service were normal in all aspects. They returned with all types of disabilities due to the trauma of war. Society readily began to realize that something had to be done for these recruits, since they were not responsible for their disabilities. This positive attitude toward treatment for these disabled recruits was captured by parents of children with disabilities and they began to demand treatment for their disabled children.

FORMATION OF NATIONAL PARENTAL GROUPS

Parents have formed national advocacy groups to advance the course of individuals with disabilities (go to www.nichcy.org/pubs/genresc/gr2.htm for a list of associations). These groups have been instrumental in lobbying for the rights of disabled individuals in the courts and at state and congressional hearings. Due to their efforts, many federal and state laws have been passed.

ROLE OF FEDERAL LEGISLATION

Federal legislation has significantly improved the educational opportunities for children with disabilities. As indicated, parents were instrumental in having these federal mandates passed. Section 504 of the Vocational Act of 1973 prohibited the discrimination of children with disabilities. The U.S. Congress aided school districts to comply with Section 504 by passing the Education for All Handicapped Children Act, Public Law 94-142. PL 94-142 specifies how Section 504 guidelines should be implemented. Parental involvement in the referral, identification, placement, programming, and evaluation phases of each child's individual education is a major thrust of that law (National Council on Disability, 1995; U.S. Department of Education, 1995).

TREND IN PARENTAL PARTICIPATION

Today, parents of children with disabilities are not as actively involved as they were historically. There are several reasons contributing to the decline of parental involvement in the schools. The basic family structure has changed. The cohesive structure of earlier years is not present today. Some parents do not feel welcome in the schools; a significant number of minority parents who do not speak fluent English are present in our society (this issue is addressed in chapter 7). The bleak economic conditions have forced both parents to work or, in the case of a one-parent family, the parent must work two jobs to support the family. Some parents are critical of the performance of their children in public schools as measured by standardized tests and have called for reforms in education (Finders and Lewis, 1994; Harry, Allen, and McLaughlin, 1995).

These factors have had an impact on parents of disabled children as well. However, due to federal legislation, parental involvement in the public schools has escalated chiefly because of The Family Education Rights and Privacy Act which was passed in 1974. Chapter 5 is devoted to a discussion of the impact of federal legislation on parental involvement.

PARENTAL CONCERNS

Concerns of parents relevant to their children with disabilities cover a variety of issues. Generally, parents are concerned with the following:

- Cause of the disability. What factors are responsible for the disability? Is it hereditary? What did we do to contribute to the condition? Why us? Why did that happen to us? Is it safe to have another child? Parents generally feel that they are responsible for the disability. They constantly seek reasons for the disability by visiting different professionals to establish the cause and a cure.
- Impact on the family structure. Parents are concerned with how their child with a disability will impact the family. Will his or her presence affect their normal children? How will the disability be explained to the children, relatives, and neighbors? Are there

educational and community resources available to serve their child?

- Treatment and intervention. Many parents spend countless hours seeking treatment or a cure for the disability. Questions posed by parents may include the following: Is there some type of surgery which may assist my child? What type of treatments or interventions are recommended? Where may the needed services be located? Is drug therapy recommended? What type of community services are available? How will his or her school placement be determined?
- Prognostic outlook. Parents are deeply concerned with the future of their children. Questions and concerns frequently voiced are: Will a cure be found for our children? Will our children outgrow the disability? What will our children be like when they are adults? What are the chances, if we have other children, that they will not be disabled?

These four broad areas outlined are in no way a comprehensive review of all parental concerns. They only reflect basic concerns of parents. (Chapter 3 comprehensively addresses parental reactions and concerns.) Additionally, these categories can be subdivided into additional areas. One of the major purposes of this text is to fully investigate the aforementioned areas and to present research to answer the many questions posed by parents of children with disabilities (Green and Shinn, 1995).

SUMMARY

Family systems theory provides a framework for understanding the dynamics that are present within families. Children with disabilities and their families face a unique set of issues, as well as the usual challenges of childhood. Understanding the issues that are important to families is particularly critical when trying to develop a positive relationship between professionals and families. Both formal and informal avenues for collaboration exist. However, open communication is the integral component of developing this important collaborative relationship. In order to improve the collaborative relationship, parents must avail themselves of the training offered at family service centers. Some of the recommended training would include:

- Parenting skills
- Counseling skills
- Strategies for coping with their disabled children
- Legal rights and due process procedures
- Sharing information
- Collaborative strategies
- Sharing information
- Strategies for involvement in the school
- Promoting cultural awareness
- Reporting strategies
- Community involvement

The organization of the text is premised upon the listed areas. These areas will be fully developed and specifically outlined to assist parents and educators to use collaborative activities effectively to promote their children's education, as well as to deal effectively with problems which they may encounter in society. Additionally, the text is designed to: (1) assist parents in recognizing and accepting their children's disabilities, (2) help parents develop positive attitudes toward their disabled children, (3) identify and recognize resources and treatment facilities in the community, (4) recognize the importance of counseling, (5) work in collaboration with the school and community agencies, and (6) help parents deal effectively with their own frustrations and self-esteem.

CHAPTER 2

Parenting Skills

The parent is the child's first teacher from the moment he or she is born. The child begins to learn from his or her parent communication, social, self-help, academic, and other skills that will assist in developing his or her self-esteem. These skills will be necessary for motivating children to be successful in school (Slavin, Karweit, and Wasik, 1993; Epstein, 1989; Mink and Nihira, 1986; Taylor, 2000). The National PTA Board of Directors (1997) has adopted a parent involvement position that promotes parent participation in "every facet of the education and development of children from birth to adulthood" (Slavin, Karweit, and Wasik, 1993, p.1). This position further recognizes that parents are the principal influence in their children's lives. Parent involvement, according to the PTA, takes many forms. Parents are a key component in the field of education, from shared responsibilities for decision making for their individual child's education, health, and well-being to parent participation in organizations that address community-based needs for all children. This adoption by the National PTA Board of Directors clearly summarizes the values of parental input from the early development stages of the child through adulthood.

The importance of parenting should not be overlooked by the schools. Parents are the child's first teachers. The parental role in the family, therefore, focuses on the parent as a role model for the child. In the early formative stage of a child, the actions modeled by parents or adults are emulated by children. It is at this point in a child's life that the quality of parental behavior is critical. Parents who express warmth, happiness, consideration, and respect in their daily handling of the child are acknowledged to be assisting the child in developing a positive approach to life. Parents should provide model behaviors that they wish their children to demonstrate (Dunst, Trivette, Hamby, and Pollock, 1990). If parents do not provide guidance by personal example of their major values, it is difficult to help a child emulate desired behaviors (Cullingford, 1996).

In essence, behaviors parents wish their children to exhibit in their adult lives should be a reflection of the parents' own behaviors. The primary parental role in the family is that of being a teacher of trust. Quite often, society has witnessed many children who have no confidence in their families or themselves; hence, they choose alternate support groups as a family. Parents need to have confidence that the emotional support given to their children will enable them to cope with the demands of family, friends, school, and society.

Dealing with the confidential aspect of the child's life is one of the most essential components of parenting. At this time, children are taught to have confidence and reliance on themselves. Parents are advised to intervene in whatever practical way necessary to influence their children's behavior, to set limits, shape behaviors, and engage in mental problem-solving discussions (Whitechurch, and Constantine, 1993). Parenting, therefore, requires parents to provide skills that will equip their children to be able to function appropriately in society.

Parenting is not about beautiful things all the time. It is about good and bad, the fulfilling and the draining, the rewarding and the punishing. With respect to this, parenting practically depends on how well parents grow with their children and help their children to become positive individuals. To build this confidence, parents need to exhibit self-confidence in the presence of their children.

Respect is a major part of parenting. Parenting is a most stimulating job that requires wisdom, sensitivity, strength, and endurance. To be effective, parents must respect their children as human beings. In some cases, children turn to undesirable elements because their parents do not set appropriate models for them to emulate. The mind-set of children is conditioned primarily by how their parents respect or regard them (Caldwell, 1997).

Children need to be interacted with and talked to with as much respect, courtesy, and consideration as you would expect for yourself. Yelling at children has a deteriorating effect on them. To receive respect and cooperation from children, parents should respect their individual rights.

Love and discipline are key elements in the art of parenting. Although it is advisable for parents to love their children, it must be expressed in ways that are beneficial for their children and comfortable for the parents. Discipline is a form of love, and parents should learn how to use it to avoid letting love for the child cloud the responsibility of parenting.

Communication is a tool for good parenting. Parents who communicate well with their children create, in a practical form, a direct channel for closeness and development of a positive self-concept, which will be needed for later school success (Solo, 1997). Children who experience all or part of the aforementioned elements develop confidence about themselves that carries over to many other situations or difficulties that they may face. A woman who experienced good communication and a warm relationship with her own parents always looks forward with confidence to her own mothering, and there is every likelihood that she will pass her good experience on to her children.

The importance of parenting in this family relies on commitments, providing warmth and nurturing for all members, and encouraging the development of strategies for dealing with difficulties. The challenge in parenting is to relate to children with disabilities as well as to children without disabilities in manners and ways that stimulate their potentialities for growth and provide appropriate opportunities for experiences that develop these potentialities. Parenting skills in various cultures differ. Educators and teachers should be aware of the various culture styles and adjust instructional programs and school activities to reflect diversity (Hindle, 1998; Okagaki and French, 1998; Taylor, 1997).

DEVELOPING PROSOCIAL SKILLS/BEHAVIORS

Research from social learning theory implies that prosocial learning behaviors of children with disabilities are enhanced when behavioral expectations are clearly specified and reinforced with praise, encouragement, and other positive acts by parents and teachers. (Refer to table 2.1 for specific examples.)

Table 2.1   Ninety-Two Ways to Promote Academic and Social Growth of Children with Disabilities

1. You're doing a good job.
2. You did a lot of work today!
3. Now you've figured it out.
4. That's RIGHT!!!
5. Now you've got the hang of it!
6. That's the way!
7. You're doing fine!
8. Now you have it!
9. Nice going.
10. You're really going to town.
11. That's great
12. You did it that time.
13. GREAT!
14. FANTASTIC!
15. TERRIFIC!
16. Good for you.
17. GOOD WORK!
18. That's better.
19. EXCELLENT!
20. Good job, (name of student).
21. You outdid yourself today.
22. That's the best you've done ever.
23. Good going.
24. That's really nice.
25. Keep it up!
26. WOW!!
27. Share your best work.
28. Much better.
29. Good for you.
30. That's much better.
31. Good thinking.
32. Marvelous.
33. Exactly right!
34. SUPER!
35. Beautiful work.
36. You make it look easy.
37. Way to go.
38. Superb!!
39. You're getting better every day.
40. WONDERFUL!
41. I knew you could do it.
42. Keep working on it, you're getting better!
43. You're doing beautifully.
44. You're really working hard today.
45. That's the way to do it.
46. Keep on trying.
47. That's it.
48. You've got it made.
49. You're very good at that.
50. You're learning fast.
51. I'm very proud of you.
52. You certainly did well today.
53. That's good.
54. I'm happy to see you working like that.
55. I'm proud of the way you worked today.
56. That's the right way to do it.
57. You're really learning a lot.
58. That's better than ever.
59. That's quite an improvement.
60. That kind of work makes me very happy.
61. Try another way.
62. PERFECT!
63. FINE!!!
64. Well done.
65. You figured that out fast.
66. You remembered.
67. You're really improving.
68. I think you've got it now.
69. Well look at you go.
70. TREMENDOUS!
71. OUTSTANDING!
72. Now that's what I call a fine job.
73. You did that very well.
74. That was first-class work.
75. Right on.
76. SENSATIONAL!!
77. That's the best ever.
78. Good remembering.
79. You haven't missed a thing.
80. You really make my job fun.
81. You must have been practicing.
82. Your cooperation is appreciated.
83. Good show.
84. CONGRATULATIONS!
85. Not bad.
86. Nice going, (name of student).
87. OUTSTANDING!
88. SUPERIOR!
89. Good thinking.
90. Clever.
91. Superior work.
92. Keep up the good work.

Table 2.1 provides some ways in which parents and teachers may promote academic and social growth, as well as raise the self-esteem of all children, including children with disabilities. It also shows ninety-two ways for saying to children with disabilities that they have done a good job. These words and phrases are designed to reinforce good work habits and to develop skills needed for academic and social success. Data in table 2.1 is in concert with principles advocated by Bandura (1997). Bandura's social learning theory advocates how social learning may aid parents in using parental skills.

Bandura proposed a very comprehensive and powerful social learning theory of modeling. Bandura's theory stands as the most popular theory of modeling today. One reason his theory is so popular is that it explicitly recognized that children imitate only a small fraction of all the responses they learn through observation. According to Bandura, children learn a multitude of brand new social responses simply by observing the actions of significant and salient models around them, including their parents, siblings, teachers, and playmates. Bandura calls this process observational learning and believes that this is a major way children acquire new patterns of social behavior. This theory fits into what most developmental psychologists say: from 0-7, children are learning from significant others, and from 7 to early teenage years, they are modeling and demonstrating what they have learned from others. During the teenage years, when children are looking for their own identity, they are looking to their friends and others in the same developmental stage for learning. If parents use their skills surrounding discipline and rewards during formative years, they still will be able to lovingly guide their children to adulthood without subjecting them to serious irreversible traumatic experiences. On the other hand, without parents employing good parenting skills, children may develop unacceptable social skills (Taylor, 1998).

Social learning theory implies that children learn from instruction and discipline they directly experience at the hands of their parents, teachers, and other socializing agents. Parents must give instruction to their children, establish routines, and serve as role models until their children have developed acceptable behaviors. Parents must decide when it is appropriate to transfer the locus of control from themselves to their children. Before transfer occurs, parents should be sure that their children have appropriate self-directed strategies to make independent decisions and to act appropriately on their own (Coleman, 1986).

EFFECTIVE PARENTING SKILLS STRATEGIES

Parenting is the process that develops skills needed for children to be successful in their environments. In order for parenting skills to be successful, parents need to be cognizant of techniques to employ, involving trust, respect, love, discipline, and communication. The recommended parenting skills for parents to use in directing and guiding their children with disabilities have been developed premised upon the aforementioned techniques (Naeef, 1997; Dunst, Trivette, Hamby, and Pollock, 1990; Winton, 1994; Powell, 1998; Leung, 1998).

Parents believe that they naturally know how to raise their children. Unfortunately, humans are not born preprogrammed with those child-rearing skills that will naturally help them to accurately discriminate and discern what to do when they confront a two-year-old's no's, or a seven-year-old's defiance about doing his or her homework, or a teenager's rebelliousness about obeying curfew set by the city to protect him or her from physical harm.

Parenting skills are not taught. Parents learn these skills through trial and error, strategies from their parents, information from published sources, and from specialists in the field. Parents generally use information from these sources to guide and direct the activities of their children. This is equally true for parents of children with disabilities. Most social sciences agree that parenting is a complex and dynamic process (Giannetti and Sagarese, 1997).

Whereas there is no universal set of principles for teaching parents parenting skills, parents must respond to the physical, psychological, and social/emotional needs of their children if they are to be successful in school and society. According to Taylor (1998), during the formative years, parents can promote positive and effective parenting skills for their children with disabilities through implementing the following strategies:

- Relate Tasks to the Developmental Level of the Child. Some children are eager for new tasks and experiences. Others need to be coaxed and encouraged. Regardless of how your child approaches challenges, success will be important for the development of self-concept. Direct your child toward challenges that he or she is developmentally ready for. Break down big tasks into smaller parts (e.g., if your child wants to make a garden, break down the project into easy steps— digging, making holes, dropping seeds, covering them, water). Show the child each step, but let your child do it for himself or herself.
- Build a Sense of Security and Trust. Given a loving and responsive home environment, your child will be able to establish a sense of self apart from the people and things about him or her. Patience,

consistency, and loving discipline are acts of caring, which support your child as he or she strives toward independence.

- Be Sensitive to Your Child's Signals. As an individual, your child shows unique ways of responding to new people and new experiences. Although he or she may not be able to put his or her feelings into words, he or she may need your reassurance when entering into unknown territory. Sometimes fearfulness and negative behaviors are signs that your child is not quite ready for the challenge at hand.
- Make your Child an Equal in the Family. Membership in a family involves learning to share: sharing time, sharing material resources, and sharing one another's life. As your child grows more capable, he or she should be given the opportunity to perform tasks, which contributes to the functioning of the family. Your child also needs to be shown ways to express how much he or she cares about the people that he or she loves.
- Be Aware of Your Child's Limitations. Realize that your child's present capabilities are largely determined by his or her overall developmental level. Your expectations of his or her behaviors should be based on his or her developmental age, not chronological age.
- Go from the Known to the Unknown. Prepare your child for new experiences by linking the familiar to the unknown. If your child has met the librarian and visited the children's room in the neighborhood library many times, then participation in preschool story hour is not so scary a prospect.

Other activities that parents can use at home to prepare their children may include:

- Read to your children, even after they can read independently. Set aside a family reading time. Take turns reading aloud to each other.
- Take your children to the library regularly. Let them see you checking out books for yourself, too.
- Build math-reasoning skills together. Have young children help sort laundry, measure ingredients for a recipe, or keep track of rainfall for watering the lawn.
- Regulate the amount and content of the television your family watches. Read the weekly TV listing together and plan shows to watch.

- Share telling stories.
- Model appropriate social skills.
- Praise children often.
- Have children make brooks and illustrations about themselves.
- Give children responsibilities in the home.
- Discover ways to catch children being good.
- Discuss intervention strategies with children.
- Set behavior expectations based upon the development level of children.

SUMMARY

From the very beginning, children with disabilities should have an important place within the family structure. By being responsive to children's needs, the foundation for interactive social relationships begins. The drive for independence emerges as developmental skills grow. As your child tries to do more and more for himself or herself, he or she continues to depend on you for guidance and support. Parents' delight in the small accomplishments of a child can set expectations for larger success.

Parents of individuals with disabilities, as well as all parents, have a tremendous influence and impact on setting appropriate models for developing social and academic skills. The developmental level of the child as well as developmental sequence of tasks must be considered in social and academic training. Parents can contribute significantly to their disabled children's self-concept and control through appropriate modeling strategies.

In order for parents of individuals with disabilities to be effective, change agents in promoting appropriate social and academic skills development, early intervention in health care, counseling, housing, nutrition, education, and child-rearing practices, and the like must be improved. Early intervention and parental involvement are essential for preparing children to master skills and tasks successfully.

Parental involvement is a must in the lives of children. A thorough review of the relevant literature reveals that: parenting is essential for (1) the proper nurturing and caring of children, and (2) the nourishing, protecting, guiding, and social learning that must accompany a child throughout life and through the course of development.

CHAPTER 3

Parental Reactions

EMOTIONAL REACTIONS

Parents show and display a variety of reactions to their children with disabilities (Seligman, 1991a). Some reactions are so severe that some parents need psychological intervention to cope with the situations. Some parents gradually accept the idea; however, few parents totally initially accept a child with a disability without some counseling.

The age of onset of the disability is an important factor to consider. The reaction of a parent to a child with a disability diagnosed in the fifth grade is likely to be uniquely different from that of a parent who learned after three months that the child was disabled. The manner in which data are shared with a parent can sufficiently influence parental reactions toward their children with disabilities. Information relevant to a child's disability should be shared with the parents in a friendly, warm, and professional manner, and the presenter should be sensitive to the feelings of the parents. Parents are also greatly concerned about the financial support needed to provide the necessary services for their children.

Many negative emotions may be generated from the parents concerning this issue. Parents react emotionally not only to their children with disabilities, but also from pressures applied from the community's perception of the disability. Frequently, the community's perceptions of children with disabilities may cause parents to be rejected from or not feel welcome to participate in many of the social clubs and functions. The reactions may lead to parents being isolated from the community (Clemens-Brower, 1997).

Parental emotional reactions to their children with disabilities differ greatly. Emotional reactions may range from acceptance through complete rejection of the child with a disability (Hynan, 1996). Some parents are mature enough, with minimum intervention, to accept the disability of their children. These parents attempt to provide services to aid their children.

Other parents tend to deny that their children have disabilities, and are constantly trying to find causes for the disability. They mount a continuous search to find ways in which the child may be made normal by sending him or her to various specialists to treat the disability. This type of reaction significantly impedes realistic planning for the child with a disability, since parents and family may not perceive the child as disabled, but hostile, not cooperating with the family, or plain lazy (Lian and Aolia, 1994).

Some parents (mostly males) are unable to face the reality of their children's disabilities. Adjusting to and accepting the fact that a disabled child is in the family can be a challenge for some fathers. Many become depressed or deny the fact. They constantly deny that a disability exists. Many are not informed about the cause of the disability. They make believe that the disability is attributed to some past act that they have committed, or due to inheritance. Training, education, treatment, and family relationships concerning children with disabilities are significantly affected by these reactions.

Like most people, children with disabilities do not live in a vacuum. A child with a disability needs, as do all children, a close emotional relationship with others, and these relationships must be satisfying and stress-reducing if he or she is to achieve his or her maximum potentialities. Further, as with all children, the relationships between the child with a disability and his or her parents and community are of great importance. If the parents manifest negative reactions to the child's deficient abilities, then it becomes more difficult for wholesome relationships to be established. The greater the negative reactions of the parents, the less likely it is that the child will achieve the level of emotional maturity he or she is capable of attaining. Negative reactions of the parents, thus, can adversely affect the full maturational process of the child with a disability. It is of prime importance that any emotional problems which surface as a result of the child's disability be professionally treated on a continuous basis. Systematic treatment is highly recommended since the emotional development of the child is directly related to the positive reactions of the parents toward him or her (Harshman, 1996). It is commonly known that the future psychological adjustment of disabled children greatly depends upon the emotional climate projected by the parents within the home.

IMPACT OF REACTIONS ON THE FAMILY

When a child with a disability is born or when a nondisabled child becomes disabled, most families will go through four predictable stages. These stages are similar to the reactions that an individual would go through if a family member died. The similarity between the birth of a child and the death of a family member is that in both cases there is a loss. When a child with a disability is born, some parents believe it would be easier to lose that child because of death than it is to have a child with a severe disability. With a severely disabled child, their existence and daily needs can be constant reminders of the parent's loss; thus, there is a continuing recurrence of grief. The issue of grief is outlined in greater detail later in the chapter.

All parents will react differently when they are told their children have disabilities. Some parents will live in chronic sorrow; some parents will experience chronic depression; others will reach the final stage of acceptance in a reasonable amount of time. The importance of the reaction cannot be minimized (Alper, Schloss, and Schloss, 1994). Details will be devoted to these reactions later in the chapter.

The phases parents of children with disabilities go through are as follows:

- Phase 1: The initial reactions include doubt and disbelief. The parents cannot believe the diagnosis and deny that the diagnosis is true.

    According to Kubler-Ross (1997), parents go through various stages of mourning and grief concerning the birth of a disabled child. This view is supported by Batshaw (1997); Bruce, Schultz, Smyrnois, and Schultz (1994); Lin (2000); and O'Shea, O'Shea,

Algozzine, and Hammitte (2001). Turnbull and Turnbull (2001), Bauer and Shae (2003), and Allen, Petr, and Brown (1995) remarked that the grief theory does not explain all the family members are being exposed to. They recommended that the total family should be involved in a family-centered model addressing strategies for dealing with grief and tragedy. Professionals should provide interventions which will enable parents to move from the grief stage to levels of awareness (Senge, 1990; Seligman, 1995; Kazdin, 1988; Webster-Stratton, Hollinsworth, and Kolpacoff, 1989).

- Phase 2: Awareness develops along with more feelings. Some parents frequently feel guilty. They wonder what they did that caused them to have a child with a disability; they wonder what they could have done differently. During this stage, parents feel anger. They want to know why this happened to them. Often the anger will be directed toward other people. If the anger is not controlled, the individual may become depressed. Depression will hinder the parents' ability to manage effectively (Greenbaum, 1994). Also during this phase, the parents become concerned with their feelings of ambivalence toward their children with disabilities. They feel ashamed because they have negative feelings. They are reluctant to share these feelings with others for fear they will be judged rather than understood. The issue of ambivalence will be addressed in greater detail later in the chapter.

Schaef (1992) contends that we all have our own level of truth or awareness and frequently are unaware of the attitudes of others. According to Schaef, we progress individually through levels of awareness of truth. They are:

1. Each issue has levels of truth. As one grows in awareness, his or her levels of truth deepen.
2. Each individual operates from a particular level of truth. This level of truth is his or her reality.
3. A person must fully embrace a level of truth before moving to another level.
4. Moving forward along the continuum allows an individual to better understand the concept itself, as well as the level of truth of others concerning that concept.

5. Each level is a significant break from the previous level, moving in the opposite direction. When one looks only at two adjacent levels of truth, they may give the appearance of a dualism.
6. Understanding these different levels of truth is vital to communication.

Ulrich and Bauer (2003) have added to our understanding of these four Levels of Awareness that parents go through:

Level 1: The parents become aware of the disability and may have little knowledge or experience with the disability. They may not have the necessary competencies to discuss the child's disability with professionals. During this stage, parents may deny the existence of the disability due chiefly to a lack of information concerning the condition or fear of the stigma associated with the disability.

Level 2: During this stage, parents recognize that their children have a disability. The common belief during this stage is that they can find a professional to solve the problem and demand to know strategies that will be employed to treat their children. They may also join organizations dealing with the disability of their children and read a wide range of information concerning the disability.

Level 3: In this stage, parents emphasize the need for normalization in their children's lives. They engage their children in normal activities that children within their age range experience. During these transformational experiences, if their children cannot adequately perform the tasks, parents may argue for a reduction in the task.

Level 4: In this final stage, parents become cognizant of the fact that their disabled children need assistance. According to Vander Klift and Kunc (1996), parents and professionals recognize the value of equal work and emphasize the mutual benefits that come from celebrating diversity. Disabled children are taught about themselves and their disabilities. Children are prepared and taught to be self-advocates.

Professionals and parents should understand that parents may not be on the same level of awareness as they are. This can result in miscommunication. Professionals should counsel and provide parents with information and strategies relevant to the various levels. Professionals should ascertain which level the parents are on and provide information to improve their attitudes; all parents should not expect to be on the same level. The ultimate aim is to move parents as rapidly as possible to Level 4.

- Phase 3: During the third phase, the parents do much bargaining, associating a number of "If only I could" statements. This phase usually lasts for a long time. The parent is attempting to find excuses for the disabling condition. In some instances, the mother may attempt to associate something she has done to cause the disability. Through appropriate counseling, the parents will come to accept the disability and cease making "If only I could" statements. The length of time for the parents to stop making negative statements will depend on the amount of family support from siblings, husbands, and extended family members.

- Phase 4: In this final phase, parents acknowledge that they have a child with a disability and are willing to accept him or her. Once this phase has been successfully met, the parents are open to treatment. Various types of therapeutic treatment may be instituted. The length and time of therapy will depend upon family and community support, and their involvement in the child's education, religion, social support, and acceptance of the disabled child into the extended family. A major part of the intervention will be through counseling. To be effective, counseling sessions should involve the total family, including the extended family. Total involvement of the entire family will give the parents needed emotional support as well as assisting the family in understanding how to deal with the problem presented by the disabled child.

EFFECTS ON FAMILY MEMBERS

Having children with disabilities has an effect on the whole family, including having an effect on marriages. Some spouses are unable to tolerate or appreciate the variations in dealing with stress and divorce may result. In other families, differences are recognized and spouses turn to others for their needs to be met. In the latter case, the marriage is likely to stay intact. Siblings are also affected by having a child with a disability in the family (McLouhlin and Senn, 1994). Children fear that they can catch what their brother or sister has. They may also have many questions that need to be answered. Like the parents, the children need someone with whom they can share their feelings and from whom they can get accurate information and answers. Often-times, children are afraid to ask their questions and pretend everything is in order. It is important that they be periodically asked if they have any questions. To open dialogue, adults might share some of the questions and feelings they have about the child with the disability. Given support and encouragement, most children handle having a sibling with a disability well. They may benefit from the situation by becoming more sensitive and tolerant of others, regardless of their differences. Grandparents may be a valuable resource to the family by assisting with the care and supervision of the disabled child, providing that they accept the child. Some grandparents have difficulty accepting their grandchildren and may deny the disability (Seligman, 2000).

THE PRESENCE OF CHILDREN WITH DISABILITIES

The presence of children with disabilities may have a significant impact on parents and family members. Marital problems and other children within the family may be affected. The behavior of children with disabilities is greatly influenced by the reactions and attitudes of family members. In essence, the child with a disability affects the total family, and the family responses to the behaviors in turn affect the child. When children with disabilities are reared in home environments which are productive, the children's adjustment in the larger communities is usually good. Research has shown that the mother's personality and positive interactions between family members and the child with a disability were more important to the children's well-being than any other practice (Heddel, 1988; Hardman, Drew, and Eagan, 1996; Seligman, 1991b).

SIBLING INTEGRATION

Evidence tends to support the notion that siblings largely adopt their parents' attitudes toward the child with a disability. When negative attitudes and interventions are shown by the parents, siblings usually imitate those behaviors. When nondisabled siblings are made to supervise, care for, protect, and defend their disabled siblings, negative feelings toward the child with a disability may appear, because the time devoted to caring for the child with a disability is depriving the nondisabled sibling the opportunity to engage in recreational and educational activities.

Siblings of children with disabilities may constitute a risk factor and a burden for them if they are required to provide care. Additionally, they may show signs of resentment, anger, and rebelliousness when required to assist in the maintenance of their disabled brother or sister (Seligman, 2000). They may show feelings such as guilt (feeling the disability was their fault), jealousy (not getting as much attention), worry, embarrassment, increased responsibility, anger (over lack of attention), concern that the disability is contagious, and being unloved, forgotten, and slighted. It should be noted how important it is for siblings to know how "normal" feelings of sorrow, grief, fear, and the like are—whether this should be discussed in the context of the family or within a sibling support group.

It is not only extremely valuable for siblings to share their feelings with one another, but also equally as important for parents to share their own feelings with the siblings of their disabled child. Parents need to model for their nondisabled children how to deal with the many stages of the siblings development, for misconceptions about having a sibling with a disability are so easily developed. Thus, providing honest and direct information, and allowing siblings to be part of the parents' reality, is vitally important to the sibling's future.

Research has shown that siblings of children with disabilities are often more compassionate than adults and more sensitive to the needs of other people. Some parents fear that unless the sibling is engrossed in the life of the child with the disability, these sensitivities won't develop. However, researchers agree that it is OK for siblings to go away from their brother or sister at different points in their life. The ability of a sibling to find a happy balance between home/family and the world outside (away from the disabled brother or sister) is immensely important to the healthy development of a sibling as an adult (Vadasy, 1982; Markowitz, 1984).

Powell and Ogle (1985) have provided parents with a list of questions that they may employ to aid siblings in addressing their disabled brothers or sisters:

- What is the cause of the disability?
- Whose fault is it?
- Why is my sister or brother disabled? Will he or she outgrow his or her disabilities?
- How can I help him or her?
- Why is it that my sister or brother does not live at home?
- Will my sister or brother be able to go to school?
- How can I discuss my feelings about my disabled sibling with my parents?
- Why must we always do things that involve my disabled sibling?
- Why do my parents let my disabled sibling get away with so much?
- How can I get along better with my disabled sibling?
- Why am I smarter and stronger than my disabled sibling?
- How can I discuss my sibling with my friends?
- Will my friends tease me?
- Should I invite my disabled sibling to attend social functions with me?
- What does special education mean? Will my brother or sister attend?
- What is a group home?
- Who will be responsible for my sibling when my parents die?
- Will my disabled brother or sister live with me?
- Will my disabled brother or sister be able to work?
- Will my children be disabled?

These are a few questions and concerns that siblings will have about their disabled sibling.

Parents should have open discussions relative to these issues. Parents may need to seek outside and professional assistance in addressing many questions posed by their normal children. The references and appendices associated with this chapter may also offer a source that parents can contact.

Extensive information about how parents and professionals can help the siblings of children with disabilities is provided by Powell and Ogle (1985). These authors review the research literature on the sibling relationship; describe some of the special needs and concerns of siblings; describe strategies parents can use to provide information and emotional support to siblings; discuss the use of counseling; provide strategies to encourage social interaction; and discuss siblings as teachers, at school, and as adults. They also include a list of reading materials that can help children and young adults adjust to having a brother or sister with a disability. A second list gives the names, addresses, and telephone numbers of organizations that provide support to parents and siblings of children with handicaps (refer to www.nichcy.org/pubs/genresc/gr2.htm and appendix B).

One such organization is the Sibling Information Network, which publishes a newsletter and serves as a "clearinghouse of information, ideas, project, literature, and research regarding siblings and other issues related to the needs of families with handicapped members." In addition to disseminating information, the network provides a way for members with similar interests to contact each other. Another such organization is Siblings for Significant Change. It is a sibling membership organization that disseminates information, conducts conferences and workshops, and promotes greater public awareness of the needs of persons with handicaps and their families.

As indicated, sibling initial reactions will be influenced by the approach utilized by the parents in relating the problem associated with the disability. One important consideration in this respect is the age of the sibling in relation to his or her ability to grasp the meaning of those factors related to disability and the capacity to understand the ramifications (Stoneman and Berman, 1993).

If a parent has strong ties with any particular family member, how that member handles the situation will significantly influence what course of action the parent will take, and perhaps even affect the future relationship between them.

The conclusion that can be drawn is that the reactions of the extended family will influence and contribute to the attitudes of the parents both initially and on a continuing basis. What is necessary here is love, understanding, assistance, and encouragement by the family toward the parents and ultimately to the child with a disability. With the family's support, the parents will be able to take some comfort in knowing that the family is interested in both them and the child. The parents are looking for strength during this crisis. The family's encouragement and support just may be the catalyst that is needed to assist the parents in adjusting to their problem (Wells, 1997).

THE EXTENDED FAMILY

Social factors have a great deal of influence on the adjustment process that parents will make concerning their disabled child. These factors usually do not bear upon the initial reactions of the parents but they do affect the later decisions and coping techniques in conjunction with those of the physician, extended family, and religious affiliation.

The parents obviously place great emphasis on what society feels toward their child with a disability, particularly the community segment to which the child belongs. Frustrations are increased when the parents attempt to project what they perceive as society's expectations of them, their abnormal child, and the course of action that should be taken. The integration process of the views of society and the extended family, in relation to the parents, places added strain on the parental perceptions of the child and may, if these views tend to be polarized, create conflicts as to the proper course of action. Parental acceptance or rejection of their child with a disability is thus compounded by the attitudes they hold as well as those attitudes and the value systems expressed by the social environment (Clemens-Brower, 1997). (Refer to chapter 12 for additional information.)

"The presence of a disabled child has an impact on the entire family. The increased responsibility and demands on time that accompany meeting the unique needs of the special child often disrupt and erode family ties. Sibling as well as parents frequently experience mingled feelings of concern, dismay, and very often guilt." The chapter focuses on easing the strain of having a disabled brother or sister and how parents can handle sibling relationships effectively so that each family member has the opportunity to function in a climate that fosters growth, compassion, and bondedness. Research conducted by Vadasy (1982) and Markowitz (1984) have provided exclusive evidence that fathers' involvement in promoting positive attitudes toward the disabled is crucial. They conducted a two-hour Saturday discussion session with fathers and their disabled children. The fathers had an opportunity to discuss a variety of issues concerning their disabled children. Games, activities, and guest speakers were invited to supplement activities that the fathers could use with their children. Data from this research activity was used to develop a curriculum by the University of Washington, involving Supporting Extended Family Members (SEFAM).

Parents and siblings should be continually educated with information relevant to the needs of children with disabilities in the social environments. A first step should be for the community to assess the needs of children with disabilities. A second step should be to develop programs based upon the assessed needs. A third step should be to identify appropriate physical and human resources to augment the program. A final step should be to build with the program an evaluation design to determine the effectiveness of the program.

PERCEPTION OF PARENTS TOWARD DISABILITY

When parents recognize the extent to which their child is disabled, they attempt to seek the cause of the seeming tragedy which has beset them. Two types of motivation seem to underlie this search. The first and more rational approach is a hope that in discovering the etiology of the disorder, a way might be found that will cure the disability and prevent the occurrence of it in any future children they may have. Additional motivation for the research probably stems from an ardent wish for relief from a heavy burden of responsibility and guilt. One way or another, a great many parents feel that the blame for their child's disability rests with them (Greenbaum, 1994). They may, for example, be concerned because they allowed the baby to roll off the bed or failed to call a physician when he or she was ill. Still others harbor the memory of an unwanted pregnancy, sometimes even of a deliberate attempt to abort the unwanted fetus. In many parents, the most primitive kinds of thinking determine beliefs about the etiology of the disability. Sometimes the child with a disability becomes the focus of all past wrongdoings of which the parents feel ashamed. Parents who thus blame themselves for their child's disability suffer an additional burden which takes its own trail.

Some parents see a connection not only between the child with disability and pre- and extramarital transgressions, but also unusual intramarital sex practices and intercourse late in pregnancy. The conflict is proliferated when the parent sees the child with a disability as an extension of himself or herself. Ryckman and Henderson (1965) wrote that there are six areas of meaning involved in the parent-child relationship, particularly as it relates to the ego-extension view. Although these views were written over three decades ago, they still have relevance for today's parents. These areas are:

- The parent considers the child as a physical and psychological extension of himself or herself.
- The child is a means of vicarious satisfaction to the parents.
- The parents can derive some measure of immortality through their children.
- The child is involved in the concept of a personalized love object.
- There is a parental feeling of worth in responding to the dependency needs of the child.
- The parents can express negative feelings about the limitations and demands of child rearing.

PARENTAL REACTIONS TOWARD DISABILITIES

Some of the common reactions of parents to their children with disabilities include: (1) not realistically accepting the problem; (2) self-pity; (3) rejection of the problem; (4) guilt, shame, and depression; (5) ambivalence; (6) optimism; and (7) dependency. Many of these reactions may be closely associated with the four phases summarized earlier (Shea and Bauer, 1991; Friend and Bursuck, 1996).

Not Realistically Accepting the Problem

Some parents have developed a common defense against combating anxiety by not realistically accepting the fact that they have a child with a disability. Fathers tend to defend and use other excuses for the child's behavior. Fathers have a difficult time accepting an offspring who is not normal. They feel that these children are not an extension of themselves. Initially, most parents of children with disabilities show some type of denial to their children's disabilities. Some parental denial is short term, others deny their children's disabilities for a prolonged time. There are many factors associated with parental denial of their children with disabilities (Shea and Bauer, 1991; Friend and Bursuck, 1996; Greenbaum, 1994; Hynan, 1996; Hardman, 1996; Alper, Schloss, and Schloss, 1994). A major factor exists when the parent attempts to hide from himself or herself the reality of the fact that his or her child is disabled. This type of behavior impedes constructive and realistic planning for the child. Parents showing this type of behavior are in need of professional assistance in dealing with their problems.

Self-Pity

If parents are not able to develop an objective view toward their children with disabilities, self-pity is likely to develop. Questions frequently posed by parents reflecting self-pity are: What have I done to deserve this? Why me? Have I committed a sin? Why did God do this to me? Without appropriate counseling, parents may become embittered and anti-God.

This type of parental behavior may be attributed to the parents' associating the disability with some past action that he or she has been involved in, and that he or she is being punished by having a child with a disability. Until this self-pity reaction is reversed, little constructive planning can be developed to assist the child, because the parents believe that they are responsible and no amount of intervention will help.

Rejection of the Problem

Rejection of the problem is used as a defense or an excuse to deny the existence of the child. Many parents never particularly accept the child's disability. They may accept the results from the diagnosis but do not accept the prognostic implications. They believe that the disability is not permanent and that a cure will be found; they continually seek and search for professional assistance in eradicating the disability. The parent is not usually cognizant of the child's need for psychological adjustment to the desire to make him or her normal. Severe emotional reaction may develop within the child, such as a reduction in his or her self-worth and image.

Guilt, Shame, and Depression

Most parents of children with disabilities experience some guilt or shame. Guilt refers to the parents' self-condemnation, self-blame, personal disappointment, and a low self-image. These reactions by parents are designed to not recognize or compensate for their feelings of hostility and rejection created by having a child with a disability. Feelings of guilt may result in a lifetime of suffering for the parents. Shame is displayed by parents in several ways. Shame refers to how parents think that other individuals will react and what they will say about having a child with a disability. Many parents become social rejects because they cannot successfully cope with having a child with a disability. Some move constantly from neighborhood to neighborhood to avoid establishing direct relationships. Society's reactions to many parents of children with disabilities have forced them to place their children in public and private institutions. As indicated earlier, parents who experience guilt and shame often need professional assistance in order to successfully cope with their reactions. Delaying seeking professional assistance will only compound the problem and impede programs for educating the child with a disability.

Ambivalence

Negative reactions may occur when parents realize that the condition of their child cannot be reversed and the disabilities are permanent. Negative reactions vary from wishing that the child was never born or wishing that the child would die, unacknowledged hostility, and rejection. These ambivalent feelings promote reactions of guilt, which may lead to overprotection and an attempt to deny or compensate for hostile feelings, causing the parent to feel ashamed (Nicholas and Bieber, 1996). Ambivalent feelings toward children with disabilities can result in parents making unrealistic demands upon the children or becoming less tolerant of mistakes made by the child with a disability. As with most reactions, parents will need professional assistance to overcome negative overtones.

Optimism

Many parents are optimistic about their children's disabilities. Many are constantly searching for some remedy to eradicate the disability. They take their children from clinic to clinic, from one professional to another. They have not come to grips with the reality that the condition is irreversible. They simply refuse to admit that the child is permanently disabled. They do not believe that diagnostic evaluations are reflective of future (prognostic) evaluations. They believe that one day their child will be normal.

Dependency

A mother and her child with a disability may develop self-perpetuating patterns of mutual dependency. Unknowingly, the mother may develop overdependency in the child with a disability. When a parent devotes a significant part of himself or herself to the care of a child with a disability, a pattern of mutual dependency may exist. Both child and parent become dependent upon each other. Excessive care, supervision, and protection given the child by the parent may promote dependency. If care is not taken, the parent will make serving the child the center of his or her life. When dependency on the part of both parent and child persists over a period of time, the trend is difficult to reverse. Thus, increasing mutual dependency between mother and child does not promote independence and interferes with constructive programming for the child.

Attempts were made in this section to highlight some of the common reactions that parents show toward their children with disabilities. Many parents will need professional counseling and treatment to overcome many of the negative reactions projected. Chapter 4 has been reserved to outline specific treatment modalities to assist parents in working successfully with their children with disabilities.

IMPACT OF GRANDPARENTS

Grandparents may be a valuable resource to the family by assisting with care and supervision of the disabled child. Grandparents' experiences and knowledge may be used to offset many of the problems imposed by the disabled child. They may also assist in transporting the children to services provided by the community, as well as providing emotional support to the parents. Most grandparents will rise to the occasion and assist the family in any area needed. There are, however, some grandparents who have difficulty accepting their disabled grandchildren and may deny that a disability exists (Seligman, 2000). Those grandparents who voice strong negative reactions toward the parents and their grandchildren cause discord in the family unit. These grandparents will need psychological intervention to enable them to overcome negative behaviors (www.nichcy.org/pubs/genresc/gr2.htm provides sources that grandparents can contact for information).

BONDING AND UNITING FAMILIES

Since disabilities are often difficult to detect, prior to their identification, families may be intolerant of their children's behavior. Even after disabilities are identified, deficits in children's academic and behavioral skills and unsatisfactory school experiences may contribute to increased levels of parental stress (Dyson, 1996). An inadequate understanding of their children's disabilities may lead parents to believe their children's failure is due to a lack of ability, stubbornness, willfulness, or lack of effort. Research findings by Chapman and Moersma, as cited in Walther-Thomas, Hazel, Schumaker, Vernon, and Deschler, 1991; Meirer, as cited in Walther-Thomas et al., 1991; and Siegel, as cited in Walther-Thomas et al., 1991, all support Dyson's view. Consequently, parents may develop inappropriate expectations or overprotective or indulgent behaviors that could have a negative impact on the child's success.

Some useful strategies to employ in bonding families:

- Keep the family unit concerning services and support in the community available to aid the disabled individual.

- Do not place undue burden on normal siblings to care for their disabled siblings.
- Involve the total family in counseling and therapeutic treatment in order that they may be understanding and be sensitive to the needs of the disabled child.
- Develop procedures for dealing with sibling rivalry.
- Explain to the sibling the nature and cause of the disability.
- Involve the total family in activities; denote role and responsibilities that the disabled child is able to perform.
- Provide strategies and activities for normal siblings to react with their disabled siblings.

SUMMARY

The age of onset, intensity, and complexity of the disability and financial resources of the parents are some factors associated with how parents will react to the disabilities of their children. Most parents react negatively to the birth of a child with a disability. Generally, children with disabilities are perceived as a disappointment and a direct blow to the ego of most parents.

When parents begin to relate their own past to the reason for having children with disabilities, the consequences may be devastating. They may assume that they are being punished for some act which they committed. These strong emotions impede constructive assistance that might normally be given to the children and may lead to defensive behaviors on the part of the parents. These behaviors frequently result in a denial of the existence of a disability and are associated with a term called "defense mechanism."

Parents have few problems maintaining a defense mechanism approach while the child is young; they simply keep him or her out of the public view. All they have to do during the early years is to convince themselves that there is no disabling condition in their child. As the child becomes older, it becomes extremely difficult to keep the child hidden from the public view, due to school and situations in the community. Strategies which operate during the early years will no longer suffice. Additional strategies must be enacted to maintain the self-deception of the parents. At this point, the parents may need professional services to aid them to cope with the reality of the situation.

The immediate and extended family should be involved in counseling. Families should be provided with current diagnostic information relevant to the child's disability, as well as strategies for dealing with their attitudes and negative feelings. The counselor must deal with the family's multiplicity of fears and anxieties of guilt and shame displayed by many parents. Attempts should be made to reduce the tensions imposed by the child with a disability through providing activities which will increase the tolerance levels and modify the behaviors of the family members. Parents should be provided with information to help them understand that some children with disabilities can potentially become independent adults. (Refer to chapter 4 for recommended counseling techniques.)

Counseling Parents

Effective counseling techniques can do much to inform parents about the nature, extent, and implications of their children's disabling conditions. Further, many of the emotional strains, conflicts, and resulting unhappiness can be significantly reduced with professional counseling strategies. A first step should be to conduct a needs assessment of the parents. Once conducted, teachers and educators will have factual data for conducting counseling sessions to reduce, minimize, or eradicate problems.

Table 4.1 was constructed as a sample to elicit information from parents relevant to securing information and/or services for their children with disabilities. Once the data in table 4.1 are analyzed, responses may be categorized, ranked, or assigned priorities. Informational sessions and conferences may be scheduled to address the problems in a variety of individual and group sessions as reflected in chapter 10. Parents need detailed information explained in laymen's terms on treatment, intervention, and diagnostic evaluations and etiological information concerning their children. Information relevant to community facilities and services, intervention and treatment, education, related services, and other technical services should be made readily available to them. They should be made aware that their problems are not unique. Many parents have children with disabilities and are seeking ways to assist them.

TREATMENT

Diagnosis and counseling are continuing processes which should begin simultaneously. It is of prime importance that professional staff members

Table 4.1   Needs Assessment for Parents of Children with Disabilities

Name_____

Address_____

Child's Name_____

Teacher_____

Dear Parent:

We need your assistance in order to plan appropriately for your children. Please complete the survey and return it to the school as soon as possible. There are no right or wrong answers. We want your opinions on the questions listed.

  Please use the following scale in rating your responses relevant to information you need:

very much = 5, much = 4, neither = 3, little = 2, none = 1.

1. How can I aid the professionals who work with my child?
   1 2 3 4 5
2. Relationships between brothers and sisters.
   1 2 3 4 5
3. Ways of explaining disability to children, relatives, and others.
   1 2 3 4 5
4. What reward system can I use at home?
   1 2 3 4 5
5. How can I judge motor development?
   1 2 3 4 5
6. Physical, medical, and social needs of my child.
   1 2 3 4 5
7. How is my child evaluated and assessed?
   1 2 3 4 5
8. What can I do at home to help my child?
   1 2 3 4 5
9. What can I do to help my child's social and physical development?
   1 2 3 4 5
10. How infants grow and develop . . . what's normal?
    1 2 3 4 5
11. Parent-professional conferences—How can I contribute?
    1 2 3 4 5
12. Arrival of a new child in the family
    1 2 3 4 5
13. How does language develop?
    1 2 3 4 5
14. How can feeding and mealtimes be easier?
    1 2 3 4 5
15. What services are available in the community to aid my child?
    1 2 3 4 5
16. List and rate any other type of information needed.
    1 2 3 4 5

involved in the diagnostic process also be included in counseling. The importance of including parents from the inception to the conclusion of the diagnostic and treatment process cannot be overemphasized. Diagnostic information is of little use to parents unless it can be adjusted to fit into the parents' short- and long-range plans for care of the child. Parents should participate in present and future treatment plans. (Refer to appendix B for specific treatment modalities.)

Since most parents with children with disabilities suffer from some emotional conflicts, guidance and counseling are deemed important if the child is to be effectively treated. Parents must change their method of viewing the child or they will develop ego defense mechanisms such as denial, repression, or a guilt complex. Parents must be helped to deal with their feelings. Unless professional help is given, there exists a great likelihood that the emotional problems of the child will increase. For the best results, both parents should be included in the counseling process (May, 1991; Johnson, 1990; Atkinson and Juntunen, 1994).

Through various guidance and counseling techniques provided by diagnostic clinics, parents can be given professional information about their child. The information, if properly introduced, will do much to change the parents' attitudes about their child with a disability. Support and guidance by the clinic's professional staff are of vital importance in teaching the parents effective methods of dealing with the child as well as their own emotional problems. The diversity of parental problems negates that many specialists be involved in the counseling process, depending upon the unique needs of the parents. This involvement can be proliferated by including the parents in the educational process through assisting in school-related projects and guidance for helping their children with school assignments. It is of prime importance that this type of relationship be evident if the child with a disability is to achieve maximum benefit from his or her school program (Casas and Furlong, 1994).

INITIAL IMPACT

Research findings have consistently shown that virtually all parents experience some anxiety when a child with a disability is present in the family

(Seligman, 1991a). There are special problems faced by parents of children with disabilities. Parents go through many states of adjustment to the fact that their child has a disability. Awareness of the fact confirming the disability may likely cause intense subconscious anger on the part of the parents, and development of an innate pattern of parental rejection of the child. Chapter 3 explores the many dimensions of awareness. Parents often have difficulty coping with these feelings. Even the most mature parents find these subconscious reactions troublesome. While parents differ in their initial reaction, most display helplessness, grief, or guilt in varying degrees. The passage of time does not always ameliorate this condition.

The initial impact of a child with a disability can be severe and profound; parental coping can be unsuccessful or incomplete; and repeated crises may arise (Bristor, 1994). Many parents may thus suffer from poor mental health. Some of the mechanisms by which this might come about have already been indicated. For most parents of children with disabilities, there is a lack of acceptance of their child. Often the child with a disability is perceived as an intruder, and his or her relationship with his or her parents is frequently fraught with frustration, doubts, fears, guilt, and anger. These barriers combine to prevent the healthy integration of the child with a disability into the family structure (Turnbull and Turnbull, 1993).

In order for most children with disabilities to be successfully integrated into the family structure, parents will need some form of counseling. Counseling will enable the parent to view the child in a different perspective. Unless professional help is given, there exists a great likelihood that the emotional problems of both child and parents will increase. Professional personnel can serve a valuable function in showing parents how to deal effectively with their children with disabilities. It should be noted that all professionals are not trained to counsel parents of children with disabilities; however, they can serve as agents in the referring process.

COUNSELING TECHNIQUES

Theoretically, the professional therapist or counselor is the ideal person to counsel parents. The psychological problems, although different in focus, should be amenable to traditional therapeutic techniques. (Additional information is provided in appendix B.) However, there are some who are hindered by their traditional approach to therapeutic problems. Many times, parents require assistance immediately and a flexible approach involving prolonged contact may not be necessary. Research findings have indicated that short-term therapy for crisis intervention can produce effective results. The psychological state of the parents, their age, number of children, and sex of the child with a disability are some of the factors that will determine the type and degree of counseling. Therefore, the counselor/therapist should be highly trained and competent in his or her field in order that he or she might appropriately guide the parent (Bradley, Knoll, and Agosta, 1992).

Counseling for parents of children with disabilities is not designed to eradicate all of the problems that parents encounter with their children; rather, it is to provide strategies for the parents to deal more effectively with problems related to having children with disabilities.

ROLES OF PROFESSIONALS

Based upon the nature and extent of the disability, many parents may be counseled by professionals from several disciplines. Counselors should be trained to be active listeners. They must give the parents sufficient time to present their cases. Parents should be encouraged to discuss their problems and identify areas in which they need assistance, the type of services their children have had, and the expectations they have for their children's future (Brandt, 1998; Friend and Bursuck, 1996).

As indicated, many parents of children with disabilities do not understand the professional jargon used in describing most disabilities. Many parents do not understand the language used by many professionals and are frightened by the complexity of these terminologies. Effective counseling techniques and strategies should include using the vocabulary and communication level of the parents. Professionals should adapt and modify their approaches based upon the parents' level of understanding. Parents should be assured that their children will be treated as individuals, not as cases or statistics.

Parents also need counseling in accepting their children's disabilities. Counselors should provide strategies for dealing with the shame and guilt shown by many parents. Counselors and educators should be aware of the intense social pressure experienced by these parents. Some parents may become defensive and hostile due to social pressures as well as unsympathetic counselors. Counselors and educators should be patient and show understanding, acceptance, and empathy when counseling parents. By using this approach, counselors can reinforce certain behaviors of parents and reject others without forming judgmental biases or condemning relevant parental statements concerning their disabled children (Muir-Hutchinson, 1987; Turnbull and Turnbull, 1990; Gartner, Lipsky, and Turnbull, 1991; Bradley, Knoll, and Agosta, 1992; Turnbull and Turnbull, 1993).

THE ROLE OF EDUCATION AND GUIDANCE

The major role of educators in the treatment and guidance of parents of children with disabilities is to provide correct knowledge and information. When in doubt, educators should refer parents to appropriate professionals. The educator's role is not to counsel parents, but merely to direct and recommend them to professionals.

Professionals must establish the emotional levels of parents before effective treatment can be initiated. Some parents have a high level of acceptance, while others have a low acceptance level. Professionals must assess the level of acceptance and provide appropriate intervention and treatment (Shea and Bauer, 1991; Dettmer, Thurston, and Dyck, 1993).

ETIOLOGY OF THE DISABILITY

As indicated throughout this chapter, parents need to be fully apprised of the etiology and the extent of the disabilities of their children. They also need to know the extent and depth of the disabilities, the amount of sensory acuity in tact, the nature and types of treatment needed, prognostic information, and the availability of community resources. Parental understanding of the etiology of their children's disabilities provides them with a realistic view of the limitations and assets of the children. This understanding on the part of the parent can lead to realistic intervention and planning (Amlund and Kardash, 1994; Blacker, 1984; Turnbull and Turnbull, 1993).

School personnel should refer parents, in a timely manner, to the appropriate agency and well-trained and competent professionals to serve their disabled children. Early intervention and services are crucial for the child's development and the reduction of stress within the family unit. When parents discover that their children have a disability, they need time to adjust and make decisions relevant to interventional strategies for the care and treatment of their children (Darling, 1979; Gibbs and Teti, 1990; Liewellyn, Dunn, Fante, Turnbull, and Grace, 1996; Murphy, 1990).

COUNSELING FAMILIES

It has been projected throughout this chapter that the total family must be involved in the counseling process if it is to be successful. Skilled professionals certified in their respective disciplines should conduct the counseling. Educators who are not certified in counseling should not attempt to conduct sessions. The educator or teacher's role should be to provide support to the family. Coleman (1986) suggested that some parental problems are beyond the teacher's competencies and should be referred to appropriate professionals. He listed the following conditions:

- Parents experiencing a period of unusual financial difficulty, marital discord, or emotional upheaval.
- Parents routinely expressing feelings of helplessness or depression.
- Parents feeling unable to control their child.
- Parents reporting that the child is habitually in trouble with juvenile authorities.
- Parents chronically appearing to be under a high level of stress.
- Parents imposing on the teacher's time at home or school with their personal problems.

Although Coleman suggested the aforementioned conditions in 1986, they still have relevance for today. Parents have varying counseling needs. Some will be defensive, and others will be resistant to treatment because of previous treatment. Counseling techniques are designed to reduce and minimize these types of behaviors.

The total family should be involved in any treatment. Family therapy should be continued throughout the lifetime of the child and the counselor should be aware of community resources and services in the community so that he or she might make appropriate referrals. Counseling should help the family set realistic goals for their children with disabilities, as well as acknowledge their own expectations for their children.

Family therapy is designed to assist parents in understanding and coping with problems imposed by children with disabilities. Both the child and the family must be included in an affective therapy treatment program. Fine and Carson (1992) wrote that a problem is best understood and affective therapy adapted when the problem is seen as an adaptation of the child's relationship within the family.

EMOTIONAL NEEDS OF THE PARENTS

As discussed in previous paragraphs, parents display a wide range of emotional problems. The emotional reactions of parents should be fully assessed before treatment or intervention is attempted. Frequently, parents are not aware of the consequences of their emotional reactions on the child, the school, and the family. Professionals should assist parents to understand the nature, cause, and result of their psychological defense, and indicate how this defense can be minimized. The parents should be made to understand that they are not alone, but that many other parents have similar problems. Parents should be encouraged to react and participate in parent groups designed for parents of children with disabilities. Parents sharing similar problems can do much to eliminate individual problems of parents (Shea and Bauer, 1991).

Parental problems may be addressed individually or in groups. The therapist must assess the best approach for the parent. This research believes that some parents might initially be treated individually, but the long-range plan should be to involve the parents in group activities where common views can be shared and discussed. This view is supported by a preponderance of research. Group activities have proven to be highly effective for educative and guidance sessions. Additionally, group activities may serve as a method where valuable procedural methods may be shared by each parent. These group activities enable parents who have similar problems (Atkinson and Juntunen, 1994; Bradley and Knoll, 1992; Muir-Hutchinson, 1987; Coleman, 1986; Shea and Bauer, 1991).

GROUP AND INDIVIDUAL PSYCHOTHERAPY

Some parents' emotional problems are so severe that they may require group or individual psychotherapy to deal with them (Shea and Bauer; 1991; Blacker, 1984; Coleman, 1986). The more negative and withdrawn the parent is, the more likely he or she is to react in a negative way to the additional problems projected by the child with a disability. Parents who have these severe emotional reactions cannot be successfully treated through education and counseling alone. They are in need of specific treatment designed to reduce or minimize the emotional problems. Some parents may profit significantly from group psychotherapy, whereas others will need individual psychotherapy. Once assessed by the therapist, the major type of psychotherapy will depend upon the emotional problems of the parent as well as his or her personality makeup. Treatment is designed to assist the parents to achieve a satisfactory level of functioning and adjustment by learning to cope and to tolerate their symptoms. Detailed types of psychotherapy are beyond the scope of this text. The readers are referred to any basic text on psychotherapy techniques and strategies.

SUMMARY

The goals of counseling parents of children with disabilities are basically those techniques used to counsel any group. There are no separate groups of counseling techniques used to counsel parents of children with disabilities. Some modifications or adaptations of the methods employed may differ, but the basic counseling techniques and principles remain the same. Parents of children with disabilities need information relevant to their children's intellectual, social/emotional, and physical deficits, and how these deficits have impacted their disabilities. They need information relevant to community agencies and facilities which may provide care and treatment to their children, interpreting diagnostic information and terminology, dealing with accepting their children's disabilities, and strategies for involving the immediate and extended family in the counseling process. Skilled and competent counselors are needed to provide professional services to parents of children with disabilities.

Counselors or therapists have a wide variety of strategies and techniques to employ to assist parents in dealing effectively with their children with disabilities. The techniques used are based upon the assessed needs of the parents, such as group and individual psychotherapy. Therapists are trained to determine the nature and extent of the psychotherapy to be employed to assist both the child and the parents to successfully cope with problems imposed by the disabilities.

CHAPTER 5

Impact of Federal Legislation
on Parental Involvement

The passage of federal and state legislation was necessary to guarantee parents equal education opportunities for their children with disabilities. Historically, parents and associations involved with disabled individuals were responsible for state and federal legislation as well as court cases involving the education of their children. Their actions and involvement made a significant impact on practices and procedures for educating children with disabilities (Hardman, Drew, and Egan, 1996).

Two of the most importance court cases affecting the education of children with disabilities are: *Pennsylvania Association for Retarded Children v. the Commonwealth of Pennsylvania* in 1972 and *Mills v. Washington, D.C. Board of Education*. Both cases dealt with the right of disabled children to full access to a free and appropriate education. Parents and The Association for Retarded Citizens were responsible for the success in these court cases. Success of the court cases was responsible for passage of various state and federal legislation. The state and federal legislation outlined specific ways for parental involvement in the education of their children.

Several federal laws were enacted based upon the success of the court cases. Public Law 93-112, Section 504 (the Rehabilitation Act of 1973), established equal rights for all individuals with disabilities. Section 501 of the same act forbids federal departments and agencies from discrimination in employment based upon handicapping conditions. Section 502 sets standards for eliminating architectural, transportation, and attitudinal barriers confronting handicapped individuals. Section 503 mandated that federal contractors and subcontractors refrain from discriminating against handicapped individuals in employment and promotion practices (Shea, and Bauer, 1991; National Council on Disability, 1995).

Public Law 93-380 is designed to protect the educational rights legislated in Public Law 93-112. The major components involve: (1) expenditure of federal money to implement the law; (2) development of a state plan to ensure procedural safeguards for the identification, evaluation, and educational placement of handicapped children; (3) placement of exceptional children in the least restrictive educational setting capable of meeting their needs; and (4) use of parent surrogate as an advocate when the parent cannot be located.

The Buckley Amendment to Public Law 93-380 was legislated to protect the rights and privacy of students and parents. It mandated that schools cannot release information on a child without parental consent. The amendment also gave parents the right to examine school records and to challenge irrelevant information (U.S. Department of Education, 1995).

The federal laws laid the framework for the establishment of national policy, which set standards regulating federal, state, and local policies governing educational services and programs for handicapped children and their parents. Public Law 94-142 combined and made these policies operational on the national level, mandating a free, appropriate public education for all handicapped children (Turnbull and Turnbull, 1996).

PUBLIC LAW 94-142

Public Law 94-142 and other federal legislation have mandated that parents be involved in planning educational experiences for their children with disabilities. The Individualized Education Plan (IEP), which is part of P.L. 94-142, and P.L. 105-17 mandated parental involvement, from initial identification to placement of children with disabilities into educational settings. (Refer to appendix C for a summary of P.L. 105-17.)

The emphasis on P.L. 94-142 and subsequent revisions are the requirements that parental consent be obtained for any decisions made in the IEP process. Also, that parents always be informed of any steps taken in the IEP process, whether they concern pre-referral, referral, evaluation, service, treatment, progress, annual review, and/or modifications of the IEP. Parental consent is the voluntary agreement of the parent or guardian after being apprised of all information in a comprehensive form. Parent awareness and approval are essential.

The summer of 1997 also saw the passage of the new Individuals with Disabilities Education Act (IDEA), which is the major federal program for educational and related services for physically and emotionally disabled children. The new version of the law clarifies issues such as discipline, mediation, parental involvement, and the provision of related services.

PARENT PARTICIPATION IN ELIGIBILITY PLACEMENT AND ASSESSMENT DECISIONS

Under the old IDEA, parent participation was not required for making decisions regarding a student's eligibility for special education and related services. Under the new legislation, parents are specifically included as members of the group making the eligibility decision. (Refer to appendix C for additional details.)

THE NEW IDEA

Parent participation in placement decisions is similarly required. Under the old legislation, parents' involvement in deciding the placement of their child was not required. The new IDEA clarified the parents' right to be involved in such decisions. (Refer to appendices D and E for additional readings.)

Increasing the involvement of parents in the education of their children is a national goal for policy makers in both general and special education. One of the National Education Goals states that, "By the year 2000, every school will promote partnerships that will increase parental involvement and participation in promoting the social, emotional, and academic growth of children" (National Education Goals Panel, 1994, p. 1). In the Individuals with Disabilities Education Act Amendments of 1997, Congress emphasized the rights of parents to participate in decisions about their children's education based on the belief that "strengthening the role of parents and ensuring that families of such children have meaningful opportunities to participate in the education of their children at school and at home" can improve the education of children with disabilities (Section 601 © (5) (B)).

IDEA delineates several levels of parental rights regarding involvement in special education programs for students ages three through twenty-one: consent, notification, participation in educational decisions about their children, and participation in policy making. For example, before conducting an initial evaluation to decide if a child qualifies for special education services, local education agencies (LEAs) must obtain parental consent for the evaluation. LEAs must notify a child's parents of evaluation procedures that the district proposes to conduct. LEAs must give parents an opportunity to participate in the development of their child's individualized education program; parents must also be involved in decisions about the child's educational placement. When there is a disagreement about identification, evaluation, or placement of their child, parents (or the LEA) may request a due process hearing. As an example of parent involvement in policy making, IDEA requires that each state establish an advisory panel for providing policy guidance with disabilities, and the panel must include parents of children with disabilities (U.S. Department of Education, 1998b, 1998d).

The Part C program for infants and toddlers has an especially strong emphasis on family centered service delivery, recognizing the need to provide services for all members of the family, not just the child with a disability, to promote child development. IDEA requires that each infant or toddler with a disability and his or her family receive a multidisciplinary assessment of the child's unique strengths and needs and the services appropriate to meet those needs; a family directed assessment of the resources, priorities, and concerns of the family; supports and services necessary to enhance the family's capacity to meet the infant or toddler's developmental needs; and a written individualized family service plan. The latest revisions to IDEA was recently approved by the House of Representatives. The Council for Exceptional Children (CEC) is noted below.

Despite widespread opposition from CEC and other disability groups, the House approved its bill to reauthorize the Individuals with

Disabilities Education Act titled "Improving Education Results for Children with Disabilities Act."

While CEC supported some of the bill's provisions, the negatives far outweighed the positives. CEC opposed the bill's discipline provisions, the lack of mandatory full funding for special education, and the absence of support for special education research, technical assistance, and other special resources. CEC also was concerned about the bill's procedural safeguard provisions, which were intended to reduce special education lawsuits as well as the amount of special education paperwork.

The discipline provisions in the bill are particularly problematic, as they strip many of the provisions in IDEA which protect students with disabilities and ensure they receive an appropriate education. The bill's diminished discipline protections said:

- Schools would not need to determine whether or not a student's behavior resulted from his or her disability.
- A child's placement might be changed if he or she violated the school code. IDEA now says the placement of a student with a disability may be changed if a child brings a weapon or drugs to school.
- Schools do not need to perform a functional behavior assessment on students with disabilities who exhibit inappropriate behavior.
- While schools must provide educational service for students with disabilities who are suspended or expelled, the schools are not required to follow the student's IEP.

CEC is pleased to report that the bill's amendment to enact a model voucher program was defeated. CEC worked diligently to defeat this (CEC Today, 2003). The next law, P.L. 110-117, No Child Left Behind (NCLB) Act of 2001, was also designed to promote parental involvement in the schools. It permits parents to find alternate types of education for their children if satisfactory progress is not made in public schools.

According to NCLB, local school systems must notify parents if a teacher who is not highly qualified is teaching their children. Presently, this act applies only to Title 1 schools. A highly qualified teacher is one who holds a valid standard professional certificate, advanced professional certificate, or resident teacher certificate. However, certification does not make a teacher highly qualified.

Parents must be notified of the school's probationary status, and within thirty days of the school being placed on probation, the local superintendent must submit a corrective action plan detailing the behavioral intervention that will be employed within the probationary period to address the school problems. Each year that the school remains in a probationary status, the local superintendent must submit a corrective action plan to the state and notify the parents.

These legislative actions were designed to improve parental involvement and participation in their children's education. That comprehensive law gave parents direct and immediate authority to find alternative meaning of assessment and education for their children. (Specific details concerning the law may be found in appendix F.)

ROLE OF THE U.S. DEPARTMENT OF EDUCATION

To support parent involvement, the U.S. Department of Education, Office of Special Education Programs (OSEP), funds seventy-six Parents Training and Information Centers and ten Community Parent Resource Centers to provide training and information to parents of toddlers, children, and youth with disabilities and to the individuals working with these parents. The programs provide assistance and support to thousands of parents and families every year. Their goal is to empower parents to become effective advocates for their children with disabilities. In 1998, Congress appropriated over $18.5 million for these efforts.

In addition to the Parents Training and Information Centers and Community Parent Resource Centers, OSEP funds a number of model demonstration projects and research institutes in the parent involvement field. One example is the Beyond the Barriers project at the University of New Hampshire Institute on Disability. This project explores new models of community-initiated and family centered approaches to meeting the needs of young children with disabilities. Another example of OSEP's investment in parent training is Partners Plus, a model demonstration project which involved families in the design, implementation, and evaluation of respite care to serve children with disabilities from birth through age eight.

Some parents do not avail themselves of the research concerning their rights and the training designed to improve their participation and involvement. Federal laws and studies conducted by the U.S. Department of Education have eliminated many of the barriers which impede their involvement. In spite of these changes, some parents elect not to participate because they are not aware of the removal of these barriers (Finders and Lewis, 1994; Harry, 1992; Sontag and Schacht, 1994; Turnbull and Turnbull, 1996; U.S. Department of Education, 1994; Ypsilanti Public Schools, 1998). Barriers that impede parental involvement, such as language, culture, education, and employment, still exist. Strategies for dealing with some of the barriers have been adequately addressed by several authors. Hoover-Dempsey and Sandler (1995) wrote that there are several decisions that parents make before becoming involved in their children's education. The authors suggested the following factors: (1) the view of their role and involvement in education, (2) the role that they will play in assisting their children at school, and (3) the amount of time which will be required for their involvement in school. Other factors which may influence parental participation involve school personnel behavior.

Many local programs have demonstrated success in increasing the percentage of parents involved in the education of their children with disabilities. Factors found include establishing interpersonal relationships among parents and school personnel, providing professional development to familiarize service providers with the techniques for and importance of involving families, instructing families about their rights under IDEA, and using specific strategies to train and elicit active parent involvement (Cheney, Manning, and Upham, 1997; Salembier and Furney, 1997; Turnbull and Turnbull, 1990). Other factors that may inhibit parental involvement by school personnel include: (1) ignoring parental concerns, (2) not attending scheduled meetings, (3) not preparing for the meeting, (4) not seeking parental input, (5) purpose of the meeting was not well defined, and (6) not explaining technical language. These behaviors may be a particularly important influence on the involvement of racial/ethnic minority parents.

Kalyanpur and Rao (1991) found that some educators exhibited disrespect for minority parents' opinions and focused on racial/ethnic minority children's deficits; others disregarded cultural differences that character-ized parenting styles. Harry, Allen, and McLaughlin (1995) reported re-duced levels of involvement over time for African-American parents with children in early intervention programs. While these parents were gener-ally satisfied with preschool programs, they became increasingly con-cerned about stigma, classroom environment, and curriculum issues. IEP development offers another opportunity for parents to become involved in their children's education.

Special education offers many specific opportunities for parental in-volvement, including participation in initial and subsequent evaluations and annual IEP meetings. Some studies document differences in the level and types of involvement between parents of students with and without disabilities. Salisbury and Evans (1988) found that mothers of children with disabilities were "offered more opportunities to be in-volved, were more satisfied with their involvement, and felt more able to influence their child's education" than mothers of children without disabilities" (p. 268).

IEP INVOLVEMENT

When parents attend IEPs and other team meetings with school per-sonnel and professionals, a concerted effort must be made to keep the conference on a level which parents can understand so they can par-ticipate in the discussion about their child. According to Hardman, Drew, and Egan (1996), IDEA mandated the following rights for par-ents:

- To consent in writing before the child is initially evaluated.
- To consent in writing before the child is initially placed in a spe-cial education program.
- To request an independent education evaluation if the parent feels the school's evaluation is inappropriate.
- To request an evaluation at public expense, if a due process hear-ing finds that the public agency's evaluation was inappropriate.
- To participate on the committee that considers the evaluation, placement, and programming of the child.

- To inspect and review educational records and challenge information believed to be inaccurate, misleading, or in violation of the privacy or other rights of the child.
- To request a copy of information from the child's education record.
- To request a hearing concerning the school's proposal or refusal to initiate or change the identification, evaluation, or placement of the child or the provision of a free, appropriate public education.

Parental participation in developing IEPs is mandated by federal laws. (Refer to appendices C and D.) These laws cannot dictate that educators display positive attitudes toward parents. Research findings have consistently shown that negative attitudes toward parents can have a diverse affect upon their participation in IEP meetings. Educators should set the team culture by ensuring that parents are accepted as team members (Briggs, 1997; Dabkowski, 2004; Cloud, 1993; Lamorey, 2002; Horn, 1992). In essence, parents should not be collectively seated in the back or side of the conference room.

The schools have not done an effective job in meeting the federal mandates. Educators must think of an experiment with innovative ways of involving parents in the schools. Over the last several decades, the school has had a difficult time in establishing effective partnerships with parents. Much of the fragmentation has occurred because of non-involvement, hostility, or parental indifference towards the school (Harry, Allen, and McLaughlin, 1995).

If IEP team members feel that they do not have enough information to answer the above questions, then tests and other evaluative procedures would be conducted in order to gather specific information needed. If, however, they feel that sufficient data exist to address these questions, then the school system is not required to reevaluate the child. Parents must be notified of that determination, as well as their right to request that their child be reevaluated anyway. If parents request such a reevaluation, the school must conduct it. An important change in the law requires that parents give their consent before any reevaluation of the child may be conducted. If parents fail to respond to the school's request for consent, however, the school may under certain conditions proceed without it.

In order to ensure that the rights and privacy of parents and their children with disabilities are protected, federal regulations directed all state and local school districts to develop procedural safeguards for parents and their children. Due to changes in the various amendments to federal legislation, safeguard procedures have been slightly modified to meet the letter of the law. As a result, procedural safeguards are reported for both the old and new IDEA.

PROCEDURAL SAFEGUARDS: OLD LAW

Public Law 94-142 and its amendments give parents the right to "Procedural Safeguards" and the right to "Due Process" instituted for them. (Refer to appendix G for a parent due process checklist.) These procedural safeguards address the following areas:

- Records
   1. Parents have the right to examine all educational records concerning their children. These records contain the following kinds of information:
      a. Information about identification and evaluation of their children.
      b. Information about the educational placement of their children.
      c. Other information about providing a free, appropriate public education.
   2. Both the state education agency (SEA) and local education agency (LEA) must maintain a list of the types and location of information collected, maintained, and used, and must make this list available to parents upon request.
   3. An additional record must be kept of all personnel who have had access to the information collected. This record must include the name of the individual, the date, and the purpose for which the information was sought.
   4. Any personally identifiable data, information, or records collected by either the SEA or the LEA must be kept confidential.
   5. Both the SEA and the LEA have the right to charge a fee for copies made of this information, providing that the charge is

reasonable and does not prevent the exercise of rights by any party. No fee can be charged for search or retrieval of any information.

6. At any point, parents may request an amendment to the informational record kept on their child. The education agency must respond within a reasonable time to the request for an amendment. If the agency chooses not to make the amendment, they must inform the parents of their right to a hearing to challenge the record. If at the hearing, a decision is made to amend the record, the LEA must inform the parents in writing about the decision. If the decision is not to amend the educational record, parents still have the right to place an amending statement in the record. This statement will be maintained as though it were part of the original record.

7. All agencies must obtain written parental consent before any identifiable information is disclosed to anyone other than authorized personnel, or before that information is used for any purpose not required by law. Should there be a refusal of parent consent, the information cannot be disclosed.

8. Before any information is destroyed, a reasonable effort must be made to notify parents of their right to a copy.

9. At the parents' request, the SEA and LEA must destroy any personally identifiable data after it is no longer needed. A permanent record may be maintained which can only include the following information:

a. Name
b. Address
c. Phone numbers
d. Grades
e. Attendance record
f. Classes attended
g. Grade level completed
h. Year completed

- Assessments
Another area in which procedural safeguards must be maintained concerns the evaluation of children.

1. All children receiving special education services must have an educational evaluation.

2. Parents or guardians must give their written permission before their child receives an educational evaluation.

3. No single evaluation procedure can be the sole criteria for making program and/or placement decisions. Information from other sources must be considered, including information concerning physical condition, educational history, and adaptive behavior in home and school.

4. Assessment practices must not be racially or culturally discriminatory.

5. If the parents feel that their child has not had access to a fair assessment, the parents are entitled to obtain an independent evaluation at public expense. However, the LEA may initiate a hearing to show that its assessment is appropriate. If the final decision at the hearing is that the LEA assessment is appropriate, the parents still have the right to an independent evaluation, but not at public expense. Parents should exercise caution regarding independent evaluations because they can be very costly and this expense becomes the parents' responsibility if the decision at the hearing is that the LEA assessment was appropriate.

6. All rights which parents have must be available to the student when he or she reaches the age of eighteen.

- Program Planning

1. Parents have a right to know about their children's educational program. That is, parents must be notified in writing before there are any changes or attempts to change their children's educational identification, evaluation, or educational placement. Parents must be notified in writing that an Admission, Review, and Dismissal Committee (ARD Committee) is meeting to discuss their child, and that they may attend the ARD meeting. The parents must be notified early enough so that they can arrange to attend, and the meeting must be held at a time and place which is convenient for the parents. The parents may bring

whomever they wish to the meeting. Their notice must tell
them:

   a. The purpose of the meeting.
   b. The time and location of the meeting.
   c. Who will be attending.

2. The IEP is a written account of the educational programs and
   services, which the school is going to implement for the child.
   If the parents agree to the individualized educational program,
   the parents are required to sign the IEP. The school then must
   provide those services which are identified in the IEP. If parents
   ask for a copy of the IEP, the school is required to send them
   one.
3. Any information which the parent receives must be in the primary language or primary model of communication (for example, sign language). The IEP law requires that ARD Committee
   meetings and IEP meetings be held within a certain period of
   time, and that those programs and services identified on the IEP
   begin with certain timelines from initiation to annual review.

• Hearings
  If for any reason parents or guardians feel that their child is not
  being provided a free, appropriate public education, or if there is
  any disagreement between the parents and the local education
  agency regarding identification, evaluation, or educational placement, the parents or guardians have the right to a "due process
  hearing."
  Due process simply stated means fair procedure. Under the law,
  schools must use fair procedures in all matters regarding parents and
  students. Due process is one of the most important constitutional
  rights of parents and students. A due process checklist appears in appendix G.
  The rights specified will assist parents in staying on top of decisions about their children. While a due process hearing is their
  right, it can be an exhausting process. Before proceeding on this
  route, parents should have tried to resolve differences through

every other means—by being as well prepared and persuasive as possible with teachers, specialists, and administrators. If conflicting points of view cannot be resolved except by a due process hearing, parents should prepare their cases as thoroughly as possible. Parents may wish to receive advice or other assistance from any one of a number of sources including the State Department of Education, recognized associations representing disabled people, or established advocacy groups, or they may want legal consultation. The school system must advise parents of sources of free or low-cost legal aid.

The following points ensure the implementation of due process procedures for everyone:

1. The law states that local hearing is to be commenced and completed as quickly as possible, and in most states, means no later than forty-five days after there is receipt of a written request for a hearing.
2. Parents have the right to be notified in writing about the decision reached as a result of the local hearing. This written decision must be rendered within five days of the hearing and written notification of this decision must be made to the parents within five days. If parents are dissatisfied with the decision, they may appeal the decision within thirty days to the State Department of Education, for a hearing before a three-member board of independent hearing officers which will conduct an impartial review within thirty days of receipt of a written appeal and render an independent decision. These timelines operate in most states.
3. Should the decision by the State Hearing Review Board not be agreeable to the parents, they have the right to take civil action in the State or United States District Court, or any one of the three common Law Courts of the Supreme Bench.
4. The hearing shall be impartial. That is, it must be conducted by someone not employed by the agency responsible for the child's education or care. For example, any Local Education Agency employee may not serve or be considered an Impartial Hearing Officer.

5. Parents or guardians have the right to legal advice or counsel and to be accompanied by counsel at this hearing. Parents may also be accompanied by individuals who have special knowledge or training with respect to the problems of their child.

6. Parents, either themselves or through their counsel, have the right to present evidence and to question witnesses. They also have the right to compel the attendance of any witnesses with special knowledge or training about the problem of their child.

7. Both parties to the hearing have the right to prohibit the introduction of any evidence which has not been disclosed to them at least five days prior to the hearing.

8. When it seems appropriate, the child himself or herself has the right to be present.

9. When the parents or guardians wish, the hearing may be open to the public.

10. Parents have a right to a written or electronic verbatim record of the hearing at reasonable cost.

One question often raised is, What happens to the children while these decisions are pending? According to the law, the children have the right to stay in the educational program where they were originally placed before any action began. If the parents or guardians of the children are applying for initial admission to a public school program, the children may be placed in that program until all the proceedings have been completed, if the parents or guardians agree to that placement. During any of these proceedings, the educational program which is agreed upon must be provided at no cost to the parents/guardians. As with the IEP, the law requires a certain time within which these hearing procedures must take place. (See appendix H for strategies to employ when a child's behavior is a manifestation of his or her disability.)

NEW SAFEGUARD PROCEDURES

The new law (IDEA) added specific requirements regarding safeguard procedures for parents. A copy of the procedural safeguards available to the parents of a child with a disability shall be given to the parents, at a minimum:

1. upon initial evaluation;
2. upon each notification of an individualized education program meeting and upon reevaluation of the child;
3. upon registration of a complaint under subsection (b) (6).

Contents

The procedural safeguards notice shall include a full explanation of the procedural safeguards, written in the native language of the parents, unless it clearly is not feasible to do so, and written in an easily understandable manner, available under this section and under regulations promulgated by the Secretary relating to:

1. independent educational evaluation;
2. prior written notice;
3. parental consent;
4. access to educational records;
5. opportunity to present complaints;
6. the child's placement during pendency of due process proceedings;
7. procedures for students who are subject to placement in an interim alternative educational setting;
8. requirements for unilateral placement by parents of children in private schools at public expense;
9. mediation;
10. due process hearings, including requirements for disclosure of evaluation results and recommendations;
11. state-level appeals (if applicable in that state);
12. civil actions; and
13. attorneys' fees.

A. If the child's parent/guardian disagrees with a determination that the child's behavior was not a manifestation of the child's disability or with any decision regarding placement, the parent/guardian may request a hearing. The state or local educational agency shall arrange for an expedited hearing in any case described in this subsection when requested by a parent/guardian:

1. In reviewing a decision with respect to the manifestation determination, the hearing officer shall determine whether the public agency has demonstrated that the child's behavior was not a manifestation of such child's disability consistent with the requirements of paragraph (4) (C).
2. In reviewing a decision under paragraph (1) (A) (ii) to place the child in an interim alternative educational setting, the hearing officer shall apply the standards set out in paragraph (2).

   Placement during appeals. When a parent requests a hearing regarding a disciplinary action described in paragraph (1) (A) (ii) or paragraph (2) to challenge the interim alternative educational setting or the manifestation determination, the child shall remain in the interim alternative educational setting pending the decision of the hearing officer until the expiration of the time period provided for in paragraph (1) (A) (ii) or paragraph (2), whichever occurs first, unless the parent/guardian and the state or local educational agency agree otherwise.

B. Current placement. If a child is placed in an interim alternative educational setting pursuant to paragraph (1) (A) (ii) or paragraph (2), and school personnel propose to change the child's placement after expiration of the interim alternative placement, during the pendency of any proceeding to challenge the proposed change in placement, the child shall remain in the current placement (the child's placement prior to the interim alternative educational setting), except as provided in subparagraph (c).
C. Expedited hearing. If school personnel maintain that it is dangerous for the child to be in the current placement (placement prior to removal to the interim alternative education setting) during the pendency of the due process proceedings, the local educational agency may request an expedited hearing. In determining whether or not a child should be placed in another setting, the hearing officer may suggest an appropriate place.

The old IDEA was addressed earlier in the chapter. The new IDEA increased parental participation in eligibility decisions, placement, prior written notices before decisions are made, and written notices to parents in their native language (The National Information Center for Children and Youth with Disabilities, 1998; U.S. Department of Education, Individuals with Disability Education Act Amendments of 1997).

In essence, the purpose of safeguards and the due process requirements are to ensure as much as possible that all parents/guardians be an essential part of planning education and services for their children with disabilities. In the event that parents/guardians elect to participate in the planning process, the school should have records to show that attempts were made to involve them. In most school districts, parental involvement is sought in four areas:

- At the time of referral for special education: Parental notification of the meeting is usually required before any type of assessment is conducted.
- At planning conferences: Parental involvement, through their consent for approving services for their children with disabilities, is expected. If parental consent is not given because they believe the services are not appropriate, due process procedures may be implemented.
- In finalizing the educational program: Parental endorsement is needed to approve any significant changes in the student's program or related services.
- In phasing out special education or related services: Parental permission is needed to modify or cancel any special education service.

If the parent is dissatisfied with the school district's plans or the related services being provided, the parent may request an impartial due process hearing. At such a hearing, the parents and school officials may be represented by legal counsel. When a request for a due process hearing is made, an impartial hearing officer is appointed by the state education agency, and a formal hearing is held at which both sides present evidence and a verbatim transcript of the proceedings is kept. The impartial hearing officer evaluates the evidence and issues a ruling. If the parties do not wish to abide by the ruling, a state-level hearing may be requested. The impartial hearing officer makes a recommendation to the chief state school officer, who issues a ruling that is binding on all parties involved. The only recourse available to a parent or a school district beyond the state-level hearing is to take the matter to court. The process outlined above is accurate with minor variations for nearly all of the fifty states.

The due process procedure makes no presumptions of who is right or wrong in a conflict. The impartial hearing officer's role is to hear both sides and render a decision. Although the major purpose of the due process is to protect the rights of children and their parents, frequently judgments and decisions are made not supporting the parent. The impartial process is far from perfect for the following reasons:

- The process assumes that the impartial hearing officer is trained and competent in special education matters and understands the process.
- Many parents are not familiar with the process and do not know procedural safeguards mandated by law.
- Many parents do not want to get involved in a long and time-consuming process to prepare for a hearing.
- Parents who receive a favorable ruling feel that they have created negative feelings in the school district by having their cases supported.

The impartial hearing process is not perfect, but it is a first step in the due process for parents and reduces the number of special education cases going to court. Another approach in reducing the number of court cases is to train and inform parents about special education by developing partnerships between professionals and families.

DEVELOPING A PARTNERSHIP BETWEEN FAMILIES AND PROFESSIONALS

During the past twenty-five years, a significant shift in philosophy has occurred regarding the relationship between families of children with disabilities and professionals that serve them (Winton, 1994; Turnbull and Turnbull, 1996). Unlike the past, today's professionals consider the family a unit, instead of solely focusing on the mother-child dyad; they also understand there are family issues beyond those related to the child that must be addressed to effectively serve children with disabilities. Now professionals consider not only the needs of the family but also its strengths when developing educational programs that meet the child's needs. This philosophical shift has influenced the development of special education legislation and the relationship between families and professionals.

Involvement of families in decisions about their child's education is a central component of family-school collaboration (Turnbull and Turnbull, 1996). Consequently, the role that families can have in the education of their child with disabilities has evolved since the passage of P.L. 94-142. Families of school-aged children served through the IDEA, Part B, have tended to be less involved in decisions than those of infants and toddlers served under Part H. Although families of school-aged children served under Part B are entitled to participate in their child's IEP meeting, many do not. A recent longitudinal study conducted in a large urban and primarily minority school district found that parent attendance at IEP meetings decreased over a three-year period (Harry, Allen, and McLaughlin, 1995). In contrast, family participation is at the core of the Part H program. This emphasis is evident in many ways. One example is the importance given to families at the individualized family service plan (IFSP) meeting for infants and toddlers with disabilities. During these meetings, families are an integral part of the process of designing the IFSP. This perspective is, in part, an outgrowth of the systems perspective of human development which emphasizes that children with disabilities do not exist in a vacuum. To comprehend the impact of the disability, one must gain an understanding of the context of children's lives (Turnbull, Turnbull, and Shankon, 1995).

This module describes some of the changes that have occurred in parent-professional partnerships. It addresses a systems perspective of human development. This issue has been summarized in great detail in chapter 1. The remaining sections discuss the type of partnerships that have developed as a result of IDEA.

FAMILY COLLABORATION IN IDEA, PART A

In 1986, Part A of IDEA stipulated that a family centered approach be used in serving eligible children from birth to age three. Also, a commitment to the parent-professional partnership is embedded throughout the Part A regulations. Part A established the IFSP and required that professionals collaborate with families when developing a plan for the child, consider the entire family when deciding on services, and choose services that strengthen families. As part of these requirements, the IFSP documents the family's resources, priorities, and concerns related to the development of the child (34 CFR 303.344(b)).

In an attempt to measure the degree to which early intervention services are being implemented in a family centered manner, McBride, Brotherson, Joanning, Whiddon, and Demmitt (1993) conducted semi-structured interviews with fifteen families receiving early intervention services and with fourteen professionals. A major finding of the study was that time a shift toward family centered practices had occurred. All of the families stated that professionals showed concern for the family, not just the child with disabilities. Also, the professionals articulated that implementing the IFSP requirements changed their professional practice orientation from child focused to family focused. However, when describing their practice, five of the fourteen professionals discussed goals that were still based on a child-focused orientation. The study also examined the families' role in the decision-making process. Four families deferred decision making to the professionals, and three families chose to share the role. Ten families believed they could learn the most about their child by observing the professional and answering questions, and more than half the families described their role in the decision-making process as having the final veto power. Finally, many of the families stated that their emotional well-being had improved through contact with professionals who showed concern for their emotional needs and with other parents who were in a similar situation.

Another study (Bailey, Palsha, and Simeonsson, 1991) found that professionals were concerned about their changing roles. Results of a survey of 142 professionals working in early intervention programs in two states showed that professionals perceived a moderate level of competence in their ability to work with parents and a higher level of competence working with children. However, as a group, they considered their role of working with families as important. Their primary concerns were how family centered practices would affect them personally and whether they had the skills to engage in such practices. This study also suggests that the level and type of training given to professionals can significantly influence parent-professional relationships.

FAMILY COLLABORATION IN IDEA, PART B

The relationship between parents and professionals may change when children with disabilities turn three and begin preschool. For most families, the setting in which services take place changes from the home to the school. Regularly scheduled private home visits between families and professionals end. Children are served within a group setting, and parents may be invited into the child's classroom. They may take on the role of parent helper or observer. Also, school districts may transition to an IEP to develop goals and objectives for the child instead of using an IFSP to address the needs of the child and the resources, priorities, and concerns of the family. Therefore, the goals and objectives tend to become more child centered than family centered.

Typically, parents of children in primary and secondary special education programs are given less support and have less input into their child's education than parents of children from birth through age five (Winton, 1994). However, there are both informal and formal ways (e.g., IEP and individualized transition plan (ITP) meetings) to encourage parent involvement and thereby increase collaboration. Informal involvement includes the many opportunities for parent-teacher communication. This can include written notes between school and home, parent involvement in the classroom and extracurricular activities, telephone contact, technology options such as the Internet, and conferences (Turnbull and Turnbull, 1996). Increasing this communication to include the accomplishments of the child as well as the child's needs is an important part of developing collaboration.

OSEP recognizes the importance of the role that families need to play and is taking steps to promote an increase in the participation of families served through IDEA, Part B and Part H. A four-step plan to strengthen the working relationship between families and schools has been proposed. It includes: (1) increasing involvement of families in decision-making, (2) improving information available to families, (3) linking families to other resources and supports in the community, and (4) reducing adversarial dispute resolution by using mediation (U.S. Department of Education, 1995, appendix I).

THE CHALLENGE OF TRANSITION

There are several important factors to consider when providing services to families. One, as mentioned earlier, is to have an understanding of the family's perspective in order to develop a collaborative relationship between families and professionals. Another is the understanding that one of the most important factors in families' lives is the attainment of certain milestones. Often these life milestones are used to determine when services should be given. These milestones or transitions that occur during one's lifetime can be traced in a variety of ways. Two of the possibilities, as described by Mallory (1996), are developmental transitions and institutional transitions. Developmental transitions are associated with the maturational milestones an individual reaches in life, such as learning to walk or talk during the first years of life, reaching puberty, childbearing, and having children leave home. Institutional transitions mark the changes of moving from one institutional setting to another. They include events such as entering daycare; elementary, middle, or high school; college or military service; and the workforce (Morningstar and Turnbull, 1995, 1996).

Brotherson, Berdine, and Sartini (1993) and Morningstar, Turnbull, and Turnbull (1996) indicated that the transition from secondary school to adult can be very difficult for students with disabilities and their parents and families, especially when the case management, education, and related services provided through IDEA have expired. During this transition, parents must be taught effective strategies for facing this dilemma.

The timing of when to administer services can be as influential on the family as the services themselves. Social policies have emphasized institutional transitions, which are often independent from the developmental transitions. This can have negative effects on individuals with disabilities and their families. For example, the individual experiencing the transition may lose his or her locus of control and transition from setting to setting, based on institutional transitions that are dictated by social policies such as laws and regulations. The likelihood of this happening increases if the individual has a disability and an assumption is made that the individual is less capable of making his or her own decisions (Mallory, 1996). However, if there is an open dialogue and a partnership between families and professionals, the likelihood of the family or individual losing control is reduced.

Two institutional transitions in special education are the transition from IDEA, Part H, to IDEA, Part B, at age three, and the transition from school to post-school activities. These are formal opportunities for parent-professional collaboration. The Part B regulations contain provisions for a smooth transition that take place while the individual is served through Part B or ready to exit any or all Part B services (34 CFR 300.344(c)) and 300.346(b). The Part B regulations stress parent participation during IEP meetings as well as during transition periods (34 CFR 300.345). Fostering positive interactions during these meetings is especially important. Studies and testimony have shown that schools try to comply with legal mandates and procedures but have not made the effort to foster empowerment through collaboration (Green and Shinn, 1995; Turnbull and Turnbull, 1996; National Council on Disability, 1995). However, strategies for involvement are being pursued. They include increased efforts to involve families in the assessment process (Winton, 1994) and using collaborative conference techniques to increase parent and student participation.

Parent involvement can have a critical effect on the transition process from school to post-school activities. A study by Morningstar, Turnbull, and Turnbull (1996) found that families greatly influenced decisions made by students with disabilities. With regard to the transition process, students' perspectives about their vision for the future, how to plan for the future, and their self-determination were all influenced by their families. Most of the students based their career plans on input received from career planning courses in school. Although the IEP process requires transition planning (34 CFR 300.346(b)), with the current format used during IEP meetings, the majority of the students found the IEP process irrelevant. Morningstar et al. suggested that parents' and extended family members' viewpoints be incorporated into the IEP process in a more meaningful way.

SUMMARY

Parents have historically provided the force behind major changes in the field of special education. They formed local, state, and national organizations to promote the welfare of their children. They actively petitioned local, state, and federal agencies to legislate changes. Their efforts greatly assisted in passing federal legislation designed to improve the educational opportunities for all children with disabilities.

The most recent federal legislation actions (P.L. 105-17 and P.L. 107-110) have mandated the involvement of parents in the planning and implementation of individualized education programs as well as ensuring that procedural safeguards for parents are fully explained. These laws and court cases have had a significant impact upon regular and special education programs and related services.

Federal legislation also mandated that collaborative efforts be conducted between parents and professionals. Parents were no longer to sit passively and have professionals dictate educational plans for their children. The law gave parents the right to be active participants in all assessment, placement, educational, and transition services. The legislation clearly indicated and validated that involvement of parents and families in decisions about their child's education is a central component of family-school collaboration.

CHAPTER 6

Techniques for Improving Parental Involvement

Sontag and Schacht (1994) contended that there are a variety of ways that parents of children with disabilities elect to become involved in their children's education. Involvement may be launched on several fronts, between home-based activities and school events. Research findings concerning the extent to which parents participate show that three-fourths of the parents were involved in the decision-making process. Approximately one-half of all parents provided a variety of services by supplying information to other parents, coordinating services for their children, providing transportation to therapy centers, attending meetings and conferences, volunteering for a variety of school-related services, such as being actively involved in individualized education plan (IEP) meetings, assisting in evaluating special education services, supervising homework, and addressing behavior problems presented by their children (Sontag and Schacht, 1994; Harry, 1992).

According to Lynch and Stein (1982) and Turnbull (1983), historically the involvement of parents in the education of their children has not been active. Fiedler (1986) identified seven levels of parent involvement, from least to most active. They include: (1) attendance and approval of teacher priorities, (2) sharing information, (3) suggesting goals, (4) negotiating goals, (5) collaboratively analyzing and monitoring implementation, (6) joint programming, and (7) independent programming. These factors will be discussed in greater detail in chapter 10.

Parents of children with disabilities are less likely than other parents to participate in general school functions which conflict with their work schedules. Hoover-Dempsey and Sandler (1995) have provided some reasons for poor parental participation. They listed the following factors:

- Specific domains of parent skills and knowledge;
- Demands placed upon parents' time and energy;
- Working full time during the day; and
- School hours conflict with work schedules.

Several researchers claim that children's age and competence affect the nature and type of involvement of parents. Data supports the notion that parents' support for assisting their children in school decreases as involvement declines (Hoover-Dempsey and Sandler, 1997; Lareau, 1989; Salisburg and Evans, 1988; Stevenson and Baker, 1987; Yanok and Derubertis, 1989).

Concerning parental involvement in early education programs, Gavidia-Payne and Stoneman (1997) stated that perceptions of family functioning such as problem solving, communication, roles, involvement, and actively associating with other school functions were significantly related to parental participation in early prevention programs. In another study involving parents and young children with developmental delays, Coots (1998) found that parents who actively participated in home-based and school-based activities were more aware of child professionals who could assist them, familiar with school activities, knowledgeable of various ways of assisting their children, aware of the responsibilities of schools in educating their children, and aware of the importance of achievement of their children. The study also indicated that the higher the educational level of the parents, the more involved they were with school-based and home-based participation.

Parental involvement is a widely accepted practice among proponents of education. Parents can serve as partners to the teacher in the child's academic program. Henderson (1988) summed up the importance of parental involvement in the schools by stating that parents are a school's best friend. She listed several statements which have major implications for involving parents in the school: (1) the immediate family, not the school, provides the first instruction for the child; (2) parental involvement in their children's education improves the child's chances for later academic success; (3) parental involvement is most effective when it is comprehensively planned; and (4) the earlier parents become involved in their children's education, the more likely they will be involved throughout the child's academic career.

It is incumbent upon the school to understand and appreciate the importance of parental and family involvement in order to improve family/school cooperation. Individuals with disabilities cannot successfully reach their optimum level of functioning unless their parents become actively involved in their education (Taylor, 1998). Significant benefits can be derived from involving parents at any level.

It was commonly thought that parental involvement should be its strongest in the early school years, where strong foundations can be established. This view is expressed by many educators. Educators also support parental involvement and collaboration at the middle and secondary levels. Research indicates that parental support is cumulative and the earlier parents are involved, the more successful the school experiences are (White and White, 1992; Finn, 1998; Epstein, 1995; Davies, 1996; Swick and Broadway, 1997).

To be effective, parental involvement must be launched on two fronts, the home and school. Involving parents with their children's education at home augments the learning process, providing that learning strategies are collaboratively addressed by both teachers and parents. Achievement of students tends to accelerate when both teachers and parents agree on common goals and objectives to be achieved. Parents can be instructed to focus on school readiness skills and specific objectives which nurture learning.

All children benefit when parents are involved in the school; this is especially true for children with disabilities and minority children. The education level of parents should not be a prerequisite for involving parents in the school. There are many nonacademic tasks that parents can perform. All children are pleased and proud to see their parents involved in the school (Wang et al., 1996; Floyd, 1998; Clark, 1993).

Both the home and the school have a significant impact on students' attitudes. Attitudes are mostly formed at home during the early years and are reinforced by the parents as the child matures. If attitudes are not reinforced by the school, negative ones may surface and impede the achievement of students.

DEVELOPMENT OF SCHOOL POLICY

Parental involvement in school policy is essential if the school is to meet state and federal mandates involving parents. Chapter 10 is devoted to this topic. Parents should serve on all the major policy-making bodies in the school, not just the PTA. Parents should be involved in choosing textbooks, curriculum development, developing curriculum guidelines, social committees, and serving as resource individuals. Parental involvement appears most effective when parents are directly involved in all school activities that have a direct impact on their children. Parents can be effective when they define the conditions under which they serve. Specific ways should be articulated on how parents can participate in the education program. Some in-service training may be needed by parents to effectively participate in the education program (Thompson, 1998; Miller, 1998; Potter, 1996; Ohlrich, 1996).

Brandt (1998) wrote that schools cannot meet the challenges of reforms without first doing a better job of establishing rapport and connecting with parents and the public. Strategies must be developed to reestablish public support for the public schools. The Education Commission of the States—in concert with new schools—conducted a parental survey to determine views toward education. Results supported that people wanted change, but could not agree on what type or the extent of change that was needed. In order to bring about effective changes and reforms in education, views and perceptions of parents much be an essential part of the formula.

The following strategies were recommended by the Education Commission of States (1996a):

- Listen to people first, talk later.
- Expect to fail if you do not communicate well with teachers.
- Make involving parents and the community a top priority.
- Be clear about what it means to set high standards for all students, and what it will take to achieve them.
- Show how new ideas enhance, rather than replace, the old ones.
- Educate parents about the choices available to them.
- Help parents and other community members understand how students are assessed and what the results mean.

Sergiovanni's views (1996) supported the Education Commission of the States' position in that he argued that both the what and how of student learning should be decided by teachers and parents, because that is the essence of a democratic community and because the give-and-take of such discussions is what produces understanding and trust. Authenticity is essential in promoting trust between stakeholders. It is what parents desire most from the school (Rich, 1998). Educators assumed that parents expected them to be professional and businesslike, but parents actually want the opposite. Parents from all levels complained about educators talking down to them (Education Commission of the States, 1996b).

Over the last several decades, schools have had a difficult time establishing effective partnerships with parents. Much of the fragmentation has occurred because of noninvolvement, hostility, or parental indifference toward the school. Many schools serving parents of children with disabilities consider them a nuisance, unproductive, uneducated, lacking social graces, and not well-informed on education and social issues. The relationship is further strained when parents internalize negative behaviors displayed by the school. They frequently view the school as an unacceptable place, which has no interest in them as individuals. There must be a total shift in this paradigm. The school must accept these parents and provide training and assistance in desired areas if the child's educational experiences are to be effective. Parents may also reinforce the academic and social skills taught at school by teaching them at home. They may also provide the school with valuable information concerning developmental issues, safety concerns, community resources, and demonstrations. Additionally, they may serve as resource individuals.

Effective parental involvement programs acknowledge the fact that parents are a child's earliest and most influential teachers. Attempting to educate the child without parental support is akin to trying to rake leaves in a high wind.

COLLABORATIVE EFFORTS AT SCHOOL

The National Association for the Education of Young Children (NAEYC) has advocated programs to develop closer support between parents and teachers. Program goals should be developed in collaboration with families and the school staff. Parents should be equal partners in formulating, implementing, and evaluating the effectiveness of programs for their children. It is commonly recognized today by the school that parental involvement is a necessary ingredient in the education of their children.

In order to improve parental involvement in early childhood programs, Powell (1998) stated that the process requires conceptual and structural provisions that enable all staff to maintain meaningful connections with families. The following provisions are recommended:

- Early childhood programs serve families, not children alone. All policies should consider the impact that they have on the family as well as incorporate information from the family and the direct involvement of family members.
- Program practices in relating to parents must be in tune with widespread demographic changes, especially the characteristics and circumstances of families being served by the program. The cultural values, lifestyles, and customs of the families must be considered, respected, understood, and carefully integrated within the program.
- Parent and teacher confidence in each other is the foundation of healthy relationships. Strategies must be implemented to assist in training parents and using the expertise of parents in the education programs. Using this approach, a twofold purpose is accomplished: (1) Parents are assured that practices are safe and conducted by competent teachers, and (2) teachers are assured that parents' strengths and competencies have been identified and used appropriately within the educational program.
- Relations with parents should be individualized in a way that informs staff of the understandings of the work with each child. Ways of achieving the goals and objectives for children should be clearly articulated by teachers and parents. Parents and teachers should agree about content, resources, curricula, evaluation, and specific ways for achieving the stated goals and objectives of the program.
- Programs should actively acknowledge parents as persons. The dignity of all persons should be respected, regardless of class, in-

come, education, racial, or cultural values. The interests and needs of parents must be considered in any program.

- Parents' beliefs may be as important as basic support for facilitating parent participation in meetings and other activities. Parents should be encouraged to participate in meetings. Their suggestions and recommendations should be considered in making decisions relevant to educating their children.
- Definitions and assessment of the quality of an early childhood program should be made to give greater attention to parents' perspectives and to the program practices with parents and families. Parents have seldom been involved in defining and evaluating the scope of programs. They have valuable input to give and must be permitted to share their views. It is important that these views be reflected in programs.
- Professional education and credentials should promote skills in relating to parents. Professional certification of teachers must be imposed. Part of the certification of teachers should be competencies required for effective work with parents, which is the major purpose of this text. Innovative strategies should be in place to increase parental involvement in the school.

PARENTAL INVOLVEMENT IN THE SCHOOL

According to Kelley, Brown, Butler, Gittens, Taylor, and Zeller (1998), parental involvement in their child's school has been improved through looping. Looping is a process of addressing the student's behavioral and social development. On the first day of school, the student, the parent, the teacher, and the administrator implement a contract for optimal learning. The agreement specifies the roles each participant will play in the performance of the child. The process has shown a decrease in suspensions, an increase in attendance, and a healthy bond among parents, teachers, and administrators.

Parents should feel welcome at schools and should be used to augment the school program by serving as volunteers. Children are proud to see their parents involved in the schools, performing a variety of tasks. Roles of parents within the school should include more than cutting out posters, making bulletin boards, making photocopies, and

participating in bake sales. Rather, they should be included in virtually all aspects of the school program. Schoolwide involvement
should include, but not be limited to, participating in evaluating programs, conducting surveys, acting as team leaders, selecting textbooks, developing courses, developing standards for dress codes, developing new report cards, and developing technology plans.

Many of the aforementioned tasks can easily be accomplished
through what Cavarretta (1998) referred to as shared decision making—
parents, teachers, community leaders, and administrators working in
teams to resolve issues surrounding students' educational needs. The
planning team is also empowered to assist in developing the school's
curriculum and other support services needed to achieve the goals and
objectives of the curriculum.

Cavarretta (1998) summed up some problems associated with shared
decision making: It can be hard to sell to entrenched staff members who
have developed their own styles of operation; shared decision making
may challenge individuals in their comfort zone; and the so-called experts' viewpoints may be contested and challenged (refer to chapter 8
for additional information on sharing).

Parental involvement in the school can also be expedited through
scheduling periodical conferences. This will provide opportunities for
the teachers to assess the parents' skills and completeness for working
in the classroom. As the parents become familiar with the academic
programs at school, they may reinforce the skills taught to their children at home. Under supervision, the parents may develop or establish
an academic program at home to augment the school's program.

Armstrong and McPherson (1991) informed us that parental involvement is essential in assisting the school in developing appropriate
social and educational skills for individuals with disabilities. He concluded that involving parents in academic social skills homework
makes transferring of skills functional and realistic for children with
disabilities. The school should assure that parents are involved in:

- the assessment process
- instructional planning
- decision making
- evaluation

- identifying related service needs
- selecting parenting skills
- planning for support learning at home
- strategies for parental education
- ways for becoming better advocates for educational reforms

Hoover-Dempsey and Sandler's model (1995) focused on parental involvement in educating children with disabilities. (Refer to chapter 10 for additional details concerning the five steps.) The model concludes with a summary of the literature reviewed concerning parental involvement. In 1996, a National Household Education Survey was conducted concerning parental involvement in the school. Data from the survey indicated that 89 percent of the families had participated in some school-based activity. Ninety-six percent of the families who had disabled children between ages six and eleven had participated. Views concerning parents of young children's involvement in school-related activities are expressed by Lareau (1989), Mink and Nihira (1986), Salisbury and Evans (1988), Stevenson and Baker (1987), and Gavidia-Payne and Stoneman (1997). These authors concluded that children's ages and competence affect the level of parental involvement.

The nature and type of school-related activities also affect parental involvement, such as the amount of activity designed to assist the child, convenience of scheduled times, value placed on participation activities, in-service training, coordinating services, observing their children during therapy, program planning, tutoring children, and serving on policy-making bodies with the school. These factors and more have been documented to improve parental involvement in school-related activities (Sontag and Schacht, 1994; Hoover-Dempsey and Sandler, 1995; Coots, 1998; Gavidia-Payne and Stoneman, 1997; Robbins and Dunlap, 1992; Trivette, Dunst, Boyd, and Hamby, 1995; McNeil, Eyberg, Eisenstadt, Newcomb, and Funderburk, 1991).

BENEFITS TO CHILDREN

A significant body of knowledge exists which supports the notion that parental involvement promotes students' achievement (Epstein and

Hollifield, 1996; Chavkin, 1993; Eccles and Harold, 1993; Epstein, 1989, 1991, 1996; Henderson, 1987; Hess and Halloway, 1984; Hobbs et al., 1984; U.S. Department of Education, 1994). A study conducted by The National Center for Education Statistics (1998) found there were positive relationships between the father's involvement in school-related functions and school success.

Other benefits of parental involvement according to Hoover-Dempsey and Sandler (1995) are:

- Children may acquire skills beyond school-related subjects.
- Children may be motivated to do well in school.
- Involvement will assist parents in securing appropriate education for their children.

Research findings by Ames (1992) were similar to those found by Hoover-Dempsey and Sandler. The author contended that for children with learning disabilities, parental involvement had a positive impact on their academic ability. Research findings by Mundschenk and Foley (1994) claimed that children whose parents were involved in their education have a positive attitude toward learning, develop patterns for studying, and complete required homework. When parents model appropriate behaviors for their children, they are communicating that school is important and children tend to imitate these behaviors in school, and in other settings (Switzer, 1990; Cordisco and Laus, 1993).

ROLE OF THE SCHOOL

The school can promote or inhibit parental involvement in the school. Many schools have developed innovative plans for increasing the number of parents of disabled children involved in school functions. Some of the creative ways include:

- Provide professional development to parents.
- Teach families about their rights under federal regulations.
- Expand the parents' role to academic services such as tutoring children, working with groups, helping children with homework, reading to children, chaperoning, and going on field trips.

- Use specific strategies to encourage participation.
- Plan with parental input.
- Use plain language that parents can understand.
- Show respect for all minority groups.
- Seek and request information from parents concerning instructing and treating their children.
- Adjust meeting schedule to accommodate parents' schedules, such as attending PTA and IEP meetings.
- Employ and use the expertise and competencies of parents in the instructional program by providing direct instruction to children (Hoover-Dempsey and Sandler, 1995; Cheney, Manning, and Upham, 1997; Turnbull and Turnbull, 1990; Kalyanpur and Roa, 1991; Switzer, 1990; Callahan, Rademacher, and Hildreth, 1998; Mullin, Oulton, and James, 1995).

The school can also inhibit parental involvement by not listening to the parents and not involving them in the decision-making process, by not requiring school personnel to attend meetings, by presenting irrelevant information at meetings, by using technical language, by planning meetings at an inopportune time for parents to attend, and by not making parents active participants in school-related functions (Salembier and Furney, 1997; Harry, Allen, and McLaughlin, 1995).

PARENTAL INVOLVEMENT IN THE CLASSROOM

As outlined earlier in the chapter, parents who conduct academic tasks in the classroom should receive some type of advanced preparation and orientation. During this orientation, parents should be provided with the school's mission, philosophy, and educational program. Additionally, they should be apprised of: (1) class schedules, (2) school calendars, (3) official meetings, (4) resources and supplies, (5) extracurricular activities, (6) in-service training and provisions for working parents, (7) conference schedules, (8) food and snacks, (9) evaluation and progress reports, and (10) advanced notices of services needed. Many parents can serve as valuable resources. Some have expertise and competencies in selected areas, which can support the academic program (Graft and Henderson, 1997; Ohlrich, 1996; Miller, 1998; Thompson, 1998; Floyd, 1998).

IMPROVING THE INFRASTRUCTURE PLAN

Attempts have been made throughout this chapter to denote the importance of involving parents in the total school program. It is believed that to achieve this goal, the infrastructure of the school must be changed to educate and prepare parents for a variety of duties. Recommended activities and strategies should include:

- A comprehensive understanding of the learning process by parents
- A committee consisting of some parents to assess parental needs in the school
- Development of syllabi to address the goals and objectives in the various school programs
- Recommending procedures for training and educating parents on their roles and functions in developing an infrastructure plan
- Development of an assessment plan to evaluate the effectiveness of training and the infrastructure plan
- Assigning duties and responsibilities for implementing strategies and the infrastructure plan directly into the instructional plan in the classroom

PARENTAL INVOLVEMENT IN THE EDUCATIONAL PROCESS

The selection of content for any unit should be based on three broad considerations: (1) the significance of the content in attaining the purpose of the particular unit, (2) the importance of the content to society, and (3) the needs and interests of the learners. Curricula experiences, to be effective, must cover experiences under the three basic domains: cognitive, affective, and psychomotor. Parental resources should be sought, and if parents have any experiences in the listed domains, they should be employed.

PARENTAL INVOLVEMENT IN IMPROVING
ACHIEVEMENTS OF THE CHILDREN

The importance of involving parents in developing and constructing curriculum has been recognized for many years, yet their direct involvement has not been clearly evident in the school. A systematic plan is needed by teachers to assist parents in raising the achievement of their children. The following suggestions are recommended for teachers to employ to assist parents in helping their children. Teachers should encourage parents to:

- set a definite time for study each day with no interruptions;
- provide the proper environment;
- provide the materials needed;
- require the student to organize school materials;
- require a daily list of homework assignments;
- provide support and guidance, if the child becomes discouraged or frustrated.

There is no universal agreement on the impact of parental involvement in school engagement and student achievement. In-school engagement is defined as attending conferences, doing volunteer work, and attending school events, to name a few. Some research has shown negative results, others have shown some positive results (Finn, 1993; Ho and Williams, 1996; Taylor, 1996; Wolf, 1998; Whiteford, 1998).

A recent Reader's Digest poll revealed that strong families give children an edge in school. Children who socially participate with family functions scored higher on tests than those who did not. The survey also revealed that strong family ties improved self-image and confidence in children. The family is the cornerstone for success in later life. Parent education appears to play a role in how well the student performs in school.

The quality of family life appears to be a significant factor in all the groups. Children with disabilities from intact families performed better than those who lived only with their mothers. Strong family ties appear to reduce some of the anxiety faced by children with disabilities. Children with disabilities from families who attended church also scored higher on tests.

In a similar study, Plunge and Kratochwill (1995) found that parents of children with disabilities in preschool through fourth grade also exhibited high rates of participation. Results showed that 85 percent of parents were actively involved in the IEP meetings and signed the IEP. More than 70 percent of parents indicated that they often talked with the teacher about their child's progress in class, received information about how to teach their child at home, and received information about their legal rights. Other findings showed that fewer parents volunteered in class (42 percent), had a home visit (30 percent), attended parent meetings (22 percent), or helped evaluate the school's special education services (19 percent). A study conducted by Harry et al. (1995) of African-American parents' involvement in educating their children with disabilities reported high levels of participation in home-based activities assessed by the teacher.

Special education offers many specific opportunities for parental involvement, including participation in initial evaluations and annual IEP meetings. In a study conducted by Salisbury and Evans (1988), it was found that mothers of children with disabilities, regardless of the severity of the disability, were "offered more opportunities to be involved in school, were more satisfied with their involvement, and felt more able to influence their child's education" than mothers of children without disabilities (p. 268).

PARENTAL INTERVENTION AT HOME

In support of the author's views, parental involvement has been proven to be highly correlated with student achievement. Research findings have shown that differences in children's performance could be directly attributed to specific parental behaviors and interventions. High achieving students usually had parents who constantly interacted with them, created conducive home environments, provided emotional support to their children when they encountered failure, assisted children in managing and organizing their time, and actively involved themselves in their children's homework, literacy, and reading at home (Wang, Haertel, and Walberg, 1993; Finn, 1993, 1998; Masten, 1994; Penn and Lee, 1992; Astone and Lanahan, 1998; Taylor, R. D., 1996; Taylor, 1997, 1998; Ho and Williams, 1996; Edwards, 1992, 1995).

Additional research by the authors listed supports the view that children whose parents regularly converse with them on school-related matters perform better academically than children whose parents do not discuss school issues. The relationship between parent-student is significantly improved when there is joint parent-student decision making.

COMMUNITY INVOLVEMENT

Research has shown that community involvement and action can be powerful allies in transforming schools. Community involvement with the schools has been credited with: (1) improving the physical conditions and resources which support learning in the schools; (2) raising the attitudes and expectations of parents, teachers, and students; and (3) improving the depth and quality of the learning experiences of students through collaborative planning (Hatch, 1998; Shirley, 1997; Murnane and Levy, 1996; Vargas and Grose, 1998).

It is essential that parents be involved and informed about progress made toward achieving reforms. Parents are more likely to become associated with the school if educators develop a strong and trusting relationship with them. The bond can be further strengthened through making frequent contacts with the parents, conducting seminars, and sponsoring social events developed by the community.

It is important that the community assist parents as much as possible because of the emotional impact on the family. Services provided to parents by the community will impact to some degree how children with disabilities will develop, as well as provide strategies for family members to deal with the disabilities. The most important act a community can provide to families is a willingness to listen and understand what the parents are experiencing. It is essential for parents and siblings to have someone to whom they can express their feelings and receive support.

The need for direct involvement of parents and communities has been advocated by Atkinson and Juntunen (1994). They reported that school personnel must function as a school-home-community liaison. Casas and Furlong (1994) wrote that parental participation and empowerment in the community must be increased. Encourage parents to visit with other parents of children with disabilities. Most communities have support groups for parents who have disabled children. Organizations dealing with the specific disability of the child can also be helpful to the family (e.g., The Association of Retarded Citizens, United Cerebral Palsy Association). Go to www.nichcy.org/pubs/genresc/gr2.htm for a list of additional associations.

Parents need to be reassured that they are competent individuals. Encourage the parents to have a life of their own, to go out and to enjoy themselves. Offer to baby-sit so that the parents can have a period of relief. Encourage parents to use respite care facilities where children with disabilities can be cared for while parents go out, go on a trip, or run an errand.

Parents should use a variety of community resources to promote social and academic experiences, through direct participation with their children with disabilities. Participating in community activities is one way for children to have fun while gaining practical experiences with peers (Taylor, 1998). Many communities offer a variety of activities designed to build social and academic skills, such as:

- preschool story hour at the library
- water play and swimming lessons
- children's films
- holiday parades
- holiday parties
- supervised play at "tot lots"
- dance classes
- children's exhibits at museums
- special events at shopping malls
- community outreach centers
- community fairs at neighborhood schools

Parents need not only community support, they also need reliable information from professionals involving their children with disabilities.

PARENTAL GUIDELINES FOR PROMOTING SOCIAL AND ACADEMIC GROWTH

Individuals with disabilities like all children have developmental milestones in their social skills. This sequence permits parents to work with their children where there are developmental problems and to pattern the learning of social and academic skills in a more predictable manner. It is commonly agreed that parents should be provided with as much information as possible concerning their children with disabilities. Heddel (1998) recommended the following guidelines for communicating diagnostic information to parents:

- Parents should be told as soon as possible, preferably by a doctor. This information should be communicated in an appropriate place, such as an interview room or an office.
- There should be no casual observers—this is a private matter.
- Both parents should be told at the same time. It should not be left to one parent to inform the other.
- The newborn should also be in the room, if possible.
- Parents should be given time and an opportunity to ask questions, even though they may be confused and at a loss for words.
- Another interview should be scheduled, not more than a day or two later.
- Parents should be encouraged to bring questions that will inevitably come up in the interim, and should be told that another person having experienced the specific type of disability will be at the next meeting to help answer questions and suggest some sources of help. Information is also needed on strategies that parents can employ in working with their children with disabilities at home.

SUMMARY

From the very beginning, children with disabilities should have an important place within the family structure. By being responsive to children's needs, parents build the foundation for interactive social relationships. The drive for independence emerges as developmental skills grow. As your child tries to do more and more for himself or herself, he or she continues to depend on you for guidance and support. Parents delight in the small accomplishments of a child and can set expectations for larger success.

Parents of children with disabilities, as well as all parents, have a tremendous influence and impact on setting appropriate models for developing social and academic skills. The developmental sequence of tasks must be considered in social and academic training. Parents can contribute significantly to their children with disabilities' self-concept and control through appropriate modeling strategies as outlined in chapter 2.

In order for parents of children with disabilities to be effective, change agents in promoting appropriate social and academic skill development, early interventions in health care, counseling, housing, nutrition, education, and child-rearing practices, and the like must be improved. Early intervention and parental involvement are essential for preparing children to master skills and tasks successfully. This view is strongly endorsed by the National PTA.

According to the National PTA: "Over 30 years' research has proven beyond dispute the positive connection between parents' involvement and student success. Effectively engaging parents and families in the education of their children has the potential to be far more transformational than any other type of educational reform" (1997, p. 5). Parent and family involvement in their children's educational experiences is directly linked to student learning and motivation, quality schools, and effective reform strategies (Watkins, 1997; National PTA, 1997). Students whose parents are involved in their schooling demonstrate advanced academic achievement and cognitive development (Herman and Yeh, 1980).

There has been strong support from the federal government to include the family in the early educational process of their children. Parental involvement permits children to successfully manipulate their environments. The federal government created guidelines for the educational community for developing and implementing comprehensive, coordinated, and multidisciplinary interagency programs for early intervention services for infants, toddlers, and their families (Gallagher, 1998).

The role of parental participation in the education of their children with disabilities, according to much of the research in the field, has shown limited participation between the parents and the school. This view has been interpreted by many to imply that parents simply had no interest in the education of their children and participation at best was positive (Lynch and Stein, 1987). Several factors may contribute to lack of parental participation and involvement. Many parents do not feel welcome in the schools. They believe that they have little to offer in the education of their children. Cassidy (1988) reported that problems with scheduling, transportation, and knowledge of instructional program (IEP) procedures are partly responsible for poor parental participation. Parents must be actively involved in all aspects of planning, including assessment, instructional planning, program evaluation, and monitoring programs. Special efforts are needed to develop better working relations from diverse parent groups (Lynch and Stein, 1982; Turnbull, 1983; Fiedler, 1986).

The role of parents of children with disabilities in the schools must supersede the mandates of P.L. 94-142 and its amendments. Parents must feel that they are welcome in the school and be given responsibilities concerning planning and collaboration with teachers, and they must become involved in policy making. Parents should have an active role in the planning and instruction of their children and function as advocates for them if children are to profit significantly from their school experiences. Schools should experiment with various ways of improving parental participation, since parents are the foremost educators of their children.

CHAPTER 7

Promoting Cultural Awareness

Parental cultural and language backgrounds should be taken into account when planning conferences and meetings. A lack of understanding of culture and language differences can have a negative impact upon the meeting, resulting in prior goals not being achieved. Educators should provide a parent liaison with similar cultural and language backgrounds to assist in eliminating or reducing barriers to parental participation and involvement. The concept of shared vision should be evident and parents should have an active part in the decision-making process (Walker and Singer, 1993; Horn, 1992; Cloud, 1993; LaMorey, 2002; Berry and Hardman, 1998).

School-family relationships and communication can be improved through culture sensitivity. Results from research conducted by Harry (1992), Sontag and Schacht (1994), Sileo and Prater (1998), Turnbull and Turnbull (1996), and Taylor (2001) revealed that minority parents were dissatisfied with professionals' ability to appreciate and understand cultural differences. It was further indicated that through workshops and in-service developments, educators and professionals can learn about strategies and techniques to learn more about cultures in their communities and recognize their own cultural bias.

To test the above concepts, Blue-Banning, Summers, Franklin, Nelson, and Beegle (2004) designed a study using focus groups to conduct detailed interviews with families of disabled individuals from diverse cultural and language backgrounds, using qualitative research methods. Interviews were categorized and common themes listed. Themes reported included: (1) communication, (2) commitment, (3) equality, (4) skills, (5) trust, and (6) respect. Indicators were listed for each of the reported themes. In summary, the study showed that professionals need to listen and incorporate family stories concerning effective collaboration strategies, and parents need to be cognizant of professionals' views. For details of this study, the reader is referred to Blue-Banning and colleagues (2004).

Strategies should be developed or in place to permit families with different cultural and linguistic backgrounds, to fully participate in the schools. Many children who have disabilities are taught in unproductive classrooms. In a recent study conducted by Harry (1992), it was revealed that, "services for disabled individuals need to be based upon the needs of children, rather than upon their disabilities. Many minority disabled children already have the burden of battling stigmatizing labels as they struggle to move into the mainstream of life in their communities. Any system which shows that cultural differences are devalued by an educational system designed to identify deficits rather than strengths is at best erroneous or worse malicious" (p. 246). Variables such a socioeconomic status, education level, and length of residence in the country should not promote stereotyping beliefs relevant to cultures (Wayman, Lynch, and Hanson, 1990). Hyun and Fowler (1995) provided examples on how cultural awareness can be enhanced by exploring one's own cultural heritage and examining the attitudes and behaviors that are associated with one's own culture. Teachers must become familiar with the child's culture and community (Powell, 1998).

In concert with Powell's view, McGoldrick and Giordan, (1996) revealed that culture means different things to different cultural groups. These researchers believe that professionals need to be apprised of unique family characteristics in order to understand the richness of various cultures. Most cultural groups, according to the authors, are combinations of multiple groups.

If limited English is spoken, the school should have an interpreter present. An ideal person might be a leader in the cultural community, provided that the individual can speak and interpret both languages. In planning for meetings and conferences, the following steps are recommended by Hyun and Fowler (1995) and Langdon and Novak (1998):

- Decide with the parent who will participate.
- Encourage parents to bring people who are important to them.
- Send a written notice of the meeting in the parents' native language.
- Determine whether families need assistance with childcare or transportation.

Following the aforementioned steps will show respect for the parents and recognize their individual differences and cultural values. Parents need to feel that their cultural styles and language are valued knowledge, and that this knowledge is needed and welcomed in the school. The school can assist those parents by providing training programs to assist them in understanding their roles in planning and understanding their rights as mandated under federal legislation (see appendix G for some strategies). Any training program, to be successful, must incorporate the language and culture of the parents in order to prepare them to participate and contribute to the educational planning of their children (Gorman and Balter, 1997; Thorp, 1997).

Creative and innovative ways relevant to family involvement must be experimented with to improve parental involvement, especially for parents of children with disabilities (Mansbach, 1993). Factors such as: (1) diverse school experiences, (2) diverse economic and time constraints, and (3) diverse linguistic and cultural practices all combine to inhibit parental involvement. Diversity should be recognized as a strength rather than as a weakness.

DIVERSE SCHOOL EXPERIENCES

For parents whose home language or culture differs substantially from the norm may be exposed to conflicting expectations about acceptable modes of behavior. This is particularly true for parents of children with disabilities. Some culturally shaped learning is not within the acceptable

ranges for most schools. Parents confronted with so-called normal behaviors frequently remark that the behaviors of their children with disabilities are not accepted by the schools. If the schools are to effectively
serve the needs of parents from diverse cultures, radical reforms and
strategies must be developed to address the following as advocated by
Cross (1988):

- an awareness and acceptance of ethnic differences;
- self-awareness of one's personal culture;
- recognition of the dynamics of differences;
- knowledge of the family culture;
- adaptation of skills.

In summing up Cross's (1988) provisions, it should be readily recognized that changes are needed in how educators define cultures.
Strategies are also needed to address ways of adapting ones perception
toward various cultures. Educators must develop sensitivity to parents
who exhibit behaviors which are foreign to our culture and modify and
adjust the academic program to compensate for cultural differences.
The school must change the basic Eurocentric model in use out of respect for cultural diversity.

DIVERSE ECONOMIC AND TIME CONSTRAINTS

Many families of children with disabilities have limited funds, due to
factors such as the high cost of health care and maintenance. Due to
the constant care and needs of a disabled child, only one parent can
work—usually the father, if one is present in the home. Another factor deals with the type and nature of the employment. Many parents
of children with disabilities hold low-paying jobs, chiefly due to their
lack of educational training. Money earned is used to maintain the
family from day to day. These economic conditions in the family frequently take priority over concerns related to the child's education.
Thus, activities related to school, such as homework, attending meetings, volunteering, or involvement in any school activities are not
considered important by some parents. In essence, many parents feel

that the times spent with academic matters are secondary to employment. Educators should consider the aforementioned and attempt to structure activities to include parents in the schools. The notion of employing some of these parents as lunch aides, crossing guards, paraprofessionals, consultants, and resource individuals should be considered.

DIVERSE LINGUISTIC AND CULTURAL PRACTICES

Parents are accustomed to certain ways of acquiring and transmitting information. These methods are usually different from those expected by the school or less adaptive in different cultural contexts. Parents may be relatively unprepared to learn new ways of expressing themselves in languages and cultural experiences different from their own. The schools should recognize and appreciate the cultural and linguistic styles of parents. Misunderstood cultural and linguistic practices can lead to misjudging the parents' language and culture style as inappropriate (Taylor, 1998).

The school should highlight the notion that each culture and language has made significant contributions to the world. Establishing relationships and activities for parents from diverse cultural and language heritage should be encouraged and supported by the school. Multiculturalism and diversity should be accepted and respected (Atkinson and Juntunen, 1994; Casas and Furlong, 1994; Taylor, 1997, 1998).

The aforementioned research has clearly indicated the need for direct work with parents of children with disabilities. School personnel must act as a school-home-community liaison between all aspects of the multicultural environment.

PROMOTING CULTURE AWARENESS

According to Hyun and Fowler (1995), cultural understanding and awareness may be expedited by the school by developing strategies for educators to examine their own attitudes and values associated with their own and other cultures. This serves to reinforce the concept that cultures are more alike than different; there are several commonalties

among cultures. Specific strategies may be developed by the school to
improve cultural awareness of parents with children with disabilities.
Some strategies may include interviewing parents and family members,
examining their official records to verify experiences and competencies, clarifying one's attitudes toward diverse cultures, utilizing resources relevant to various cultures, developing associations with various groups and members of diverse culture groups to access materials
in languages other than English, and recruiting teachers from the same
cultural background as the children to be served.

The school should stress that each culture style is different; however,
there are similar characteristics which operate across all cultures. It is
incumbent upon the school to recognize cultural styles and how styles
determine one's behavior. School activities should reflect the richness
and contribution each culture has made to improve the human condition.

According to Sontag and Schacht (1994), a critical aspect of school-
family communication is cultural sensitivity. Minority families report
dissatisfaction with school personnel's ability to appreciate and understand cultural differences and languages. Through in-service workshops
and professional development, teachers may learn about different cultures, recognize their own cultural bias, and understand how cultural
traditions and beliefs affect interactions between parents and school personnel (Sileo and Prater, 1998; Turnbull and Turnbull, 1996). Based upon
the discussion above, school personnel may access materials for parents
in languages other than English. Employing teachers from the same
racial/ethnic background as the school's parents and children may also
enhance communication.

Barnwell and Day (1996) contend that language may interfere with
establishing rapport between the teacher and the parent. This is especially true when the parent and teacher speak different languages, or
English is not the parent's native tongue. The authors listed some
strategies to improve communication between teachers and parents
from different cultural groups. They include: (1) being familiar with
special terminology in other languages, (2) speaking in a positive tone,
(3) avoiding being judgmental, (4) making sure that parents understand critical information, repeat information if necessary, (5) providing time for parents to give suggestions for solving the problem or to

give justifications as to why the problem exists, and (6) presenting in-formation to the family in their native tongue. (Refer to appendix I.). Establishing relationships and activities for parents from a diverse cul-tural and language heritage should be encouraged and supported. Mul-ticulturalism and diversity should be accepted and respected by all (Atkinson and Juntenen, 1994; Casas and Furlong, 1994; Taylor, 1997, 1998, 2003).

Norton and Drew (1994) wrote that people of diverse cultural back-grounds have perspectives and beliefs regarding disabling conditions that may differ from those of the majority culture. The research also in-dicated that parents from some cultures have great difficulty accepting disabilities due to religious beliefs and values. The school must take these factors into consideration when planning educational activities for parents.

SUMMARY

Many parents, but especially parents of children with disabilities from minority groups, can find school an intimidating place (Lynch and Stein, 1987). Participation may be promoted by planning activities and inviting parents to school activities involving cultural experiences of their children. Cultural sensitivity on the part of the school is necessary if it is to effectively relate to the parents. Diversity should be recog-nized as a strength rather than as a weakness. Parents need to feel that their cultural styles and language are valued knowledge, and that this knowledge is needed and welcomed in the school. The school can as-sist those parents by providing training programs to assist them in un-derstanding their roles in planning for their children. Any training pro-gram, to be successful, must incorporate the language and culture of the parents in order to prepare them to participate and contribute to the ed-ucational planning of their children.

It is of prime importance that school personnel understand different cultural experiences and how they may impede or impact behaviors (Simpson, 1996). Language for example, can interfere with the rapport between the school and the parent, especially in cases where different languages are spoken or the parent has limited language ability. In cases of this nature, a translator or interpreter should be present (Barnwell and Day, 1996). Equally important, school personnel should avoid rapid speech and complex and technical language when conferring with parents. All information given to parents should be in their native tongue. School personnel should become familiar with resources in the community that may assist them. (Refer to www.nichcy.org/pubs/genresc/gr2.htm and appendix I.)

Collectively, some researchers attribute student success to parental involvement despite the adversities posed by poverty, minority status, or native language (Finn, 1993; Masten, 1994). In essence, some children succeed in spite of the environment when their parents are actively involved in school activities. On the other hand, deprived environments can have a significant impact on the achievements of children with disabilities; for instance, a home without any interesting books to read to the disabled student. Students from such deprived homes may not have the skills to be successful in reading or completing school assignments (Edwards, 1995). The educational program of the school is strengthened when the cultural values of the parents are considered in educational planning.

CHAPTER 8

Sharing Information

Parents possess information about their children which often is invaluable to the educational process. Finders and Lewis (1994) indicated that in addition to basic knowledge and information concerning their children, parents may have competencies in specific areas that they can share relevant to the instructional programs. Schools which have an open environment, and openly encourage sharing by parents, increase and enhance services offered to children with disabilities.

Covey (1989) discussed the importance of communication in parents sharing information. A first step would be for school personnel and parents to discover ways to understand each other which may lead to shared responsibilities. Communication between home and school is essential in planning effective programs for children with disabilities. A systematic shared plan improves communication and collaboration.

The following strategies are recommended by the Ohio Developmental Disabilities Planning Council (2004) for improving sharing with the home:

- At the beginning of the school year, send home a school handbook for that year. Include names and telephone numbers for community resources, parent mentors, support groups, extracurricular leaders, and parent-teacher organization (PTO) leaders. Clearly inform parents on how to get in touch with their child's teacher.
- Provide a district calendar to each family for the school year. It should indicate holidays, school events, school board meetings, PTO meetings, school telephone numbers and addresses, and

names and numbers of staff at district level and school board members.

- Exchange a daily or weekly notebook or log between home and school. Teachers generally use this technique for students who have an identified disability. However, it is useful for working on a specific goal with any child because the school and home can then reinforce each other's efforts.

- Provide parents with a preview of upcoming topics and assignments so that they can help their children prepare for those assignments or activities.

- Create a welcoming space in the school that contains materials for parents. It may include books, brochures, or videos on any topics in which parents have expressed an interest.

- Parents see school bulletin boards. They are an opportunity to share information about school projects. Photographs of children are eye-catchers.

- Keep a scrapbook or file throughout the year on each child containing art, photos, and written materials. Send it home at the end of the year to show progress and uniqueness. The teacher can compile the scrapbook from daily or weekly portfolios that he or she sends home to show the ongoing progress of the student. Returned and signed by the parents, the samples provide accurate communication about the child's progress and upon review make preparation for conferences and report cards easier for the teacher.

- Responses to parental surveys, done on at least a yearly basis, reveal needs, concerns, and accomplishments. Surveys allow the school to learn how the community perceives it, can point the way to improvement, and be the basis for celebration.

- Notes for students to take home, when they have achieved or tried hard, provide immediate reinforcement from school and communicate the child's accomplishments to the family.

- Decorated postcards mailed from school to home to mark attainment of goals are a special way to make the child feel proud and to receive communication from school. Businesses may agree to redeem these recognitions for food or merchandise.

- Similarly, schools can favorably recognize parents who show responsibility in helping their children achieve in school. Notes and computer-generated awards are inexpensive ways to do this.
- The school or a parent can regularly send press releases, preferably with photographs, to the local newspaper to inform the entire community of the school's programs and individual accomplishments. This task could become an established volunteer position.
- Ensure that messages from the school look inviting, nonthreatening, and attractive.
- See www.state.oh.us/Ohioddc for more information.

Parents and teachers must share information so that systematic planning and instructional procedures are realistic. Sharing information will assist parents and teachers to assess the origin, degree, type, and location of the problem (James, 1996). The primary reason for sharing information is to determine if the problem is in a school, home, or community one existing in several locations. Once the problem is identified, assistance can be made available. Another value of sharing information is for both parent and teacher to verify the information. Parents have a legal right to examine and contest any information relevant to their children. Chapter 5 addresses this issue in greater detail. Several sources may provide information for teachers and parents to share and validate: (1) cumulative records, (2) medical and social histories, (3) achievement test results, (4) mental abilities, and (5) physical growth and development.

These sources will provide a preponderance of information concerning children with disabilities and may be used:

- to share with parents their child's assessment information and describe his or her special and regular education programs;
- to ascertain parents' perceptions of their children and their exceptionality, as well as their special needs, prognosis, and educational programs;
- to determine parents' needs, desires, interests, and competencies in parenting their children and responding to their special needs.

Sharing information can lead to valuable insight on the part of both parent and teacher (Greer, 1996). A significant amount of information may be shared through a teacher-initiated conference, where parents may be given the opportunity to share relevant information concerning their children. A room free of distractions, where parents can feel free to discuss matters, should be provided. Most classrooms do not provide this security.

TEACHER INITIATED CONFERENCE

The teacher should have several general questions to pose to the parent during the interview, such as general demographics, physical characteristics, history of the disability, types of educational strategies and intervention that the child has been exposed to, personality traits, home and family behaviors, types of employment, if any, and other information not in the official school record, such as community services or out-of-state services.

Information can be collected and validated through the initial conference. Many learning and behavior problems can be addressed jointly by teachers and parents during this conference. Many problems can be posed and solved through collaboration. Teachers should be fully aware that regardless of the conditions in the home, the school cannot relinquish its responsibility in educating the child. Situations which profit from collaboration may be classified into the following categories:

- The student is not physically or emotionally available for learning. The physical or emotional problems are impeding learning; the parent or the teacher needs some direct intervention.
- The student needs additional exposure to facilitate learning. Reinforced practice at home in the content areas, social skills, and physical skills are needed to reinforce skills taught at school. Some parental training may be in order.
- The student's positive behavior should be reinforced. Strategies for reinforcing behavior should be a joint effort conducted by the school and home. Agreements should be made on the types of be-

haviors to enforce and the type and amount of rewards to be given for certain behaviors.

Based on information from the initial interview, several types of conferences may be needed. This issue has been given special attention in chapter 10. The following guidelines are designed to assist teachers in preparing for conferences and sharing information (Waler, 1998; Hamlett, 1997; Swideret, 1997).

- Acquire knowledge from other professionals involving the past performance of the student.
- Enlist information from school staff members to objectify information and observations.
- Collaborate on information with the family members, the education staff, community individuals, and specialists in the field to increase competence.
- Acquire and share information with community agencies concerning the child, once parental permission has been obtained or permission from a mentally able child over eighteen years old.
- Ethics procedures should be followed when sharing information within the school or agency. Parental permission is recommended when information from the classroom is shared with others within the school associated with the child's education.
- Impress upon professionals, nurse, counselor, administrators, next year's teacher, the importance of confidentiality.
- All recorded conference information should be available to parents upon request.
- Any information, which cannot be validated by parents, should be discussed and removed, if so warranted.
- Nonteaching staff and volunteers should be apprised of ethical standards for handling information.
- Requests for information from outside agencies or individuals not remotely associated with the child's educational program must include written permission from the parent to release such information.
- Personal and working notes should not be shared with others. The records should not be considered part of the child's official

records. Some type of safeguard should be in place to protect the records. In rare instances, personal notes may be shared if they will promote some aspects of the child's program.

- Information, which can be objectively verified or does not assist the student, should not be included in reports.
- To the best of his or her ability, the teacher should ensure that the protection and rights to privacy of those under his or her supervision are protected.

CONFIDENTIALITY

Information collected from sharing sessions and initial conferences related to children with disabilities must be treated in a professional and confidential manner. Information may not be distributed without parental permission. Parents should be assured that information revealed about their children will be treated as a private matter. Unless this is done, further cooperation and collaboration may be impeded. Every effort should be made to reassure parents that unless they agree to disclose specific information, what they tell is strictly confidential.

ROLE OF PROFESSIONALS

Professionals working with parents of children with disabilities should observe and heed confidential information not only out of the respect for the parents, but also because of laws which protect the rights of parents (refer to chapter 5). Consequently, many aspects of confidentiality are being reviewed and reexamined by professionals. Some of the strategies employed by professionals to apprise parents of their rights include conducting workshops and symposia on the subject. Educators need to examine their strategies for assuring confidentiality of information and take a new look at the ethics which underpin their practices.

Strickland and Turnbull (1993) may provide standards for educators to employ. They articulated that public agencies must obtain parental consent before releasing personally identifiable information to anyone other than officials of the agency. Several safeguards were listed to protect the confidentiality of information:

- Each public agency shall appoint one official with overall responsibility for ensuring confidentiality.
- Training must be provided to all persons collecting or using personally identifiable information.
- A list must be compiled and made available for public inspection by each agency containing the names and positions of all employees within the agency who may have access to personally identifiable information.

When the agency no longer needs the information, it must inform the parents that they have the option to request the destruction of the information. A permanent record without regard to time constraints, involving demographic and academic information, may be maintained. If parents have access to electronic equipment, the school can establish effective communication with them by:

- Creating an up-to-date telephone hot line that parents can call to get school information. If necessary, provide this service in different languages.
- Taking video pictures of children succeeding in school for them to share at home. (It may be necessary to obtain permission at the beginning of the school year from parents to do this.)
- Sending recorded audio tapes home with students with messages from the teacher or of the child reading. Leave room for parents to record a response message on the tape.
- Schools can share information and programs when they host a computer night at school. Parents come to learn what computer programs students use in the classroom and how they can help to follow up or individualize the activity at home.
- Contacting radio stations to help publicize school events.
- Record student achievement and activities for broadcast on the local cable TV channel.

- If parents have an electronic mail address, students and teachers can learn to use this method of communicating with home (www.state.oh.us/Ohioddc/).

IMPACT OF INFORMATION EXPLOSION

Parents who have access to the Internet may share and find information from other parents who have disabled children. The technology is a unique way of reducing isolation and finding support worldwide, as well as providing many resources for dealing with specific problems presented by having disabled children.

Technological advances and the information explosion age have made confidentiality of information an issue of concern for the relationships between individuals and institutions giving professional services and the client being served. Information electronically stored on children with disabilities can easily be retrieved by individuals other than professionals involved with the child or family. This has created serious problems in protecting privacy and human rights. Some of the changes responsible for a lack of security in confidential information may be attributed to the following factors:

- Demands on accountability for the quality of services and third-party payment practices require extensive information and personal data about individuals served. Many people not involved in direct service to clients are employed in the data gathering and evaluating process. Consequently, people know more about other people's affairs.
- Modern technology has not only made vastly increased collections of data possible, but that data is now available and easily accessible.
- Public concern is growing with the belief that professionals work in the best interest of individuals they serve. People are questioning how professionals use the information they gather about children with disabilities.
- There is increased public awareness from parents that information constitutes power. Those who know about children with disabili-

ties and their families have the power to use the information as
they wish.

• The "Rights" movement now includes the Right to Privacy, which
expresses the nation's concern about information gathered and
kept by institutions serving the disabled. Those records have the
potential for a far-reaching impact on the lives of students with
disabilities and their families. Parents can find out what information is kept and can challenge the accuracy of that information.
Schools must make ethical, logical, and responsible decisions
about data collection and storage to ensure the confidentiality of
information entrusted to them.

PRIVACY LAWS

In general, educators are in agreement with the aims of the various privacy laws. They recognize that abuses can occur in both public and
private institutions. They are equally concerned with the fact that, in order to render quality service over a long period of time, schools must
gather and share information with other professionals. It is illegal and
unethical not to protect the privacy of parents by sharing information
without parental approval. It is also unethical, though not illegal, to
withhold information from other professionals who need that information to work effectively with parents of children with disabilities.

The Code of Ethics of the National Education Association adopted
by the 1975 Representative Assembly states that, "Educators . . . shall
not disclose information about students obtained in the course of professional service . . . unless the disclosure serves a compelling professional purpose or is required by law" (Section 8, Principle 1).

Guidelines are needed by the National Education Association similar
to those posed by the American Psychological Association to assist educators in protecting privacy of information gathered through conferences
and collaborative efforts. Educators are mandated by law to secure information and to release information with parental approval. Assuring
confidentiality of information does not direct teachers and professionals
not to disclose information about students, but directs and requires teachers and professionals with certain constraints to share information with

professional individuals who need it to provide quality services to the parents of children with disabilities. Educators should be fully apprised that P.L. 94-142 guarantees confidentiality in the disclosure of information that may unnecessarily identify a student as having a disability.

SUMMARY

Most educators would agree that parents are the first teachers of their children. This view was supported by federal and state regulations, giving parents the ethical and legal right to be totally and completely involved in the education of their children. This includes sharing and validating information. Legal mandates for parental involvement have been articulated in chapter 5. At this point, an overview of the Buckley Amendment will summarize parental involvement relevant to releasing and challenging information in their children's reports.

THE BUCKLEY AMENDMENT

The Buckley Amendment to Public Law 93-380 protects the rights and privacy of all students and parents. This legislation states that schools cannot release information or a child's record without parental consent. The amendment establishes parents' rights of access to their child's school records and the right to challenge information in the records they deem inaccurate or inappropriate.

Sharing information and initial conferences are essential to educational planning and conferences. Information gained through the sharing process can be used to develop collaborative agreements between parents and teachers. Specific techniques for using shared information in collaboration are fully outlined in chapter 10.

CHAPTER 9

Reporting Progress to Parents

Reporting the progress of children with disabilities to parents requires some modification in the regular grading procedures. Modifications should be based upon the unique disability and interest of the child if needed. Many children with disabilities will not need any modifications in the grading procedures used. Any modifications made should resemble the regular grading system as much as possible. Strickland and Turnbull (1993) concluded that maintaining similar grading procedures for all students can serve to protect the student's right to confidentiality.

Federal and state regulations mandate that student records be safely stored and parental permission be obtained when records are transferred. There are numerous ways of storing records, such as in folders, file cabinets, and computerized data storage. Regardless of the method of storage, administrators should have a plan for safeguarding them. This plan should reflect local, state, and federal guidelines as well. Additionally, procedures should be adjusted based on new policies, litigation, and legislation at the local, state, or federal levels. The *Federal Register* (1997, p. 42478) states:

> Federal regulations specify the requirements relating to school records. First, the school must inform the parents when personally identifiable information is no longer needed to provide educational services to the child. Second, such information must be destroyed at the request of the parents. However, a record of the student's name, address, phone number, grade, attendance record, classes attended, grade level completed, and year completed must be maintained without these limitations.

Parental permission is needed to destroy school records associated with the education of the child. Parents may request the destruction of records for a variety of reasons, including safeguarding measures, confidentiality, and use of records. These reasons are not inclusive. Administrators should caution parents concerning the long-term consequences of destroying records and employ specific criteria for destroying records based on local, state, and federal policies.

REPORTING TO PARENTS

It is incumbent upon the teacher of children with disabilities to develop effective reporting procedures for informing parents of the progress of their children. Reports to parents can also improve communication between the home and school. There are several reporting techniques that teachers may employ to inform parents. These techniques are chosen based upon the disabilities, needs, and interests of the children with disabilities; they are by no means inclusive.

- Anecdotal Records. Anecdotal records may be used to show progress of students. A permanent type of folder, such as a spiral notebook, should be used to keep information. All relevant information concerning the student can be listed and categorized. Information listed in anecdotal records may provide information needed to justify a change in the student's academic program. Teachers should attempt to be subjective in their interpretation of behaviors.
- Work Samples. Work samples provide a way to compare a student's performance between time periods on any area or areas in his or her academic program. Students can plot their own progress by using work samples. Parents can also have an objective method to gauge their children's progress in school.
- Checklist. The teacher records critical behaviors he or she has observed in the educational setting. Information is forwarded home to the parents. The parents' signature denotes that they have read the information included in the checklist. Collective strategies can be developed by the teacher and parents to reduce or eliminate the

undesirable behavior or, in some instances, to promote positive behavior.

- Newsletters. A newsletter is an excellent communication device for apprising parents about school issues and special events to be conducted at the school. The newsletter is also useful for notifying parents that their cooperation is needed for certain school functions.
- Daily or Weekly Report Cards. These report cards inform parents about the academic progress of their children. Parents have an opportunity to respond to the report cards and to indicate ways in which they can assist the child or to make other relevant comments.
- Telephone Calls. Most telephone calls to parents are negative; instead, the teacher should have frequent positive remarks to make.
- Award System. This system awards children for their accomplishments. The nature of the disability and the interest and needs of the children are considered. No group standards are employed. The child becomes his or her own yardstick and is awarded based upon achieving his or her individualized behavior.
- Use of Cameras and Videotapes. The behaviors of students are recorded. The recordings and pictures may be used with the permission of parents. The recordings and pictures may be used by the teacher and parent to reinforce positive behaviors or to remediate negative behaviors.
- Use of Computer Technology. This technology affords rapid reporting to parents, providing the parents have the necessary computer hardware and software and are versed in their uses.
- Home Visits. Conditions in some communities do not make home visits an attractive option to many teachers. In spite of poor community conditions, some teachers visit homes. If home visits are conducted, however, they should be done before dark and another individual should accompany the teacher.

One of the first strategies advocated by Shea and Bauer (1991) is that teachers should contact the family as soon as possible using some of the listed techniques outlined earlier. The benefits of this contact can be immeasurable in that parents can: (1) inform the teacher about changes in the developmental sequence of the child, which may have an impact upon school performance, (2) assist the teacher in understanding the student's performance outside of the school, which may have an impact upon performance in school, (3) shed light on cultural differences which may be impeding the instructional program, and (4) assist in re-inforcing skills learned at school, monitoring homework. Reporting data recorded and forwarded to parents should provide for parental dis-agreement. Any disagreements can be addressed at conference time (James, 1996; Voor, 1997).

GRADING PRACTICE

Several research studies have examined the grading practices of schools related to children with disabilities. Generally, these studies have shown that the reform movement and the public outcry for im-proved grading practices have had a significant impact. When standard grading practices are employed, children with disabilities are most likely graded lower. A study of mainstream children with disabilities in the sixth and eighth grades found that these children felt helpless in their attempts to earn higher letter grades, but blamed themselves for the low grades (Selby and Murphy, 1992). Normal standards were ap-plied in grading these students. Putnan (1992) found that teacher-made tests in the sciences, social studies, math, and English did not address higher thinking or critical-thinking skills. The questions were fre-quently written using the multiple-choice format and asked at the knowledge level. Questions written at this level do little to stimu-late critical-thinking skills for children, especially those with disabili-ties. The major question that administrators of special education programs may face concerning grading students with disabilities is whether or not a different standard should be used in grading them. In our opinion, grading children with disabilities and reporting progress of children with disabilities to parents may require some modification in the regular grading procedures. Administrators can make modifications based on the unique disability and interest of the child if needed. Many children with disabilities do not need any modification in the grading procedures used. Any modifications made should resemble the regular grading system as much as possible. Strickland and Turnbull (1993) concluded that maintaining similar grading procedures for all students can serve to protect the student's right to confidentiality. State guidelines contain little information on grading. Most states give local school districts the authority to decide on how children with disabilities will be graded. However, some states are reviewing their grading policies.

Administrators must develop effective reporting procedures for informing parents of the progress of their children with disabilities. A first step will be for administrators to examine state and local regulations concerning grading practices.

Parents have the right of securing information relevant to the function of their children in school. The legal aspects of parents' rights have been addressed in chapter 5. The teacher's major responsibility is informing parents how well their children have progressed within a reporting period. Reporting periods should describe children's progress accurately and objectively. Teachers need to describe in narrative terms and provide samples of classwork so that the parents can make their own assessment of their children's work (Potter, 1998; Green, 1998).

Teachers, as indicated, have several avenues for reporting children's progress to parents. Before forwarding a report home or conducting a conference, educators should prepare an outline and include information which will reflect significant aspects of the child's behavior. Communication should be clear and concise. Language usage must be on a level which the parent can understand; If English is not the native language, attempts should be made to report to the parent in his or her native language. If this is not feasible, an interpreter should be available so that parents may effectively participate and interact with the educator. Progress reports for children with disabilities are usually long narrative descriptions of behavior, constituting numerous pages. To summarize the total report would take too much time, so the educator should select parts of the report which he or she wishes to discuss or forward home to the parents.

Frequently in conferences, educators and teachers have special concerns. These concerns may be completely independent of the information covered in the report. To avoid this type of encounter, educators should seek from parents their special interests. Another approach would be to have a planning meeting and to set the agenda at that time, or the educator can seek permission to explore an issue which in his or her opinion is common to the parents (Goldring and Hausman, 1997). Chapter 10 describes the various types of conferences and the importance of collaboration. Parents should keep in close contact with the school, regularly check their children's homework, and frequently send notes to school inquiring about the progress of their children. Parents displaying these traits are usually familiar with the school's program. These parents do not need a full conference or reporting period. Educators can simply review the major parts of the report and enlist comments from the parents. On the other hand, parents who do not frequently visit the school or keep in contact with school personnel will need additional time and information concerning the school's program and reporting system.

Most parents like a reporting system which covers all of the aspects of human behavior in the academic, social, emotional, and physical domains. Additionally, they seek information relevant to classroom behavior, normative data on performance, progress reports on growth in all areas, and preferred learning styles. As outlined earlier, some parents will need detailed information concerning the above. Others who are well informed will need little information. Educators will have to decide upon the best structure for reporting the information to the parents. Chapters 6 and 10 provide some insights.

ACADEMIC PERFORMANCE

The school should decide upon the frequency of the reporting period: it may be weekly, monthly, quarterly, or every semester. Regardless of the reporting period, parents of children with disabilities, as well as all parents, are concerned about their children's academic performance in the basic skills as well as in other subjects. Teachers should provide objective information to parents in the academic areas through conferences and the reporting period. Parents should respond to the progress report. Collectively, parents and teachers can plan to develop strategies for improving the performance or plan to upgrade or remediate the deficit areas. Planning may take place using a variety of approaches already articulated. It is the opinion of this author that a face-to-face conference is the best approach. The conference approach permits both teachers and parents to openly discuss their feelings and to come up with a collective plan to address the child's problems.

SOCIAL/EMOTIONAL DEVELOPMENT

Social/emotional competency is an important aspect of interrelationships (Taylor, 1998). The experience of interacting with others is necessary for all children, especially for children with disabilities. These children need to be acknowledged, noticed, valued, respected, and appreciated by others, and to be aware that others want the same from them. Social/emotional competency is the sum total of one's ability to interact with other people, to take appropriate social initiatives, to understand people's reactions to them, and to respond accordingly (Taylor, 1998; Woeppel, 1990; Bryan, 1990). Children with disabilities must learn to appropriately interact with others. Social/emotional skills are a continuous process; parents need to know how their children's competency measures up and how they deal with their frustrations and approach new learning tasks. The teacher's progress report can indicate needed interpersonal skills to encourage and those to limit. Parental responses and practicing social skills at home can do much to augment the teacher's social skills program.

PHYSICAL DEVELOPMENT

Many children with disabilities have severe physical problems due to deficiencies in bones, nerves, muscles, and other organs. Consequently, they are restricted from participating in many activities. Teachers should provide parents with detailed descriptions of physical activities the child can perform and provide as many physical activities as possible to assist in maintaining and developing whatever physical strength the child has. During reporting times, the teacher should discuss with the parents the strengths and weaknesses observed and a unified plan for meeting the stated activities for the child (Taylor, 1999).

Once the academic, social/emotional, and physical traits have been appropriately assessed, the next step for teachers and parents is to decide what strategies are to be implemented to achieve the stated objectives in each of the three major areas. The classroom is an excellent place for the child to demonstrate behaviors in the mental, physical, and social domains (Taylor, 1999).

CLASSROOM BEHAVIOR

Teachers need to make known to parents methods and procedures that will be employed to evaluate the child's behavior and performance. This assessment requires professional judgment on the part of the teacher to accurately and objectively report the behavior. Detailed knowledge of development norms in the areas of intelligence, social/emotional, and physical development are needed in order for the teacher to make a valid report on the child's classroom behaviors. Parents should have an opportunity to observe the child in the classroom. They should plan with the teacher strategies for improving or modifying the behavior. When communicating with parents relevant to classroom behaviors, the teacher can compare performance of the child with another child of the same age. However, some caution is in order. Children of the same age with disabilities and having the same disabling conditions may perform well above or below the normative group. The recommended approach would be to use the child as his or her own yardstick and assess his or her learning styles to progress over a certain time frame.

During reporting and conference time, the teacher should discuss with the parent the procedures used to evaluate the child, noting reasons why the child is performing above or below the expected age level of his or her peers and how the learning style was assessed. It is essential, during the conference, that the teacher accents the positive behaviors of the child and encourages the parent to reinforce those behaviors at home. Strategies should be discussed to minimize or eradicate negative behaviors. Before ending the discussion, reporting period, or conference, teachers and parents should agree on the following:

- What can be done at school and home to increase the child's performance in all academic, social/emotional, and physical development?
- What are the timelines and location for the next conference, with a possible area for discussion?
- What community resources can we use to assist us in meeting the stated objectives?
- Do we have a plan for selecting a group leader, not necessarily the teacher?
- Who will report to parents and to those who were not present at the initial conference?
- Parents should leave the meeting with a tentative progress report on how certain strategies will be achieved.
- Parents should also be apprised of the relationship between the grading pattern and graduation requirements.

GRADUATION PRACTICES

Graduation requirements for children with disabilities differ from state to state. Most states award three types of certificates to signify completion of high school, according to Podemski, Marsh, Smith, and Price and colleagues (1995): a regular diploma, a special diploma, and a certificate of attendance. The type of diploma issued is usually left up to the individual school district.

A significant number of children with disabilities at the secondary level can earn a regular diploma. For these students, awarding a special education diploma can be a source of legal dispute. A special education diploma may signify the student was not capable of meeting the graduation requirements.

SUMMARY

P.L. 94-142 and the Buckley Amendments, Sections 513 of P.L. 93-380, mandate that information collected related to children with disabilities be treated in a professional and confidential matter and not be distributed without parental permission (*Federal Register*, 1997).

Access to records by school personnel must conform to the confidentiality safeguards:

- An administrator should be appointed to monitor the use of student records and must develop safeguard procedures for protecting them.
- Training should be provided for all school personnel regarding the use of confidentiality when using student records.
- A list indicating all professionals in the school district who have access to confidential information must be developed and maintained.
- Records must be available for auditing and inspection as required by school policies and parental permission (Strickland and Turnbull, 1993).
- Information stored electronically on children with disabilities can easily be retrieved by individuals other than school or community personnel. This may create some problems for administrators charged with protecting confidential information. Consequently, school personnel must make ethical and logical decisions about data collection and storage to assure as much as possible the confidentiality of information entrusted to them.

The teachers become the central figures in grading and reporting procedures employed in their schools. They are exposed to pressures from parents, children, and the school's grading policy for children with disabilities. The teacher becomes a catalyst in the grading and reporting controversy attempting to explain the school's reporting pattern and the unfeasibility of grading children with disabilities. Research is desperately needed to shed light on this matter. However, the school should make sure that parents understand the grading and reporting procedures employed and attempt to seek community support concerning their system.

Reports have found that children with disabilities receive deviates from school district to school district, as well as from state to state. The use of reports and grades in evaluating the progress of children with disabilities is highly questionable. Much of the controversy lies in the fact that administrators in the past had no objective or scientific system to determine the achievement of children with disabilities. The lack of specificity and objectivity of outcomes to be graded and the attitudes of teachers toward pupil interest and effort reduce the validity and reliability of marks. The value of a marking system subsequently becomes dependent upon what is being marked, who is doing the marking, who is being marked, and who interprets the marks. Furthermore, marks and accompanying competitive situations can cause many undesirable traits and attitudes to develop in children with disabilities, such as insecurity, fear, anxiety, cheating, and inferiority. These factors indicate that an objective and scientific way of evaluating the growth of these children should be instituted. Rather than group evaluations, individual evaluations based upon the unique interest, abilities, disabilities, and characteristics of children with disabilities will aid in their total development. It is recommended that the approaches outlined will better provide administrators and teachers with a model that will lead to effective evaluation of the children's achievement.

There is universal agreement that parents should be regularly informed by the school concerning their children's growth and development. The major source of conflict is how this progress should be reported. Administrators should endeavor to explain their grading systems to parents and to seek their support and approval before instituting any grading pattern. Teacher/parent conferences appear to be an opportune place to explain and seek parental approval for a marking system. When the school or agency no longer needs the information, administrators must inform the parents that they have the option to request the destruction of the information. A permanent record, without regard to time constraints and containing demographic and academic information, may be maintained (Taylor, 2000).

There are many ways of reporting to parents. Some of these include report cards, use of descriptive words, checklists, narrative or letter reports, conferences, pupil self-appraisals, informal notes, telephone conversations, information meetings, or home visits. It is maintained that as long as parents and school administrators agree upon a marking pattern, and parents understand that their children's achievement is evaluated in relation to their capacities, much of the controversy over marking will be significantly reduced. Reporting can then be viewed as a suitable method of helping parents to accept their children for who they are, to understand what the school program is attempting to accomplish, and to learn how well their children are succeeding. Reporting should help strengthen a sound relationship between home and school in the guidance of the child as well as contribute to the increased effectiveness of learning.

CHAPTER 10

Strategies for Improving Collaboration

It is evident that schools cannot effectively educate students with disabilities without support and collaboration from parents. Historically, parents were not actively involved in the schools. Several reasons may be attributed to the position taken by some parents. Over the last several decades, the school has had a difficult time establishing effective partnerships with parents. Much of the fragmentation has occurred because of noninvolvement, hostility, or parental indifference toward the school. Many schools serving parents of children with disabilities consider them a nuisance, unproductive, uneducated, lacking social grace, and not well informed on educational issues. Today, due largely to federal and state legislation and local and national parental groups serving children with disabilities, the school has been forced to involve parents in all aspects of its programs (Taylor, 1999).

Parents, as well as teachers, feel the impact of disparities between home and classroom environments (Griffith, 1998). They encounter tensions between what schools expect and do and their own practices at home, both indirectly through messages that their children bring home and directly through their own interactions with teachers and other school personnel. Materials that children bring home, often in the form of homework, inform parents about their children's capabilities and engage them in forms of interaction that they would have been unlikely to initiate on their own (Powell and Diamond, 1995; Penn and Lee, 1992; Wang, Haertel, and Walberg, 1993; Gough, 1991; Clark, 1993). Parents' perspectives on home-school incompatibility have received even less attention than those of teachers. Available evidence is largely anecdotal and typically collected in conjunction with parent-focused intervention efforts.

Parents were also discussed as critical informants in teachers' efforts to interpret their students' classroom behaviors. Efforts aimed at reducing linguistic and cultural impediments to parents' involvement in their children's early education settings were widely applauded. Those familiar with such efforts reported that parents typically respond very positively to efforts to include them. When attempts at inclusion are not considered relevant to education, awkward encounters between parents and schools can occur (Masten, 1994; Casas and Furlong, 1994; Cassidy, 1988).

Issues associated with language differences between home and school are a particularly controversial topic of inquiry that, again, has largely ignored the parents' point of view (Lynch and Stein, 1987; Cummings, 1984). Research on bilingual education, for example, has focused on children's language outcomes to the neglect of effects on children's relations with their parents. Workshop participants raised concerns about the possible threat posed to non-English-speaking parents when their child's school entry coincides with immersion in English. These parents may experience two levels of loss, one associated with the children's departure from home and the other associated with fears that their ability to communicate with their children will be compromised. It is commonly recognized that most parents will need some type of plan in order to assist their children with disabilities. Standards advocated by the National PTA organization should be strongly considered.

THE PTA'S NATIONAL STANDARDS

The National PTA organization has developed new guidelines that support the need for family involvement in the schools, premised upon the belief that parents are a child's first teacher. There is a body of knowledge which supports the notion that increased parental and family involvement leads to greater student performance. This concept is supported by the National PTA. In 1997, the association developed the National Standards for Parental/Family Involvement Program to assist schools, communities, and parental groups to implement effective parent involvement programs with the goal of improving students' academic performance (Epstein, 1995).

The standards include: (1) regular communication between home and school, (2) support in parenting skills, (3) an emphasis on assisting student learning, (4) the promotion of volunteering at school, (5) parent involvement in school decision making and advocacy, and (6) collaborations with the community to provide needed resources. These standards provided the indicators used by the National PTA to recommend the following procedures for improving parent and family involvement in the school:

- Create an action team involving all stakeholders in reaching a common understanding and setting mutual goals.
- Examine current practices; survey stakeholders' perception on current practices; modify, adapt, or make recommended changes.
- Develop a plan of improvement, based upon the data generated in bullet #2.
- Develop a written parent/family involvement policy based upon the goals and mission statement.
- Secure support and financial resources needed to achieve the goals and to support the mission statement.
- Provide professional development for school/program staff. Effective updated training is essential so that stakeholders may be abreast of the latest trends and innovations.
- Evaluate and revise plan. The plan should be a fluid document and changes should be made based upon evaluative results.

According to Sullivan (1998), using the national standards as a model will permit schools, parents, and other stakeholders to develop and implement strategies to improve students' performance and encourage students to have more positive and healthier attitudes toward learning and school. Several other suggestions have been advanced by researchers in the field relevant to parental participation and collaboration (Giannetti and Sagarese, 1997, 1998; Kines, 1999; Wilson, 1997; Graves, 1996; Shea and Bauer, 1991; Perl, 1995; Ainsworth, 1996; Mills and Bulach, 1996; Marsh, 1999; Lewis and Morris, 1998; Floyd, 1998; Hatch, 1998; Whiteford, 1998; Wolf, 1998).

TACTICS FOR IMPROVING COLLABORATIVE EFFORTS

Giannetti and Sagarese (1998) recommend the following tactics for improving parental involvement and collaboration:

- Develop strategies for making parents more welcome in the school by inviting them to share their expertise with the classroom, hosting ethnic lunches, serving as chaperones, and tutoring children in academic subjects.
- Advertise your expertise by letting parents know that you are competent in your designated areas.
- Implement an early warning system to inform parents of possible problems that children may encounter and providing strategies for correcting problems or performance before the children fail.
- Accent positive behaviors of the child rather than negative behaviors when reporting or conferring with parents.
- Find a common group to converse with parents by using their ethnic, religious, and cultural values.
- Provide a safe environment by reassuring parents than their children will be safe in the classroom. Show parents some strategies that may be employed to protect their children.
- Share with parents information that their children demonstrate in the classroom. Compare behaviors shown at home with school, such as information in anecdotal records.
- Show empathy not sympathy to parents. Empathy can assist the parents in dealing realistically with the problem, whereas sympathy appears to compound the negative aspect of the problem.
- Be an effective and fair disciplinarian by applying the consequence of behavior equally to all who disregard the established rules.
- Be a consistent role model that children can imitate and model.

The National PTA Standards and the aforementioned tactics can be effectively used in planning a supportive collaborative program. These tactics can easily be employed with parents of children with disabilities with little or few modifications.

COLLABORATIVE PROBLEM SOLVING TECHNIQUES

Collaborating with parents is a continuous process. There are several structures where effective collaborative strategies may be conducted, such as problem-solving groups and discussion groups. Most problems can be effectively addressed in conference settings (Kines, 1999; Wilson, 1997; McLaughlin, 1987; Graves; 1996; Stewart, 1996). Problem Solving Groups Bradley, King-Sears, and Tessier-Switlick (1997) provided an excellent overview of promoting parental collaboration. They stated that:

> What I discovered was, no matter how skilled a teacher, how intuitive a therapist, how caring a principal, no one can know, nor have as much stake in the unique entity that is our child, as we as parents can. Therefore, we must enter into a partnership with the school system, become familiar with the terminology, and knowledgeable about our rights and responsibilities. Having entered into this partnership, I feel confident, caring, effective, responsible, resourceful, and certainly more courageous. It's not always easy, but it is always necessary. Education is a process and we are all involved in, Whether we want to be or not we will make mistakes along the way, but we cannot remain bystanders. (p. 102)

Many parents have knowledge and skills that are valuable to the education of their children, as well as to service providers. In addition, parents may possess valuable expertise in specific occupational skills, cultural norms and beliefs, languages other than English, and hobbies. Finders and Lewis (1994) support the notion that this expertise can be incorporated into the curriculum to enhance involvement. Involvement of parents can also be improved by enlisting parental cooperation through home-based intervention related to classroom instruction.

Several states have adopted programs like Family Math and Family Science to encourage parents to participate in their children's homework. Programs that allow parents and their children to work collaboratively on a project may extend the children's learning experiences and help parents to model skills and instruct their children (U.S. Department of Education, 1994). In Ypsilanti, Michigan parents are invited to attend school with their children on the second Monday in February (Ypsilanti Public Schools, 1998). Hock and Boltax (1995) wrote that Vermont adopted a collaborative model designed to enhance collaboration between parents and school personnel in the development of individualized education programs (IEPs). IEP meetings are driven by three questions: "What do we know about this child?" "What are we going to do to help this child receive an appropriate education?" "How will we know if we are succeeding?" This approach is intended to involve families more completely in the IEP process by using open-ended questions and avoiding jargon.

Parent participation and involvement with their children may be enhanced if teachers accept and acknowledge parents' knowledge of their children's strengths and weaknesses. The view of school personnel as the sole source of knowledge of children's characteristics and instructional needs weakens parental involvement and inhibits communication, which is necessary for providing appropriate services. School personnel who encourage dialogues with parents provide a structure for expressing opinions and concerns (Harry, 1992; Sontag and Schacht, 1994).

Participation and collaborations are impeded if educators do not view parents as competent but consider them a nuisance by the school. Research findings have revealed that some parental attitudes are difficult to accept by the school and the teacher. Creative ways must be initiated by the school to assist parents in changing their negative behavior. Parent-teacher conferences have been effectively used to change negative behaviors of parents (Bank, Marlowe, Reid, Patterson, and Weinrott, 1991).

Research conducted by Finders and Lewis (1994) and Sontag and Schacht (1994) revealed that parents wanted more information concerning opportunities for participation in their children's school experiences. The model is designed to promote participation and collaboration of parents. Hoover-Dempsey and Sandler (1995) summarized the literature of parental involvement. The five levels in the model included: (1) the basic involvement decision, (2) the form of involvement, (3) mechanisms for influencing children's outcomes, (4) tempering or mediating variables, and (5) child-centered outcomes. Additional research indicates that the overwhelming majority of parents of children with disabilities are involved in their children's education through meetings with teachers, volunteering at school, helping with homework, or other school- and home-based activities.

Hoover-Dempsey and Sandler (1995) summarized parental involvement in three ways by stating that: (1) Parents may model appropriate behaviors or values for children to demonstrate at home and at schools. Research supports the principle that children will imitate adult behaviors; (2) Parents can reinforce skills taught at schools by rewarding appropriate behaviors; and (3) Direct instruction may be employed by parents to improve learning (Switzer, 1990). Direct instruction is defined by McGinnis and Goldstein (1984) as a process by which direct intervention is applied to bring about a desired change in behavior.

Additionally, skills reinforced and taught at home by parents for their children are frequently transferred to other settings (Callahan, Rademacher, and Hildreth, 1998). These authors trained parents to conduct a home-based program of self-management. Results from the program showed that both the quality and quantity of homework improved. The positive results of this program may be attributed to significant parental involvement; this statement is validated by research findings from Chavkin, 1993; Eccles and Harold, 1993; Epstein, 1989, 1991, 1996; Henderson, 1987; Hess and Halloway, 1984; Hobbs et al., 1984; and the U.S. Department of Education, 1994. In a study conducted by Hoover-Dempsey and Sandler (1995) and Herr (1983), the benefits of parental involvement in the education of disabled children may be manifested in the following ways:

- Children may acquire skills and knowledge from home, community, and school.
- Children's self-esteem may improve by succeeding in school.
- Parental involvement improves school success.

School personnel may enhance levels of parent involvement by establishing ongoing relationships with them and by teaching them about their rights under IDEA. Also, family-related factors, such as children's age, parents' competence, and parents' access to resources, may also influence the levels and types of parental involvement. Parents may also assist the school by providing direct instruction, reinforcing behaviors taught at school, and improving homework performance, which in turn will enhance the children's self-confidence and ability to do well in school.

The U.S. Department of Education has added tremendously to strategies needed to improve interaction between school personnel and parents of students with disabilities. In order to improve the level of involvement, parents should inquire about the types of services that are available in the community to serve their children. Such services as family resource centers and parent training institutes may be available to assist parents (U.S. Department of Education, 1994). Family resource centers housed in school buildings may also provide parents with a positive nonthreatening school experience. The Technical Assistance Alliance for Parent Centers' web page is another valuable resource for parents. The Alliance's page provides information on legislative issues, a newsletter for parents, a list of Parent Training and Information Centers and Community Resource Centers in the United States with links to their web sites, a database of useful information for parents, and other useful links and resources. By providing such information to parents, school personnel may alter parents' perceptions of their role with regard to their children's education.

Epstein and Hollifield (1996) contended that it would be remiss to conclude that all parental involvement yields improvement in student behaviors. Such attitudes and interpersonal relationships by school personnel may reduce parental involvement. To avoid this condition, parents and school personnel should collaborate to improve the educational opportunities of the children by accepting parents' assessment of their children's strengths and weaknesses (Harry, 1992; Sontag and Schacht, 1994).

Much of the research reported on strategies to improve parental collaboration has addressed techniques for working with individual parents or groups of parents sponsored by competent professionals. There is a body of research which involves parents collaborating and solving problems through problem-solving groups

PROBLEM-SOLVING GROUPS

Parents who have similar problems related to their children may form groups to address these problems. These groups should be designed to discuss and recommend strategies for solving the problems their children with disabilities face. The teacher should assess his or her own ability to lead such a group, and if the teacher finds he or she does not have the necessary skills or training to conduct the sessions, he or she should get a competent individual, skilled in counseling, such as a counselor, social worker, or school psychologist, to conduct the meetings. The teacher should remain in the group and participate and assist in facilitating the process.

A planned systematic approach is needed for the facilitator to conduct the meeting. A first approach is to define the problem and receive universal acceptance of its definition and identification of individuals associated with the problem (refer to appendix J for a survey form to identify problem areas). The second approach should be to develop a plan for solving the problem. Group members should discuss possible solutions and identify individuals needed, time, incident, and location relevant to the problem. Key individuals, including the teacher and parent, should be requested to provide strategies to address the problem; group consensus should be required. A third approach is to implement the plan as outlined. Specific strategies are jointly developed to assist the child with a disability. Some possible strategies may be:

- that the teacher allow additional time on task;
- that the child be placed in a different group or structure;
- that additional related services be provided;
- that a special instructional procedure be implemented;
- that support is given for homework;
- that a quiet place be provided for the child to study;
- that social skills development be enforced at home;
- that appropriate community resources be identified and used.

The nature and source of the problem will determine specific strategies to implement. The above are merely suggestions, which may or may not apply to individual children.

DISCUSSION GROUPS

Discussion groups may follow the same format employed in problem-solving groups. The nature and purposes of the groups are uniquely different. As indicated in problem-solving groups, there are some group issues and problems to be jointly solved. This discussion group is based upon problems or information which have been initially agreed upon by the group. The group assembled will discuss and reach consensus about solving a problem. Each opinion is valued and considered. The teacher may initially serve as the group leader. As structure is developed, another group leader may be selected and the teacher's role may change to a resource person. For additional information concerning the purpose, objective, and structure of discussion groups, consult Shea and Bauer (1991).

PREPARATION FOR THE PROBLEM-SOLVING CONFERENCE

According to Murphy and Dillion (1998), the room used to conduct a conference should be private, free of distractions, and accessible to individuals with disabilities. Physical objects, such as desks, should not be situated between the teacher and parent. This arrangement can impede realistic and functional interpersonal relations. A more suitable arrangement is for the teacher to sit close to the parent.

Before a problem-solving conference is conducted, there is certain groundwork or preparation needed to be made by the teacher and parent. This approach improves the collaborative efforts and greatly assists in reducing or remediating the problem presented by the child. Before the problem-solving conference, the following should be considered:

- Identification of the student's behavior which needs modification.
- Determination of what strategies the teacher will use at school.
- Determination of what the parent will do at home to reinforce the teacher's program.
- Determination of the affects of the teacher's behavior on the problems.
- Determination of the affects of the parent's behavior on the problems.
- Identification of alternative strategies for solving the problems.
- Agreement on rewards and reinforcement to use in modifying behaviors.
- Development of a joint-action plan; identification of step, timing, and human and physical resources to be implemented at school and home.

- Development of follow-up strategies and an evaluation plan to evaluate the results of the conference (Perl, 1995; Ainsworth, 1969).

THE PROBLEM-SOLVING CONFERENCE

The problem-solving conference is a technique that teachers and parents can use collaboratively to solve behavior problems of children with disabilities, once rapport has been established. In the opinion of the teacher, the parent may not have the necessary skills or knowledge to actively participate. In such a case, it is strongly recommended that the teacher train the parent so that effective collaboration can begin (Mills and Bulach, 1996; Woeppel, 1990).

Problem-solving conferences should clearly indicate to teachers and parents that the child may not have problems in all segments of his or her collegial environment. A major aspect of problem solving is to determine in which environment the behavior is occurring, such as in school, in the home, or in the community. Once the environment associated with the behavior has been identified, systematic and collaborative planning can take place. The following are some guidelines for conducting problem-solving conferences:

- Describe the behavior in objectives and measurable terms.
- Outline strategies to be used to reinforce behaviors.
- Promote the use of all available information, including information from the home relevant to the problem.
- Agree that all participants have equal rights.
- Indicate how the parents may assist in the program.
- Approve of the plan with all participants endorsing it.
- Agree upon reporting and grading policy.
- Indicate specific ways for evaluating the plan based upon the results. Some indication of the next steps to be used should be outlined.

ROLE OF THE COMMUNITY

It would be grossly negligent not to explore the role and dimensions of the community in problem solving. A desirable relationship between school, home, and community is one that is marked by a strong bond of understanding and cooperation between parents and school personnel. Parents should have a direct share in deciding what problem-solving techniques appear to serve their children best. Parents should be welcome to make suggestions for the guidance of their children. Through various channels, the school can improve collaboration for children with disabilities with the cooperation of parents and the community.

It has been commonly stated that no effective program can operate successfully for children with disabilities unless there is common understanding between various segments of the community and parents. All necessary information concerning the education of the child should be collaborated with the parent. Parents and the community should have direct input into the development of a program. For teachers and related school personnel, collaboration should involve the utilization of information from parents and community to develop instructional programs (Lewis and Morris, 1998; Floyd, 1998; Hatch, 1998).

Booth and Dunne, 1996; Carey, Ruge, Buchanan, Lowe, and Munsie, 1995; and Epstein, 1991 all concurred that effective collaboration implies more than simply establishing links with the home; rather, it requires a comprehensive and permanent program of partnership with families and communities. Marsh (1999) summarized some of the values of partnership or collaboration between the home, the community, and the school. Effective partnerships or collaboration can improve:

- school climate and programs
- family support services
- parents skills and leadership
- family and community relationships
- teacher effectiveness

Researchers, advocates, parents, and educators make a number of accommodations to enhance the extent and quality of interaction between school personnel and parents of students with disabilities. In order to maximize their level of involvement, parents may require more information on the types of services that are available for their children, their rights as parents, and the school personnel's expectations for parent involvement. Family resource centers and parent training institutes may provide parents with information about special education, community resources, parenting classes, and the like. Family resource centers housed in school buildings may also provide parents with a positive, nonthreatening school experience (U.S. Department of Education, 1994). The Technical Assistance Alliance for Parent Centers' web page is another valuable resource for parents. The alliance's page provides information on legislative issues, a newsletter for parents, a list of Parent Training and Information Centers and Community Resource Centers in the United States with links to their web sites, a database of useful information for parents, and other useful links and resources. By providing such information to parents, school personnel may alter parents' perceptions of their role with regard to their children's education. (Refer to appendices B, F, and K for specific details.)

COLLABORATIVE PLANNING

Research by Thompson (1998) clearly indicated that gaining public and professional support for the school involves developing strategies that incorporate widespread participation in the development of standards by stakeholders. Some of the strategies could be designed to assist teachers in drafting district wide standards (Education Commission on the States, 1996a).

Parental leadership skill workshops should be instituted to enable parents to become active participants in developing standards and educational decisions. Stakeholders who develop standards must share mutual commitments and responsibilities. Before enacting standards, the wider community should be informed and given its endorsement. The school must show concern and respect for all participants regardless of class, education, or diversity (Davies, 1996). This approach assures that democratic views and values are considered in educational planning.

Collaborative planning should be more than mere discussions and suggestions given by stakeholders. Rather, they should be engaged in developing strategies to bring about educational reforms and changes. Research findings tend to support that home to school collaboration is essential to the academic success of students. Collaborative arrangements increase parental decision making, and provide opportunities for school personnel to support parents in assisting their children learn. Parents who have a conceptual understanding of the subject matter taught can better assist the child and augment the teacher's teaching strategies (Whiteford, 1998; Wolf, 1998).

A unique way for improving parent-teacher collaboration is to develop teams consisting of both parents and teachers. Miller (1998) offered the following suggestions for improving parent-teacher teams:

- Be in touch long before the conference.
- Be direct and personal in arranging the conference.
- Be accommodating and try not to take no for an answer. Be flexible in setting meeting times around parents' schedules.
- Be on time.
- Be prepared with handouts and work samples.
- Be specific about problems.
- Be knowledgeable as a team about each student.
- Be welcoming.
- Be in charge.
- Be supportive.
- Consider student-led conferences, which can be very effective for positive home-school relations.
- Follow up. Hold a team meeting to develop strategies for following up on recommendations from the team and assign duties and responsibilities.

Team interaction is important and essential for improving the education of children with disabilities. This interaction can better assist the team in understanding the strengths and weaknesses of the child under study. The team may also act as an advocate for the child and assure that significant support is available to enable the disabled child to achieve his or her stated objectives.

PLANNING A SUPPORT PROGRAM

Collaboration involves planning, training, and identifying one's roles and responsibilities in achieving commonly developed goals and objectives. Several steps are advocated in order for collaborative activities to be successful. A first step should be to develop a detailed collaborative plan with timelines and general guidelines for the school year. The collaborative agreement will require a great deal of brainstorming and commitment of time and resources. A second step is to implement the agreement. A general meeting is recommended before implementation to refresh ideas and suggestions and allow for any additional relevant input. Further implementation may include the following activities:

- discussion of a film, videotape, or cassette presentation
- guest speaker(s)
- a program featuring student projects from the resource room and regular classroom
- appearances by former resource room students to discuss their experiences
- a transition meeting for students and their parents
- meetings focusing on a particular theme
- a panel of parents to share their experiences and field questions
- a "Who's Who in Special Education" meeting to introduce parents to special education support staff
- role playing of home/school scenarios followed by discussions

At the who's who meeting, a special dinner might be planned to invite all participants. A panel involving the planner of the collaborative agenda may want to conduct an informational meeting. Once the plan has been submitted, a question and answer period may follow, with the panel providing specific information to clear up any points. The panel's major objectives should be to clear up any questions relevant to the plan and to offer other parents, teachers, and community individuals an opportunity to share their concerns in a conducive and productive environment (Thompson, 1998; Casas and Furlong, 1994; Davies, 1996; Clark, 1993).

A third step should be to evaluate the effectiveness of the plan by determining to what degree the stated goals and objectives were achieved. Several data sources, such as questionnaires and surveys to teachers and parents, achievement test scores, amount and type of relevant services received, types of community resources used, and a summary of all collaboration efforts, may be employed to collect data relevant to the goals and objectives. Results from the evaluation may lead to changes and modification in the plan, if the stated goals and objectives were not effectively achieved. The evaluation may also indicate the need for additional training and selection criteria for parents, educators, and community personnel. If evaluative results are negative, the negative aspects must be identified and corrected before implementation of the plan is continued.

MODEL PROGRAMS FOR IMPROVING COLLABORATION

Lewis and Morris (1998) reported on two successful programs involving parents working in the schools, the Charlotte-Mecklenburg, North Carolina, and El Paso Public Schools. Koerner (1999) also reported on a successful collaborative program in Cobb County, Georgia. Thousands volunteered in these school districts to work in the schools, many of whom were parents.

Vermont has adopted a collaborative model designed to enhance collaboration between parents and school personnel in the development of IEPs. IEP meetings are driven by three questions: "What do we know about this child?" "What are we going to do to help this child receive an appropriate education?" "How will we know if we are succeeding?" This approach is intended to involve families more completely in the IEP process by using open-ended questions and avoiding jargon (Hock and Boltax, 1995). Volunteers serve as teachers, mentors, lunch aides, lecturers, and instructors in academic subjects; prepare materials; review textbooks; cut out materials; make telephone calls; coach games; and perform a variety of other services designed by the schools. Social events were also held to unify parents, teachers, and administrators. In addition, parental involvement included conducting mediation sessions and conflict resolution strategies, donating of goods and services, staffing the school's administrative offices, and serving on advisory boards.

Another innovative approach to parental involvement is rating teachers. Some teachers may be threatened by this process, but research by Rich (1998) has shown that parental rating can introduce new concepts and ideas by providing innovative strategies to educate the children as well as providing the basis for ongoing discussions relevant to curriculum modification. Parents rated teachers on the following:

- demonstrating enjoyment in teaching;
- setting high expectations for children and assisting children in reaching them;
- demonstrating competency in the subject matter taught;
- creating a productive and safe environment for children to learn;
- utilizing effective strategies for dealing with behavior problems in a fair and just way;
- assigning meaningful homework assignments;
- understanding the principles of childhood development;
- using a variety of communicating tools to report students' progress and needs.

The issue of parental involvement in collaborative efforts in the school should not be imposed upon them by the school. Parents must feel competent in any involvement. They should have the right to choose not to be involved when they feel that their involvement will not benefit their children or that they do not have the competencies to perform the assigned tasks. In essence, the degree of parental participation should be determined by the parents' needs and interests, not by some predetermined standards set by educators. Frequently, parents are seeking ways to contribute to the schools and be involved, but the traditional ways of participating during the school day may no longer be possible. This is especially true for families where both parents work outside the home or in single-parent families. Exploring ways to engage parents is a challenge facing many schools today. Requesting parents to work on activities at home that will support the school and do not require large investments of time is a volunteer opportunity that can fit the schedules of many busy families. A model for collaboration is presented to assist parents, educators, and the community in developing an effective collaborative plan.

A MODEL FOR PARENT-TEACHER COMMUNICATION

This chapter has focused on the importance of having a systematic plan when developing a collaboration model. According to Shea and Bauer (1991), their model is essentially a prescriptive teaching methodology. Activities emphasize positive, child-raising practice and behavior-management techniques that recognize each parent and child as an individual with unique abilities, needs, and environmental influences (see table 10.1).

Implementation of the Shea and Bauer (1991) model offers a format for providing a realistic model for collaboration and infusing, integrating, and respecting individual ideas. Additionally, the model provides a mechanism whereby communication can be expedited

Table 10.1A.   The Parent-Teacher Collaboration Model

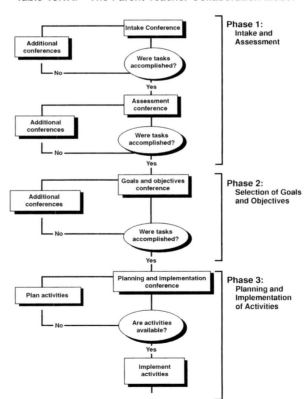

Table 10.1B.   The Parent-Teacher Collaboration Model

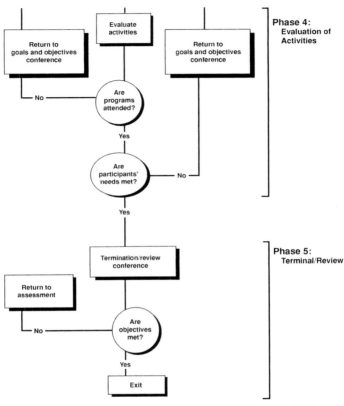

Reproduced by permission of author and publisher. For a detailed and narrative description of the model, the reader is referred to: Shea, Thomas M., and Bauer, Anne M. (1991). *Parents and Teachers of Children with Exceptionalities: A Handbook for Collaboration.* Boston, Mass.: Allyn & Bacon.

and strategies included to improve interpersonal skills. Interpersonal skills training is needed by both teachers and parents. Since teachers are the professionals, they should be aware of interpersonal skills, which will promote rather than retard communication with parents.

CONFERRING WITH PARENTS

Parents may request a conference concerning their children with disabilities for a variety of reasons. Teachers may feel apprehensive about the conference, but they should realize that, like themselves, parents also want their children to be successful, and thus view the conference as an opportunity to improve the educational opportunities for the children with disabilities. McLaughlin (1987) wrote that frequently teachers are not prepared in their training to conduct conferences, so they must learn on the job.

Parents also need to make preparations for attending a conference. According to Kines (1999), the following preparations are recommended:

- Prepare a list of topics to discuss.
- Involve the child if possible in a three-way conference.
- Be on time. It is unfair to keep others waiting; parents and teachers have busy schedules.
- Come right to the point. Clarify points to be discussed.
- Ask about class participation of the child.
- Request clarification on any issue not fully understood.
- Ask to see child's work samples.
- Talk about your child outside of school in order to inform the teacher of community and other extracurricular activities.
- Stay within the time limit. If additional time is needed, schedule another meeting or a telephone conference.
- Write a note of appreciation to the teacher, indicating the many positive things he or she has done to improve skills for the child. This can indicate an agenda for the next meeting as well.

Communication and collaboration are essential for teachers and parents if children with disabilities are to profit sufficiently from their educational experiences. According to Perl (1995), some recommended strategies for teachers to improve communication and collaboration include:

- Building Rapport—Establish the dignity and worth of the parent's contribution at the outset.
- Listening—Learn to listen actively to the parent, be attentive to responses.
- Expressing Empathy—Be aware of the nature and type of responses made by the parent, put yourself in the parent's place.
- Reflecting Affect—Attempt to reflect how the parent feels. Show empathy at the appropriate times.

- Clarifying Statements—Restate the question by asking do you mean or are you inferring a particular statement.

Parent-teacher conferences can serve useful purposes and provide invaluable information to improve the child's academic program (Fitton and Gredler, 1996; Woeppel, 1990; Edwards, 1995; Whiteford, 1998; Wolf, 1998). Consequently, a positive approach must be taken by both parents and teachers. The first step is to improve the quality of communication. Carefully planned group and individual conferences are initial ways to improve communication. A successful group conference can set the tone for the year and build a strong rapport between teachers and parents.

THE GROUP CONFERENCE

Group conferences are designed to inform a large group about relevant educational and classroom issues. Group conferences are recommended over individual conferences when general issues are being discussed. Group conferences may serve as a general introduction meeting. Specific issues involving individual children should be reserved for small and individual conferences. Some general purposes of group conferences might include:

- Acquaint parents with the school's mission, the teachers, his or her instructional program, and materials and resources used in the instructional program.
- Have a plan for involving the parents in the instructional program.
- Have a plan for using or introducing advanced technology in the classroom.
- Have a discussion on information relevant to a reporting procedure.
- Address general questions posed by parents.
- Establish protocol and a schedule for future meetings.
- Select a group leader.

A suggested format for conducting an initial group meeting or conference is reflected in table 10.2.

Table 10.2   Suggested Format for Conducting an Initial Group Meeting/Conference

1. General introduction
2. Purpose of the meeting
3. Statement and discussion of objectives
4. Examples of how the objectives will be achieved
5. Parental input on how objectives will be achieved
6. Discussing and answering any questions from parents relevant to the instructional program
7. Brainstorming on various ways parents can assist to promote their child's achievement
8. Identify specific competencies of parents and elicit their support in the instructional program
9. Conclude the meeting with a note of appreciation to parents for attending the meeting.
10. Announce the time for the next scheduled meeting

An initial group meeting as outlined in table 10.2 may have some negative consequences if the parents are not notified in a timely manner, individual needs are not met, an inconvenient time for some parents who are working has been set, and appropriate sites have not been selected. The meeting should be accessible for parents with disabilities, transportation issues must be addressed, and child care services should be available. Successful group meetings must stress the fact that parents are equal to teachers and have the right to serve on any committee to have their questions addressed in a professional manner (Rich, 1998; Perl, 1995; Steward, 1996).

SMALL GROUP CONFERENCES

Small group conferences can be productive if individuals in the group have similar interests and needs. Some of the same factors which operate in large groups also operate in small groups. Educators must decide on the group size. If the initial group becomes too large, additional small groups may be developed. There is no magic formula for determining the size of the group. Experiences, background, and competencies of the educator appear to be the best indicators for choosing the group size. Participants should be parents of children with similar problems and disabilities.

Parents should participate in all aspects of the small group conference as group leaders or resource individuals. Shea and Bauer (1991) summarized the roles and functions of small group leaders by indicating that planning lesson sequences is an important part of training, instructional, and information groups. Group leaders should be actively involved in all aspects of training. The major function of the group leader in small group conferences is to keep the group on task until the problem has been discussed and an acceptable solution has been found. It was commonly believed that since the group leader needed special competencies to lead groups, the educator was the desired person. This belief is faulty; parents who have the skills may also serve as group leaders. It is incumbent upon the educator to assist in identifying the parents who have the prerequisite skills to conduct the meeting. Once a parent leader is accepted, the educator should stay in the background and serve as a resource person only.

EFFECTIVE USE OF CONFERENCE INFORMATION

Collecting and gathering information is essential to conducting an effective instructional program for children with disabilities. Conferences are an excellent setting to collect these data. Data from the child's ecological environment should be collected and unified to give a complete profile of the child. Using this approach, the total needs and interests of the child can be successfully addressed in the instructional program. No one is better equipped than the parent in providing information on his or her child (Koerner, 1988; Graves, 1996).

Teachers must select those data sources, which are relevant to her or his instructional program. Some suggested guidelines teachers may employ are:

- Select and use information which will support the instructional program.
- Chose information which provides a clearer understanding of the student's disability.
- Identify data sources which give insight into the child's outside interests.
- Review information relevant to the family structure, family problems, and issues which may impact the instructional program, such as the child's relevant position in the family structure.

- Evaluate any special devices or program to which the child has been exposed.

Parents should know why information is needed. Most parents will freely provide information if they believe that the information provided will assist their children in any way. It is incumbent upon the teacher to maintain a professional view and assure parents that all information will be used to assist the child in achieving the stated objectives. Personal comments and reaction to information provided by parents should be carefully monitored; teachers should refrain from making personal comments relevant to the cause or the blame for the information (Sullivan, 1998).

PREPARING FOR THE FUTURE

Major problems arise for parents when their children complete secondary school. This transition can impose many problems for parents, since they will no longer have the support offered by the school. Before children graduate from secondary school, parents should be taught ways and strategies to transition students with disabilities from secondary school to post-secondary conditions (Morningstar, Turnbull and Turnbull, 1996). The school should play a major role in assisting parents as they prepare for the future.

Depending upon the degree and nature of the disability, special interventions may be needed to prepare the child to be as independent as possible. Unfortunately, many disabled children will need supervision for the rest of their lives. Parents must also plan for this reality. For those disabled children who demonstrate signs of independence, parents should teach them to: (1) take care of their own personal and social needs, (2) provide them with the opportunities to interact with a wide range of people, and (3) demonstrate appropriate social, interpersonal, and job training skills (Moon and Beale, 1984).

Wikler (1981) and Upshur (1991) articulated that the parents' role in working with the schools and local agencies is to ensure that their children's educational programs include appropriate job training and plans for future employment. The need for interagency collaborations is of prime importance in providing job training for individuals with disabilities (Smith-Davis, 1983; National Information Center for Handicapped Children and Youth (NICHCY), 1984, 1997; Health Resources Center, 1985).

These research findings describe recommended strategies for training individuals with disabilities to function successfully at work. A first step would be to make an assessment of prior job skills and additional skills needed to perform the job. The research findings also provide information about post-secondary education and identify the kind of courses, the individual plan to pursue, recreation, and residential programs. Appendix K provides additional resources and a web address for organizations that parents may contact.

VOCATIONAL AWARENESS

When helping students develop vocational awareness, parents and professionals should consider the student's abilities and interests and the labor market. During the IEP process, students are asked to consider their abilities and interests in order to provide a course of study to help them develop those abilities and interests. Questions posed may include: What is it he or she likes to do? What courses are available for him or her to take that will promote those interests? Answering these questions, the student is much more likely to connect what he or she is learning to a future career. Ideally, identifying those interests and abilities should begin in elementary school and continue on through high school.

Projections in the labor market must be considered. What occupational areas will be growing in the future? The U.S. Bureau of Labor Statistics provides information about occupations that are predicted to have the largest growth in the future. The largest areas of growth from 2000 to 2010 are projected in the service occupations (food preparation, retail sales, truck drivers), computer technology (support services as well as programmers and systems analysis), and health care (registered nurses, nurses aides, home health care). The majority of jobs in these occupations require an associate's degree or training. At the local level, employers in the health care field and building trades indicate there currently is a great need for trained workers in health fields at the local level, and the demand will continue into the future. By researching occupations that need workers, and considering the student's interests, parents and educators can help direct disabled children toward a career that they can enjoy well into the future.

VOCATIONAL PREPARATION

Academic, career, and technical courses are needed to assist disabled children gain the necessary skills needed in the world of work. According to Plank (2001), research indicates that combining academic, career, and technical courses will increase the probability of high school graduation. Boesel, Hudson, Deich, and Masten (1994) believe that science and math will aid students in problem solving, which will be necessary for future employment. Every school district offers a minimum of four career and technical programs, either on their campus or at another school district through a shared agreement. These programs can provide the basic occupational skills students need to get started on a career.

Vocational awareness and preparation begins in elementary school and continues on beyond high school. The guidance counselor, teachers, and parents are valuable resources in plotting and developing the child's educational path.

FINANCIAL ARRANGEMENT

Parents should also be apprised of the need for legal and financial support to protect the interest of their disabled offspring. Parents need to plan how this support will be provided after they are no longer alive. The plan should include: (1) finding a lawyer who is experienced in developing wills for disabled individuals; (2) evaluating the child's needs and deciding what kind of care is needed; (3) determining the amount and kind of financial support that will be needed to support the child over his or her projected lifespan; (4) planning how the funds will be transferred to the child; (5) planning legal considerations in appointing a guardian; and (6) developing strategies for living arrange-ments, such as sharing living arrangements, group home, foster fami-lies, half-way houses, and so on.

SUMMARY

Strategies for improving relationships for working with parents of chil-dren with disabilities will largely depend upon the nature and degree of the disability, the parents' degree of participation, and the establishment of rapport between teachers and parents (Ysseldakes, Algozzine, and Thurlow, 1992; Friend and Bursuck, 1996). If rapport is not well estab-lished, it is highly unlikely that collaborative activities will be successful.

Educators may employ various ways of improving communication and collaboration with parents of children with disabilities. They may use workshops, conferences, or parent study groups. These approaches, other than parent-teacher conferences, are generally group based. Par-ents who have common problems can discuss these problems as well as have experts from various disciplines address the group. The principal sets the stage for parental involvement by working with the school and community personnel. Joint planning and involvement between the school and parents can help boost the parents' self-esteem by incorpo-rating them into the educational process.

Much of the research in this chapter validated the use of intervention programs with parents. Parent intervention strategies have proven to yield sufficient benefits for affecting student behavior. During these sessions, parents are instructed in the use of instructional strategies, be-havior modification techniques, use of technology devices, counseling techniques, interpersonal skills, remedial programs, working with di-verse groups, and constructing materials, to name a few. Intervention strategies used by parents have proven to be effective in reducing a wide range of academic and behavior problems shown by disabled chil-dren, thus strengthening the skills of parents.

As another means of strengthening the parent in fulfilling their ob-ligation to children with disabilities, the schools should provide edu-cationally related counseling and family services (Christenson et al., 1997). In cases of clear educational neglect, the schools, through qualified professional personnel, should make extraordinary arrangements for preventive and compensatory educational services. As a means of strengthening special education programs, parents of children with disabilities and organized community groups should be given a responsible part in educational policy formation and planning activities.

As outlined, assisting parents and giving advice regarding a plan for care as well as decisions concerning treatment and educational placement to ameliorate the disabling conditions are all important in helping them resolve social and emotional difficulties affecting their children. Diagnostic evaluation should further assist parents in accepting the fact that their children are disabled and provide information that will assist them in meeting the day-to-day problems that will arise. It is commonly recognized that no program will be completely successful unless some parental involvement is sought and maintained. Cooperation between parents and school can aid the child greatly in his or her educational pursuits. Professional workers generally recognize that most parents have difficulty in accepting and adjusting to their children with disabilities. Consequently, without proper guidance these factors can hamper the progress and development of children.

A first step for parents in accepting their children's disabilities is to recognize the basic problem and to seek ways to face the problems or disabilities with a positive approach. The difficulty of the problem is immense for most parents. Many will need individual as well as group counseling. The school can provide some counseling for parents if their problems are not too deep-rooted. More severe problems will have to be attended to by mental health specialists. The salient point that school officials should keep in mind is that some parents have received counseling and are ready to assist in educating their children; others are not so fortunate.

Collaborative activities can meet the needs of children with disabilities by integrating the services of both the home and school in all areas of human functioning. These activities may do much to improve culture, social, and physical problems associated with the children's disabilities. Parents must become an integral part of the collaborative efforts if they are to become successful. The following guidelines are offered as a means to improve these efforts:

- Develop a plan to build trust and security among parents.
- Involve parents in the school development plan, seek volunteers in all aspects of the plan to ensure that every parent contributes to the attainment of the goals and objectives.
- Construct individual agreements with each parent so that the parent will have some responsibilities in meeting the stated goals, objectives, and IEP requirements.
- Develop strategies for identifying, assessing, using, and evaluating community resources.

Collaborating with parents and working with families are critical factors in improving communication between the home and school. Much of the improvement in communication has come about due chiefly to state and federal legislation, parental rights groups, parent empowerment, and the schools' recognition of the value of parental input in educating children. The schools have recognized the impact of such factors as poverty, race, ethnicity, family structure and transitions, and parental age on their children's development (Powell, 1995). Using the vast amount of research now available in the above areas, the schools have developed programs to strengthen parental behavior as well as revised programs to reflect cultural diversity.

CHAPTER 11

Parents' Perceptions of Placement

Inclusive education has been defined in as many ways as there are attitudes toward this educational concept. For instance, Roach (1995) defined the term as serving students with a full range of abilities and disabilities in the general educational classroom, with appropriate in-class support. Written in the opinion of Brown and colleagues (1991), inclusion is a way to implement the least restricted environment (LRE); however, it is not necessarily the regular education classroom. According to Bennett, Deluca, and Burns (1997) and Scruggs and Mostropieri (1996), the concept of inclusion is the integration of students with disabilities into a heterogeneous classroom for the entire school day. This inclusive model is typically referred to as the Regular Education Initiative (REI).

Integration of children with disabilities into the regular classroom and the reduction of special education classrooms have been issues of major concerns for parents and educators in the field for well over two decades (Katsiyannis, Conderman and Franks, 1995; Sawyer, McLaughlin, and Winglee, 1994; Baker, Wang, and Walberg, 1995; Fuchs and Fuchs, 1984). A multitude of conditions and trends have attributed to the controversy.

It is the attitudes of those involved in, or affected by, inclusive models that define and determine the impact of this practice on the individuals who will be placed in this setting. For example, Berger (1995) asserted that the process of including individuals with special needs into the mainstream classroom has become a pressing issue among those in administration responsible for the education of these individuals.

A preponderance of literature attests to the fact that most children with disabilities should be placed in inclusive classrooms. This position has created some controversy regarding inclusive versus special class placement as noted by Baker, Wang, and Walberg, 1995; Zigmond and colleagues, 1995; Borthwick-Duffy, Palmer, and Lane, 1996; Fuchs and Fuchs, 1994; Rogers, 1993; and Waldron and McLesky, 1998. The common consensus of these researchers indicated that the concept of inclusion is an excellent idea; however, it may not work for all children all of the time.

Although the preponderance of research supports the concept of inclusion, some researchers question whether or not children with disabilities can receive an adequate education in a regular classroom setting (Fuchs, 1994; Borthwick-Duffy, Palmer, Lane, 1996). According to Janko, Schwartz, Sandall, Anderson, and Cottam (1997) and Peck, Odom, and Bricker (1993), the major goal of education is to provide all children with an equal opportunity to succeed in school. Additionally, it involves placing children with disabilities in the same classroom with their normal peers (Winter, 1999). The impact of inclusion on promoting learning/achievement among disabled individuals is a source of debate within the field (Odom and Diamond, 1998; Taylor, 2000; Guralnick, 2001).

Much of the controversy may be attributed to the lack of scientific and empirical studies designed to show the impact of inclusion on achievement of both disabled and normal children (Bricker, 1995; Odom, 2000). The few studies reported yielded mixed results concerning the value or lack of value of inclusion. One of the first studies concerning the impact of inclusion on disabled children, conducted by Jenkins, Odom, and Speltz, (1985), showed no significant differences in school-related subjects and motor development between children in integrated and special education classes. However, they did report significant differences in social interaction of children in integrated classes when compared with special classes. Findings by Cole, Mills, Dale, and Jenkins (1991) and Hundert, Mahoney, Mundy, and Vernon (1998) were similar to those reported by Jenkins, Odom, and Speltz (1989).

Most of the studies that involved placing disabled children in inclusive settings versus special classes were in favor of inclusive settings.

Research findings generally reported that children in integrated or inclusive settings showed greater gain when compared with disabled children in segregated or special classes (Cole et al., 1991; Holohan and Costenbader, 2000; Mills, Cole, Jenkins, and Dale, 1998).

In summary, most of the research in opposition to inclusion states that inclusion will not work for children with disabilities due to the following reasons:

- Children with disabilities with serious problems tend to perform better in separate classes.
- There is a need to preserve the continuum of specialized programs and placement options.
- Children with disabilities enrolled in special classes performed as well as those in regular classes on curriculum-based measures.
- Children with disabilities will interfere with the progress or regular students.
- Placing children with disabilities in regular classes can lead to stigmatized labels.
- Some regular students may begin to mimic inappropriate behaviors of some children with disabilities, thus affecting learning.
- Some parents fear that services for their children with disabilities will not be available under inclusion.
- Parents of nondisabled children fear that their children would be neglected in the classroom due to special attention required for children with disabilities.
- Segregated schools are considered safe havens for some parents because they provide the specialized services needed for their children with disabilities.

VIEWS ON PLACEMENT

Teaching students with disabilities in inclusive settings is a multifaceted task that cannot be accomplished by just one person. Inclusive education happens when a team of mutually supportive players pledge to provide the best practices for a student with disabilities. Inclusive education focuses on a combination of best practices in education, including cooperative learning, peer tutoring, and community building in classrooms and schools. Teaching strategies for inclusive settings are synonymous with effective teaching strategies used in any area of education (Aefsky, 1995). Depending on the disability and level of student need, a team with unique but complementary skills should be consulted to guide, advocate for, and implement this student's educational program. More than any other element, the need for team effort to manage, deliver, and support a student's inclusive education is a drastic change for regular educators. Educators must develop a plan to integrate the life-long goals and specific needs of students with disabilities within the context of the regular curriculum (Filbin, Connolly, and Brewer, 1996).

According to Taylor (1999), collective research in support of inclusion is based upon:

- Federal legislation in support of educating children with disabilities in regular classes. The reader is referred to chapter 5, where a comprehensive review of the impact of federal legislation on inclusion is discussed.
- Research findings tend to support that children with disabilities perform academically as well in inclusive classes as separate classes.
- When provided with support, many children with disabilities are able to succeed in regular education classrooms.
- The continuum of service models is not needed in inclusive settings; children with disabilities should be placed in regular classes on a full-time basis.
- Children with disabilities will benefit from associating with their normal peers.
- Inclusion will reduce labeling of children with disabilities.
- Inclusion tends to increase interaction between students with disabilities and their nondisabled peers.

Advocates for full inclusion of children with disabilities indicate that it is the children's democratic right to be educated with their peers; integration of children with disabilities with nondisabled children enhances interpersonal skills. Other studies indicate that curricula in inclusive schools should be appropriate for different levels of disabilities and sensory acuity. There is no separate knowledge base for teaching students with disabilities. Teachers must be innovative and employ creative teaching strategies, such as learning centers, cooperative learning, concept teaching, directed teaching, and team teaching. Many adaptations and modifications will be needed in the instructional process, depending upon the amount and degree of disabling conditions present. To the extent possible, students with disabilities should be included in the learning process (Barry, 1995; Wang, Reynold, and Walberg, 1995; Baker, Wang, and Walberg, 1995; Staub and Peck, 1995; Johnston, Proctor, and Carey, 1995).

Proponents of full inclusion believe that a one size fits all approach will be disastrous for children with disabilities; it is not only unrealistic but also unjust. To correct this injustice, according to Shanker (1995), public laws addressing inclusion will need to be rewritten to fund the cost of inclusion and provide adequate training for all teachers. To give equal weight to requests from parents and referrals from teachers, teachers must be totally involved in writing the individualized education plan (IEP), and alternative arrangements should be made to temporarily place children with disabilities who are violent or disruptive in secure settings. The National Association of State Boards of Education voiced that many special education programs are superior to regular classrooms for some types of children with disabilities (Baker and Zigmond, 1990), and Fuchs, Fuchs, and Bishop (1992) and Fuchs and Fuchs (1995) reported that individualizing strategies employed in special classes are superior to the one size fits all approach observed in many regular classrooms. They supported the view that separate is better for some children with disabilities, and to abolish special education placement in the name of full inclusion is to deprive many children with disabilities of an appropriate education. The schools have little choice in seeking parental involvement concerning placement. Parental involvement is mandated by Public Law 94-142 and Public Law 107-110 to review with parents their children's IEPs.

PARENTAL VIEWS

Parental views toward inclusion are important. Parental reactions toward having their children placed in inclusive or segregated classrooms parallel the views of advocates and opponents of the measurement, which is multidimensional. In essence, parental perceptions support the statement that inclusion is no panacea for educating all of their disabled children. Their perceptions vacillate greatly between inclusion and special education placement. The disability is not the major reason why some parents do not want their children in inclusive settings. Issues such as instructional objectives, competent personnel, instructional strategies, delivery models, resources, and related services take precedent over placement. Because the issue of parental involvement is so critical to the inclusion process (Taylor, 2000, 2003), inclusion cannot be successfully achieved until the school along with parents collaboratively develop strategies concerning inclusion. School personnel must be trained to demonstrate competencies in conferencing skills and be well informed about the problems parents face as a result of having disabled children. (Specific strategies for improving teachers skills are provided in chapter 13.)

As indicated, many of the studies reported dealt with mainstreaming rather than inclusion, did not designate the type of disabilities being accessed, and mostly focused on children with mild or moderate disabilities. According to Taylor (2003), suggestions to improve results concerning the efficacy of inclusion with segregation will necessitate developing a comprehensive evaluation model—one that investigates all skill areas affected by the disability and uses multiple means of collecting information, e.g., observations, interviews, standardized instruments, and alternative approaches.

EFFECTS OF RESEARCH AND LEGISLATION ON PARENTAL PERCEPTION

The aforementioned research and the federal and state legislation discussed in chapter 5 combine to have a significant impact on parental perceptions toward inclusion. Perceptions toward inclusion are multidimensional and differentiated by several factors (Anotonak and Larrivee, 1995; Larrivee, 1992; Schmelkin, 1981; Semmel, Abernathy, Butera, and Lesar, 1991; Wilczenski, 1992).

Inclusion is an important issue because it affects virtually all stakeholders in education, including children with and without disabilities and their families, special and general education teachers, administrators, related services personnel, school staff, and the general public (Alper, Schloss, Etscheidt, and Macfarlane, 1995). Inclusion, a grassroots movement driven by parental dissatisfaction with the current delivery system and the conviction that all children should be educated together, has captured the attention of educators and the general public alike. According to Aefsky (1995), inclusion is turning the tables after fifteen unsuccessful years of teaching children in a fragmented school society. Aefsky stated that we are asking professionals, teachers, administrators, and support staff to change their roles.

Effective inclusion necessitates the involvement of parents in the planning process. By way of review, parental involvement in IEPs is mandated by law. However, many parents of children with disabilities have concerns related to inclusion. They have voiced concern about their children in integrated classrooms. Some parents are not sure that their children with disabilities are receiving appropriate services; consequently, some have elected to have their children educated in segregated classrooms (Hobbs and Westling, 1998; Westling, 1996; Hanline and Halvorsen, 1989; McDonnell, 1987). Most of the studies relevant to parental perceptions on inclusion dealt with children with mild to moderate disabilities. A study conducted by Bothwick-Duffy, Palmer, and Lane (1996) was designed to assess parental perceptions of children with severe disabilities. Parental reactions of these parents were similar to those of parents with children with mild to moderate disabilities. Regardless of the levels of disabilities, parents views of inclusion are more related to well-defined goals and objectives, the personality traits of the teachers, attitudes of staff members toward disabilities, supportive services, competent personnel, innovated instructional strategies and delivery models, resources and related services.

CRITICAL ISSUES TO BE CONSIDERED

When there is no consensus on goals or objectives, no type of placement for children with disabilities will be successful. An avoidance of clearly stated goals and objectives cannot validate the success of any placement. If clearly beneficial objectives, unique for a particular disability, cannot be identified, then the issue should not be on placement, but

rather on developing the objectives and the support services needed to
assist children with disabilities to reach their optimum levels of growth.

TEACHERS' ATTITUDES

Teachers' attitudes and expectations are critical elements in educating children with disabilities. A warm and sincere type of attitude is needed which
reflects an understanding of the disability and the recognition that children
with disabilities have the right to be treated and educated the same as normal children. This type of attitude should be demonstrated by all associated with treating and educating children with disabilities (Taylor, 1999).

SUPPORTIVE SERVICES

Supportive services and competent personnel are necessary in educating children with disabilities. Collaboration with community agencies
should be sought and encouraged. Children with disabilities will need
many support services outside the realm of the school. Competent and
certified personnel are needed to educate and treat these children. High
standards are needed for the selection of personnel. Before personnel
are assigned to work with children with disabilities, the training, attitudes, and values should be precisely delineated.

INSTRUCTIONAL STRATEGIES

Instructional strategies employed in teaching children with disabilities
should have been field tested and validated for the disability area. This
will ensure that instructional strategies will assist in minimizing and reducing the disabling conditions of the children. Staff might be well
trained to implement any type of instructional or delivery models.

RESOURCES AND RELATED SERVICES

Resources and related services are needed to complement the instructional program. Selection of resources and related services should be

premised upon the assessed needs, interests, and abilities of children with disabilities. Personnel selecting the resources and providing the related services should be competent and certified in their selective disciplines.

Additional research is needed on parental perception toward educational placement of their children with disabilities. The research conducted has indicated that parents needed additional information on the critical issues listed, parents are more concerned about these critical issues rather than placement.

SUMMARY

Historically, the placement issue was discussed in the 1970s. The issue was whether children with disabilities learned best in integrated or segregated classes. Most of the research indicates that prior to 1975, most handicapped children with mild disabilities were educated in integrated classes and those with severe to profound disabilities were educated in segregated classes. Federal legislation, P.L. 94-142 and amendments, changed this concept and gave all children with disabilities equal educational opportunities; the concept of the LRE provided all children with disabilities the opportunity to be educated with their nondisabled peers. The law provided for both types of placements, integration and segregation. Assessment data used in completing the IEP are used to determine the LRE for students with disabilities. In comparing the research over the last two decades, data still support that most children with disabilities are placed in inclusive settings (Banerji and Daily, 1995; Giangreco, Dennis, Cloninger, Edelman, and Schattman, 1993; Sharpe, York, and Knight, 1994; Staub and Hunt, 1993; Robert and Mather, 1995; Zigmond, Jenkins, Fuchs, Baker, Fuchs, Jenkins, Couthino, 1995; Alper, 1995; Mills and Bulach, 1996).

Inclusion offers the nondisabled student an opportunity to develop an appreciation for the complexity of human characteristics as well as an appreciation for individual differences. Students who have not had these experiences may be surprised to learn that, for example, speech problems that accompany cerebral palsy do not necessarily indicate limited intelligence. Cognitive impairment need not affect social development, and sensory impairment need not interfere with skill in motor activity. Additionally, students with disabilities may teach nondisabled learners to go beyond dysfunctional stereotypes. All students with behavior disorders are not aggressive, and students with learning disabilities can be highly capable in some academic areas. The advantages of inclusion have been well documented in the professional literature. In spite of the vast amount of support for inclusion, it is this author's view that inclusion is no panacea for educating all children with disabilities.

Parental perception supports the statement that inclusion is no panacea for educating all of their children. Parental perception vacillated greatly between inclusion and special education placement. The disability was not the chief reason why parents wanted their children in inclusive placements. Issues such as objectives, personnel, instructional strategies, delivery models, resources, and related services took precedent over placement.

CHAPTER 12

School and Community Interactions

Research has shown that community involvement and action can be powerful allies in transforming schools. Community involvement with the schools has been credited with (1) improving the physical conditions and resources that support learning in the schools; (2) raising the attitudes and expectations of parents, teachers, and students; and (3) improving the depth and quality of the learning experiences of students through collaborative planning (Hatch, 1998; Murnane and Levy, 1996; Shirley, 1997; Cohn-Vargas and Grose, 1998). The major purpose of school-community relations is to share information about the special education program.

It is essential that educators make parents aware and informed about progress made toward achieving reforms. Parents are more likely to become associated with the school if educators develop a strong and trusting relationship with them. The bond can be further strengthened by making frequent contacts with the parents, conducting seminars, and sponsoring social events developed by the community. Educators frequently deal with community groups and agencies and must possess effective interpersonal and community skills (Taylor, 2003).

Because of the emotional impact of disability upon the family, parents need help from the community. Services provided by the community impact to some degree how children with disabilities develop and also provide strategies to help family members cope with the disabilities (Norton and Drew, 1994). The community's most important contribution to families is a willingness to listen and understand what they are experiencing. Parents and siblings need someone they can express their feelings to and receive support from. Educators can ensure that parents' needs are heard through school-community relations designed to share information about special education with the community.

The need for direct involvement of parents and communities has been advocated by Atkinson and Juntunen (1994). They reported that educators must function as a school-home-community liaison. Casas and Furlong (1994) supported the increase of parental participation and empowerment in the community and encouraged parents to visit with other parents of children with disabilities. Most communities have support groups of parents who have disabled children. Organizations dealing with the specific disability of the child can also be helpful to the family (e.g., the Association of Retarded Citizens, United Cerebral Palsy Association).

According to Lunenburg and Ornstein (1991), educators can use the following ideas to keep parents and the community informed:

- A brochure that describes the special education program, including the district's philosophy of services to individuals with disabilities.
- Specialized brochures, each describing a specific aspect of the program.
- A parent handbook that describes the individualized education plan (IEP) process, forms, and the role of the parent.
- Articles in the district newspaper, school paper, or local newspaper.
- A special newsletter that focuses on special education news.
- Telephone contacts with individual parents and other citizens.
- Speeches to community groups or civic clubs.
- Annual reports, open houses, videotapes, and letters to groups.
- Displays at locations, such as civic meeting places and shopping malls.
- Public service announcements on radio and television describing some aspect of special education services.

Collaboration strategies can also be used effectively to promote communication. Collaborative activities can meet the needs of children with disabilities and their parents by integrating the services of both the home and school in all areas of human functioning. These activities may do much to improve culture, social, and physical problems associated with the children's disabilities. Educators must strive to become an integral part of the collaborative efforts if they are to be successful. The following guidelines are offered as a means to improve the collaborative efforts:

- Develop a plan to build trust and security among parents.
- Involve parents in the school development plan and seek volunteers in all aspects of the plan to ensure that every parent contributes to the attainment of the goals and objectives.
- Construct individual agreements with each parent so the parent will have some responsibilities in meeting the stated goals, objectives, and IEP requirements.
- Establish a citizen advisory committee and involve them in the planning.

Several authors have indicated disadvantages in promoting collaborative activities, especially advisory committees (Podemski, Marsh, Smith, and Price, 1995; Podemski and Steele, 1981):

- Advisory committees can consume a great deal of the administrator's time.
- Committee members often lack perspective and background information about educational issues.
- Special interests of individual committee members can dominate.
- Committee members may not be aware of past school practices or how the school operates.
- Committee members may not understand group dynamics or group decision-making procedures.
- Final recommendations can exceed the committee's original charge or overstep its authority.
- The committee may search for problems or issues to justify its existence.

We believe educators can overcome many of the pitfalls just listed by developing small focus groups knowledgeable about the issues under discussion whose members are willing to reach a consensus. Members of this group should have time to commit to the issues. Additionally, educators should apprise the group of any history or procedures that will assist them in reaching a consensus, provide as much assistance as possible to the group, and implement as much of the committee's recommendations as possible. Lack of implementing committee's recommendations will erode the relationship between the committee and the administrators.

Collaborating with parents and working with families are major modifications and reforms that educators can make in improving communication between the home and school. Much of the improvement in communication has come about due mainly to state and federal legislation, parental rights groups, parent empowerment, and the schools' recognition of the value of parental input in educating children. Educators have become cognizant of the influence of poverty, ethnicity, family structure and transitions, parental age, and other factors that interact with children's development (Powell and Diamond, 1995). Using the vast amount of research generated in these areas, educators have developed programs to strengthen parental behaviors as well as revised programs to reflect cultural diversity.

PROMOTING CULTURAL AWARENESS

Promoting cultural awareness encourages families with different cultural and linguistic backgrounds to participate fully in the schools. Variables such as socioeconomic status, educational level, and length of residence in the country should not promote stereotyped beliefs (Wayman, Lynch, and Hanson, 1990; Gorman and Balter, 1997). Hyun and Fowler (1995) explored how cultural awareness can be enhanced by exploring one's own cultural heritage and examining the attitudes and behaviors associated with one's own culture. Educators must become familiar with the child's culture and community (Powell, 1998). (Refer to chapter 7 for specific strategies.)

COMMUNITY AND PARENTAL INVOLVEMENT

No school program can be completely effective without the support of parents and the community. Most educators are acutely aware of the need for parents and active community involvement in the entire educational program for children with disabilities. When the school and community are genuinely interested in the welfare of the child and his or her parents, apathy and despair turn to hope and self-fulfillment, which can do much to ease many of the emotional problems experienced. Further, improvement in communication can do much to eliminate the negativism of many parents. This positive approach cannot help but assist the child with a disability in his or her educational pursuits.

A desirable relationship in the community is one marked by a strong bond of understanding and cooperation between parents and school personnel. Parents should have a direct share in deciding what types of instruction appear to serve their children best. Parents should be welcome to make suggestions for the guidance of their children. Through various channels, the educator should enlist the cooperation of parents and community agencies in designing and implementing educational programs for children with disabilities. In communities where educators work with parents and with religious, recreational, and social agencies in a constructive effort to help, the results are reflected in healthier personalities of boys and girls (Taylor, 2003).

Communities can do a great deal to make better use of their resources through a collaboration of efforts. Coordination mobilizes the skills of people to help all programs, eliminates wasteful competition, saves money, improves training opportunities, and gives invaluable assistance to the disabled child and his or her family. The school should be the key for coordinating activities in the community. Specialists in various disciplines should be consulted as needs of disabled children dictate. Some consideration should be given to the parents who may need financial assistance. Again, personnel in the schools and diagnostic centers can refer the parent to appropriate community agencies that can provide the support (Podemski et al., 1995).

Differentiation of general and specialized services is vital, not only to make ample use of community resources but also to provide the disabled child with a complete diagnosis. Services provided should include both approaches. Coordinated planning should be a well thought out process that seeks to elicit cooperation and communication among various community agencies. Some of the obstacles associated with effective community planning are: (1) lack of personnel with experience to conduct the planning, (2) decreased interdisciplinary communication due to lack of mutual respect among specialists, (3) facilities for the disabled failing to recognize that no one clinic or agency can provide the necessary services needed to diagnose, treat, and rehabilitate the disabled child, and (4) exclusion of parents from the initial diagnostic evaluation, treatment, and follow-up procedures.

The position of school personnel on a special education team headed by noneducators and the relationship of medical personnel with other members are some specific problems that should not vary as widely as they do from program to program. Understanding the intricacies of teamwork and agreeing upon its definition might clarify areas of misunderstanding. The necessity of communication within the team, or team action with parents, community members, state departments, and other programs, as well as balancing progress, morals, and democratic ideals, constitute other areas of coordination sometimes overlooked by administrators.

COORDINATION OF ACTIVITIES

Coordination of the education program for children with disabilities should exist among and between all units of the school system and community (Thorp, 1997). Effective planning for coordination calls for participation of many agencies, official and voluntary, local and regional. In order for the disabled to receive maximum benefit from community programs, activities need to be closely coordinated with the schools. Until the last few decades, the responsibility of preparing the disabled youth to assume the obligations of a mature citizen was almost exclusively that of the school. Presently, certain social and vocational services external to school, which had as their purpose the rendering of training and placement services to disabled persons of postschool age, are beginning to assist the schools in these attempts. These agencies developed separately from the school and remained at some distance until they recognized a mutuality of interests and purposes with the school. Today, the nature of the interaction between schools and other community agencies is more continuous and harmonious. The responsibility for educating children with disabilities does not rest with the elementary school alone. All levels of the public school system, parents, and community are responsible for educating all the children of all the people (Wang and Wilderman, 1996).

Regular and continuous progress of children with disabilities through the school system requires coordination of effort on the part of the community, school personnel, and teachers. The elementary schools need to be unified in purpose and procedure so that steady, continuous progress may be ensured. Despite an increase in coordination between levels of education in the public schools and a commitment to team efforts, school personnel still place too much emphasis on how to use the findings of other professionals rather than how to work to establish and improve the quality of programs for children with disabilities (Taylor, 2000, 2003).

STRATEGIES FOR IMPROVING PARENTAL INVOLVEMENT

Much of the interest and increase in parental involvement may be attributed to P.L. 94-142 and its amendments. These legislative amendments have mandated parental participation in all aspects of the child's educational program, including assessment, IEP development, placement decisions, evaluation, follow-up, and transitional services.

REWARDING PARENTS

Educators need to recognize and reward parents for their involvement. Reinforcing parental efforts can make a significant impact in working with their children (Oswald and Sinah-Nirbay, 1992). Parents employ some of the same techniques that teachers use to reinforce their children. Social and academic growth of children with disabilities may be expedited through the use of reinforcement strategies. Teachers who create a positive atmosphere for communication and collaboration with parents increase the probability of the child's success in his or her academic pursuits.

Many parents are not trained in teaching strategies. School personnel can train interested parents through observation, demonstration, and modeling. Bandura (1977) has validated the importance of these techniques. School personnel should provide ample strategies for parents to imitate. Today, school personnel realize the importance of parental involvement and understand that cooperative efforts between teachers and parents benefit the children significantly.

CONFERENCES

Both group and individual conferences have been found invaluable in improving collaboration between parents and administrators. Educators may decide on the best type of conference needed to address the needs of the children. Some problems can be dealt with successfully in large groups, others in small groups. At any rate, confidentiality must be observed once the initial conference has been held. Future conferences should be conducted regularly, agreed on by both parent and the educator. Timing of conferences is of prime importance. Conferences must be held at a convenient time for parents to attend. The length of the conferences must also be considered. Parents have other commitments, and to avoid conflicts, educators should send out conference schedules and agenda items in advance. Advanced schedules should solicit parents' commitments and suggestions. The final schedule should be modified to meet parental concerns. This approach will reinforce a sense of cooperation and openness between educators and parents. Educators must be cognizant of the individual needs of parents and plan strategies based on these needs. Various types of reinforcement or reward programs instituted should be conducted in concert with the individual needs of the parents.

IMPORTANCE OF PARENTAL INVOLVEMENT

Parental involvement is a widely accepted practice among proponents of education. Parents can serve as partners to the teacher in the child's academic program. Taylor (2000, 2003) summed up the importance of parental involvement in the schools by stating parents are a school's best friend. He listed several statements that have major implications for involving parents in the school: (1) the immediate family, not the school, provides the first instruction for the child; (2) parental involvement in their children's education improves the child's chances for later academic success; (3) parental involvement is most effective when it is comprehensively planned; and (4) the earlier parents become involved in their children's education, the more likely they will be involved throughout the child's academic career.

It is incumbent on educators to understand and appreciate the importance of parental and family involvement in order to improve family-school cooperation. Individuals with disabilities cannot reach their optimum level of functioning unless their parents become actively involved in their education (Taylor, 1998). Significant benefits can be derived from involving parents at any level.

To be effective, educators should launch parental involvement on two fronts: the home and school. Involving parents with their children's education at home augments the learning process, providing that learning strategies are addressed collaboratively by both teachers and parents. Achievement of students tends to accelerate when both teachers and parents agree on common goals and objectives. Parents can be instructed to focus on school readiness skills and specific objectives that nurture learning (Langdon and Novak, 1998).

All children benefit when parents are involved in the school, and this is especially true for children with disabilities and minority children. The education level of parents should not be a prerequisite for involving them. Parents can perform many nonacademic tasks. All children are pleased and proud to see their parents involved in the school (Clark, 1993; Floyd, 1998; Wang et al., 1996).

Both the home and school have a significant impact on students' attitudes. Attitudes are mostly formed at home during the early years and are reinforced by the parents as the child matures. If attitudes are not reinforced by the school, negative ones may surface and impede the achievement of students.

DEVELOPMENT OF SCHOOL POLICY

Parental involvement in school policy is essential if the school is to meet state and federal mandates. School personnel should insist that parents serve on all the major policy-making bodies of the school, not just the PTA. Parents should be involved in choosing textbooks, developing curriculum guidelines, forming social committees, and serving as resource individuals, to name but a few. Parental involvement appears most effective when parents are directly involved in all school activities that have a direct impact on their children. Parents can be effective when they define the conditions under which they serve. School personnel should articulate specific ways parents can participate in the education program. Some in-service training may be needed for parents to participate effectively in the education program (Ohlrich, 1996; Potter, 1996; Thompson, 1998).

Educators can promote parental involvement by adhering to strategies recommended by the Education Commission of the States (1996a, 1996b):

- Listen to people first, talk later.
- Expect to fail if you do not communicate well with teachers.
- Make involving parents and the community a top priority.
- Be clear about what it means to set high standards for all students and what it will take to achieve them.
- Show how new ideas enhance, rather than replace, the old ones.
- Educate parents about the choices available to them.
- Help parents and other community members understand how students are assessed and what the results mean.

Sergiovanni's views (1996) supported the Education Commission of the States' position. He argued that both the what and how of student learning should be decided by school personnel and parents, because that is the essence of a democratic community, and the give and take of such decisions is what produces understanding and trust. Authenticity is essential in promoting trust between stakeholders. Educators assumed that parents expected them to be professional and businesslike, and parents actually wanted the opposite. Parents from all levels complained about educators talking down to them (Education Commission of the States, 1996). Information should be provided to parents in a manner they can understand. Counseling appears to be an effective technique for providing information to parents.

COUNSELING PARENTS

Effective counseling techniques can do much to inform parents about the nature, extent, and implication of their children's disabling conditions. Further, many of the emotional strains, unhappiness, and conflicts can be significantly reduced with professional counseling strategies. Chapter 4 discusses these strategies in detail. A first step should be to conduct a needs assessment of the parents. Once conducted, teachers and educators will have factual data for conducting counseling sessions to reduce, minimize, or eradicate problems (Taylor, 2003). Information sessions and conferences may be scheduled to address the problems in a variety of individual and group sessions.

SPECIAL SERVICES

Special services should be an integral part of the teaching/learning program for children with disabilities. Disability usually denotes many associated problems. Because of these problems, educators call on specialists from other fields for purposes of evaluation and consultation. The school will not be able to provide the comprehensive array of special services required, and, therefore, arrangements should be made to use private and community services in addition to those available within the school.

Many of the disabled require medical and paramedical services. The incidence of other types of disabilities is high among this group. Because many of their problems are medical, the educator should consult each child's physician to learn how to handle possible contingencies. The disabled child from deprived settings often needs to be referred to clinics for a variety of problems because parents are often unable to handle their medical needs (Heddell, 1998; Hyun and Fowler, 1995).

Educators should promote adequate community action to meet the total life needs of all children with disabilities. This depends on the knowledge and competencies of personnel from many disciplines, which must be coordinated and utilized, and an expanded program of information and education for the general public and pertinent professional organizations.

Agencies providing services for children with disabilities should be aware of their areas of greatest professional competencies, implementation of this philosophy requires all persons to think beyond traditional approaches of individual agencies as they now exist. Program levels could be raised if special services were obtained from agencies best equipped to provide them. Barriers that make general community services unavailable to children with disabilities should be removed. The disabled should have access to all services applicable to their needs. Enriched or special services should be provided so each disabled person may develop to his or her fullest potential. Disabilities must not be seen as a single symptom, but as an array of difficulties in physical, psychological, and social areas. Because of the complexity of the problem, services should encompass a variety of professional disciplines. No single profession can meet the many needs of the disabled. The professional team should function initially as a diagnostic team, incorporating the findings of other team members in their decision process. If at all possible, the initial team should participate in the treatment and follow-up process.

Diagnostic evaluation can play an important role in the management of disabling conditions in childhood. If the diagnostic study is carried out by experts and specialists from various disciplines, referrals can be achieved more easily. The staff of the diagnostic clinic has at its disposal the information obtained in the intake procedures as well as the information requested from other hospitals and physicians. The social worker assigned to the patient usually accompanies him or her during the history-taking session. During the physical examination, it is often possible for the social worker to develop further rapport with the family. The clinical psychologist may be introduced to the family by the social worker. A conference is held between the staff members. Plans are made for needed studies and preliminary impressions are recorded. Specialized studies, such as formal psychological, medical, and orthopedic evaluations, are scheduled when indicated.

A diagnostic evaluation almost always includes a thorough review of development, social functioning, a specific history of the presenting problems, and psychiatric, pediatric, neurological, and psychological examinations. A clinic should also maintain or have access to facilities for laboratory examinations. The public health nurse can yield valuable information regarding the child's development, general physical health, interests, abilities, and relationships within and outside the family. His or her observations frequently make it possible to assess parental reaction to the child, the level of family anxiety, and the ability of the family to carry out home-training regiments. The making of a diagnostic plan and a guidance program for children with disabilities takes the combined efforts of many specialists.

Special education experts and vocational and/or regular counselors should also comprise the evaluation team. The educator should work closely with school personnel in coordinating the efforts of all those who act as resource personnel for the teacher of disabled children. With the guidance of the educators, the teacher is made more keenly aware of the factors that contribute to the growth and development of children with disabilities. The other specialists help the teacher by providing input into developing plans and activities for meeting the needs of each pupil. Joint participation of school personnel and specialists in meeting pupils' problems enables research and current findings in the field of disabilities to become a part of daily classroom teaching. Teamwork among teachers and specialists is essential for the teacher to meet the needs of children with disabilities. (Refer to appendix L for a detailed evaluation plan.)

AN INTEGRATED APPROACH TO MEETING NEEDS

The integrated approach to learning, so necessary for children with disabilities, requires that the services of specialists be coordinated by administrators and integrated with the work of other school personnel. A teacher of disabled pupils is likely to find many disabilities and maladjustments, such as speech disorders, defective hearing, poor reading ability, weak eyesight, motor disabilities, and behavioral maladjustments. The problems of disability are so intricate and extensive that many specialists will be needed in the evaluation and treatment process. Specialists in various disciplines should be consulted as the needs of the disabled child dictate (Taylor, 2003).

Because variations in the severity of disabilities come about as a result of the complex interaction of biological and environmental influences, the determination of the degree of disability is a complex problem and cannot be qualified adequately on the basis of a mere test score. It must include a careful evaluation of the medical aspects of the condition, a thorough review of the whole child—his or her social experiences, his or her family life, schooling, and social contacts—and must weigh the effects of other complicating factors such as speech disabilities or sensory or motor defects. The goals of treatment should be individual and realistic. Such goals should be based on careful evaluation. One of the major purposes of integrated services should be to improve the identification process of children with developmental problems.

Children with disabilities should be identified as early in their school life as possible by qualified experts. Early identification is necessary if the school is to give maximum help. Without early identification, many children with disabilities may be expected to fulfill unreasonable demands and expectations. Their inability to cope with situations beyond their capacities can lead to fear, anxiety, and maladjustment. When their disabilities are not known, they are likely to be misunderstood and misdirected as they attempt to meet their needs. Their behaviors may become hostile, and helping them make better psychological and social adjustments later on may become more difficult.

It would be helpful to everyone concerned if these children were identified during their preschool years. Many disabilities in very young children can be identified early. Disabled children of preschool age can first be located through referrals by parents, pediatricians, public health organizations, and social agencies. They can then be referred to psychological clinics for diagnosis. Early identification can be made by a careful and thorough case study that includes the use of tests suitable for very young children. When these children enter school with their disabilities already diagnosed, the school can better meet their needs from the beginning of their school life. The possibilities of failure, anxiety, and rejection in their experience will thus be reduced.

Accurate identification of children with disabilities, whether before or after entering school, depends on thorough, complete clinical procedures. There cannot be reliance on observation and subjective judgment alone. Symptoms of disability may be false or misleading. Passivity, aggressiveness, antisocial behavior, lack of reading ability, poor health, low marks, and defective articulation do not necessarily indicate subnormal mental development. These symptoms may be the result of negative personal and environmental factors apart from subnormal intelligence. Identifying a child as disabled solely on a subject basis may be unjust and inappropriate.

The team concept needs a prominent place in the school's organizational pattern. How effectively the team operates regarding group decisions and how carefully they sift through evidence depends to a great extent on the administrator's self-confidence and faith in the faculty. His or her ability to weave properly into the daily schedule all the diverse elements of medical treatment, therapies, testing, guidance, and special teaching, as well as social and recreational activities needed by individuals with disabilities, will test the comprehensiveness of a successful school program.

Schools can use diagnostic information to design effective programs tailored to the needs and interests of the disabled child. Evaluation findings also pinpoint modifications needed in the school curricula so the child can benefit from educational experiences. The school can plan for trained personnel, supplies, equipment, and special services based on the assessment. Teachers must employ methods and materials suited to the individual's unique pattern of needs, interests, abilities, and motivation. Properly used, this information can provide the teacher with a vehicle for individualized instruction and provide an avenue for the child to succeed in his or her educational pursuits. A first step in making diagnostic information relevant to the schools is the retrieval of accurate, descriptive data that can be used in the instructional process.

SUMMARY

Community groups should join together to plan for children with disabling conditions. Community organizations can greatly facilitate services to the disabled child. Effective diagnosis should be interdisciplinary and point the way to adequate treatment and evaluation. Parents are a prime concern in community planning and should be involved throughout the total process if the treatment is to be beneficial. Properly instituted, community planning can greatly aid the child with developmental and/or learning disorders.

CHAPTER 13

Conclusions and Implications

From the very beginning, a child with a disability has an important place within the family. By being responsive to the child's needs for comfort, play, and love, a foundation for interactive social relationships is built. The drive for independence emerges as developmental skills grow. As the child tries to do more and more for himself or herself, he or she continues to depend on parents for guidance and support. Parental delight in the small accomplishments of a child can set expectations for larger successes.

Parents of children with disabilities, as well as all parents, have a tremendous influence and impact on setting appropriate models for developing social skills, as well as all skills. The developmental level of the child, as well as developmental sequence, must be considered in social skills training. Parents can contribute significantly to their children with disabilities' self-concept and control through appropriate modeling strategies (Dewitt, 1994; DiMartino, 1990).

In order for parents of children with disabilities to be effective change agents in promoting appropriate social skills development, early intervention in health care, counseling, housing, nutrition, education, child-rearing practices, and the like must be improved. Early intervention and parental involvement are essential for preparing children to master social skill tasks successfully.

There has been strong support from the federal government to include the family in the early educational process of their children. Parental involvement permits children to successfully manipulate their environments. The federal government created guidelines for the educational community in developing and implementing a comprehensive, coordinated, multidisciplinary, interagency program of early intervention services for infants, toddlers, and their families (Gallagher, 1989; Turnbull and Turnbull; 1996; Hoover-Dempsey and Sandler, 1995; Taylor, 2000).

The role of parental participation in educating their children with disabilities, according to much of the research in the field, has shown limited participation between the parents and the school. This view has been interpreted to imply that parents simply had no interest in the education of their children (Lynch and Stein, 1987; Marion, 1981). Several factors may contribute to lack of parental participation and involvement. Many parents do not feel welcome in the schools. They believe that they have little to offer in educating their children.

Parents have played a major role during this century in improving special education services for children with disabilities. They have had support from national organizations. Refer to www.nichcy.org/pubs/genresc/gr2.htm for a list of major organizations in the United States which support individuals with disabilities. These organizations operate on the state and local levels and were chiefly responsible for lobbying for federal and state legislation, as articulated in chapter 5.

During the last three decades, federal and state legislation increased parental involvement in special education in several areas. The most significant legislation included the due process and impartial hearing procedures. These procedures were adequately addressed in chapter 5. Safeguard procedures are basically the same in all states, with minor modifications. These procedures are mandated in federal and state legislation, designed to provide parents an opportunity to advance their case and to reduce the number of court cases filed by parents or school districts.

STRATEGIES FOR IMPROVING PARENTAL INVOLVEMENT

Recommended strategies for improving parental involvement in the schools have been indicated throughout this text. Much of the interest and increase in parental involvement may be attributed to P.L. 94-142 and its amendments. These legislative amendments have mandated parental participation in all aspects of the child's educational program, including assessment, individualized education plan (IEP) development, placement decisions, evaluation, follow-up, and transitional services. Some recommended strategies include:

- Rewarding parents. Teachers need to recognize and reward parents for their involvement. Reinforcing parental efforts can make a significant impact in working with their children (Oswald and Sinah-Nirbay, 1992). Parents employ some of the same techniques that teachers use to reinforce their children. Social and academic growth of children with disabilities may be expedited through the use of reinforcement strategies. Teachers who create a positive atmosphere for communication and collaboration with parents increase the probability of the child's success in his or her academic pursuits.
- Modeling for parents. Many parents are not trained in teaching strategies. Teachers can train interested parents through observation, demonstration, and modeling. Bandura (1977) has validated the importance of these techniques. Teachers should provide ample strategies for parents to imitate, which in their opinions will improve instruction for children. Today, educators realize the importance of parental involvement and realize that cooperative efforts between teachers and parents benefit the children significantly.
- Conferences. Both group and individual conferences have been found to be invaluable in improving collaboration between parents and teachers. Teachers may decide on the best type of conference needed to address the needs of the children. Some problems can be dealt with successfully in large groups, others in small groups. At any rate, confidentiality must be observed once the initial conference has been held; future conferences should be conducted on a regularly scheduled basis, agreed upon by both parent and teacher. Conference agendas should include items other than problems children are having. The author alluded to possible items in chapters 6 and 10. Timing of conferences is of prime importance. Conferences must be held at a time when it is conducive for parents to attend. The length of the conferences must also be considered by teachers. Parents have other commitments, and to avoid conflicts,

teachers should send out conference schedules and agenda items in advance. Advanced schedules should solicit parents' comments and suggestions. The final schedule should be modified to meet parental concerns. This approach will assist in assuring a sense of cooperation and openness between teachers and parents. Teachers and educators must be cognizant of the individual needs of parents and plan strategies based upon these needs.

Various types of reinforcement strategies should be in place to strengthen parental behaviors. The type of reinforcement or reward program instituted should be conducted in concert with the individual needs of the parents.

SOCIAL AND ACADEMIC MODELS

Changes are constantly occurring in early childhood. During this rapid expanding period, children gain self-awareness and learn how to respond appropriately in different situations. Making sure that appropriate social and academic models are provided is a responsibility of parents. Children who are products of a stimulating and positive environment bring a sense of social maturity and independence to the learning environment. Research findings by Delgado-Gaitan (1991) and Salli (1991) support this important concept.

Not only are social skills important in academic areas, they are also related to socialization. Several behaviors are necessary in the socialization process, including the emergence of self-identity and self-concept. Social skills are developed through the interactions with family, school, and the community, but none are as important as the role of the parents.

Parents may stimulate social growth and development of their children in various ways. Positive activities needed for normal child development might include (Taylor, 1998) designing everyday situations for them to explore, providing activities to promote self-esteem and confidence, praising them frequently, providing support, and creating a healthy and safe environment.

Armstrong and McPherson (1991), McKinney and Hocutt (1982), and Yanok and Derubertis (1989) informed us that parental involve-

ment is essential in assisting the school in developing appropriate social skills for disabled individuals. They concluded that involving parents in social skills homework makes transferring of social skills functional and realistic for children with disabilities. Parents may assist the
schools in several ways. They may reinforce the social skills taught at
home by providing practice and reinforcement for their children. They
may also provide the school with valuable information concerning developmental issues, safety concerns, community resources, and
demonstrations. Additionally, they may serve as resource individuals
and accompany the class on field trips.

Social changes are constantly occurring in early childhood. During
this rapid expanding period, children gain self-awareness and learn
how to respond appropriately in different social situations. Making sure
that appropriate social models are provided is a responsibility of parents. Children who are products of a stimulating and positive environment bring a sense of social maturity and independence to the learning
environment. Research findings by Lareau (1987), Delgado-Gaitan
(1991), and Salli (1991) support the above premise.

A recent Reader's Digest poll revealed that strong families give children an edge on school. Children who participated socially with their
families scored higher in tests than those who did not. The survey also revealed that strong family ties improved self-image and confidence in
children. The family is the cornerstone for success in later life. Parent education appears to play a role in how well the student performs in school.

The quality of family life appears to be a significant factor in all of
the groups. Children with disabilities from intact families performed
better than those who lived only with their mothers. Strong family ties
appear to reduce some of the anxiety faced by children with disabilities, and children of families who attended houses of worship also
scored higher on tests.

Creative and innovative ways relevant to family involvement must
be experimented with to improve parental involvement, especially for
parents of children with disabilities (Mansbach, 1993; Dalli, 1991).
Factors such as (1) diverse school experiences, (2) diverse economic
and time constraints, and (3) diverse linguistic and cultural practices all
combine to inhibit parental involvement. Diversity should be recognized as a strength rather than as a weakness. Parents need to feel that

their cultural styles and languages are valued knowledge and that this knowledge is needed and welcomed in the school (Sileo and Prater, 1998; Lynch and Hanson, 1998).

P.L. 94-142 and other federal amendments (P.L. 99-457, P.L. 10-517, and P.L. 107-110) have mandated parental involvement, from initial identification to placement of children with disabilities into educational settings. Individualized Education Plan (IEP) mandates this involvement. Additional mandates and ways of involving parents have been highlighted in chapter 1. One recommended approach is to dialogue with parents in order to understand what they think can be done to improve involvement (Finders and Lewis, 1994).

Unless the aforementioned strategies are adhered to, academic and social development of children with disabilities will be impeded. The combined cooperation of both school and home are needed if social skills training is to be effective. There is an urgent need to involve parents by making them aware of, as well as training them in the use of, social skill techniques to implement at home. Cassidy (1988) reported that problems with scheduling, transportation, and the lack of knowledge of instructional programs and IEP procedures are partly responsible for poor parental participation.

The role of parents of children with disabilities in the school must supersede the mandates of P.L. 94-142 and its amendments. Parents must feel that they are welcome in the school and be given responsibilities concerned with planning, collaboration with teachers, and policy making. Parents should have an active role in planning and instructing their children and function as advocates for them if children are to profit significantly from their school experiences. Schools should experiment with various ways of improving parental participation, since parents are the foremost educators of their children (Hermanson, 1984).

INNOVATED PRACTICES

Over the last decades, the school has had a difficult time in establishing effective partnerships with parents. Much of the fragmentation has occurred because of noninvolvement, hostility, or parental indifference toward the school. Many schools serving parents of children with disabilities consider them a nuisance, unproductive, uneducated, lacking social grace, and not well informed on education and social issues. The relationship is further strained when parents internalize the negative behaviors displayed by the school and view the school as an unacceptable place which has no interest in them as individuals. There must be a total shift in this paradigm. The school must accept these parents and provide training and assistance in desired areas (Eisner, 1991; Barth, 1990; Christenson, Rounds, and Franklin, 1992).

The role of parental participation in education in general, and special education in particular, according to much of the research in the field, has been shown to be limited. This view has been interpreted to imply that parents simply had no interest in the education of their children (Marion, 1981). Several factors may contribute to the lack of parental participation. Many parents do not feel welcome in the school. They believe that they have little to offer in educating their children. Cassidy (1991) reported that problems with scheduling, transportation, and knowledge of the IEP and special education procedures were partly responsible for poor parental participation. Other researchers implied that many parents, especially minority parents, disagreed with the present classification system. Many believed that their children were misplaced, or rejected the diagnosis and assessment process used to place their children (Harry, 1992).

Parents provide the model of self-acceptance and the feeling that life is worthwhile. Also, parents who demonstrate a positive self-concept and high self-esteem treat their children with respect and acceptance and provide them with strategies for demonstrating self-advocacy skills. These skills equip children to effectively communicate their interests, needs, desires, and rights. Additionally, self-advocacy involves making informed decisions and assuming responsibilities for them. Strategies in self-advocacy include problem solving, decision making, communication skills, self-awareness, and formulating realistic and achievable goals. Providing disabled children with strategies for achieving self-advocacy skills can help them become independent and active members of society. Acquisition of these skills is essential in effective transition (Eagan, Fredericks, Hendrickson, Peterson, and Moore, 1983).

COMMUNITY AND PARENTAL INVOLVEMENT

It is commonly stated that no school program can be completely effective without the support of parents and the community. When parents and community become actively involved in the school program, the entire educational program for children with disabilities and their parents benefit. It becomes quite clear that when the school and community are genuinely interested in the welfare of the child and his or her parents, apathy and despair are replaced by hope and self-fulfillment, which can do much to ease many of the emotional problems experienced. Further, improvement in communication can do much to eliminate the negativism that many parents have developed. This positive approach is essential for helping a disabled child realize his or her educational pursuits.

A desirable relationship in the community is one which is marked by a strong bond of understanding and cooperation between parents and school personnel. Parents should have a direct share in deciding what types of instruction appear to serve their children best. Parents should be welcome to make suggestions for the guidance of their children. Through various channels, the school should enlist the cooperation of parents and community agencies in designing and implementing educational programs for children with disabilities. In communities where educators work with parents and religious, recreational, and social agencies in a constructive effort to help, the results are reflected in healthier personalities of boys and girls (Ulrich and Bauer, 2003).

Several states have adopted programs like Family Math and Family Science to encourage parents to participate in their children's homework. Programs that encourage parents and their children to work collaboratively on a project may extend the children's learning experiences and help parents model skills and instruct their children (U.S. Department of Education, 1994). This type of collaboration makes parents equal partners in achieving common goals for their disabled children.

PARENTAL INVOLVEMENT: SOME PROJECTIONS

Role of Institutions of Higher Education

In the next decade, it is projected that the colleges and universities offering programs in teacher education will be required by national accreditation agencies to include skills and strategies for communicating and conferring with parents. It is commonly recognized that parents are the child's first teacher. Teachers must be trained to employ effective strategies to fully engage the parent in all educational activities, through collaborative efforts. Many teachers of individuals with disabilities have never experienced the presence of children with disabilities; consequently, they will need the expert opinions of parents in order to develop effective intervention techniques. Colleges and universities should include in their course offerings a course designed specifically for working with parents. Practicum and hands-on experiences should be provided for students to work with parents and model behaviors demonstrated. One of the major purposes of this text is to provide strategies for training prospective special educators in colleges and universities.

Teacher training programs must prepare all teachers to work with parents of children with disabilities. Regular teachers must be exposed to the most interactive techniques in the field of special education, through increasing courses involving educating children with disabilities. The five-year teacher education program will take on greater significance if this view is supported.

The Department of Education provides a variety of funding streams to support professional development of teachers based on state and local needs; these programs do not necessarily support activities that would increase the capacity of regular education teachers to address the needs of students with disabilities. New requirements resulting from the IDEA Amendments of 1997 and P.L. 110-117 will require general educators to become increasingly skilled at meeting the needs of students with disabilities. These requirements include, for example, that general educators be included in IEP meetings, that students with disabilities be provided access to the general education curriculum, that teachers be qualified for and certified in the subjects that they teach, and that students with disabilities participate in state and local assessment programs. The Office of Special Education Programs (OSEP) intends to use data from the NCES Schools and Staffing Survey to determine if an increasing percentage of general education teachers and community service providers are receiving preservice and in-service training in special education and developmentally appropriate practices. OSEP will also support preparation programs for regular education personnel to work with students with disabilities (U.S. Department of Education, 1998a).

The amount of time that most teacher training institutes devote to training teacher candidates to work successfully with parents is minimal at best (Kaplan, 1992; Nichols, 1995; Egan, 1998; Sommers-Flanagan and Sommers-Flanagan, 1993; Taylor, 2000). Collectively, these authors agreed that teacher training programs do not provide sufficient training to enable teacher candidates to learn effective counseling and conferences techniques to meet the many challenges imposed by parents of children with disabilities.

Concerning teacher education training program, Houston and Houston (1992, p. 257) related that:

> Preparing prospective teachers to be knowledgeable about parent-conferences is too low an expectation for effective teacher preparation programs. The influence of the family on the child is too great to ignore simply having the skills to conduct parent conferences does not go beyond technical competence to tap the essence of professional preparation. The psycho/sociological influence of the family is commanding and powerful. It deserves to be placed into its proper perspective in the study of culture and society in education, as well as the techniques of parent-conferences.

INCLUSION

P.L. 94-142 and its amendments specified several major laws dealing with parental involvement, as outlined in chapter 5. The major components of placement as related to parental involvement were addressed. The law stipulated that children with disabilities should be educated in the least restricted environment (LRE). Parents were to have an active role in deciding what constituted a LRE. To many educators and parents, the LRE implies placement in regular classrooms (inclusion) for all children with disabilities. On the other hand, there are opposing views (Bilken, 1989). (Refer to chapter 11 for the controversy concerning inclusion.) It was projected that by 2002, most children with mild to moderate disabilities would be contained in the regular classroom. For those children with severe to profound disabilities, full inclusion will be gradual over the next several decades; in some in-stances, some of these children may not be fully placed in inclusive classrooms. Parental perceptions and involvement will play a major role in the inclusion issue.

AN INTEGRATED APPROACH

In this text, attempts were made to provide educators and teachers with a blueprint to follow to involve parents effectively in the schools. Strategies were also provided for parents to implement in assisting teachers and educators in educating their children with disabilities. The fact that all segments of the community must collaborate in assisting parents in providing quality education for their children has also been stressed. A desirable relationship in the community is one that is marked by a strong bond of understanding and collaboration between parents, the school, and community agencies. Parental involvement should include all aspects of the child's school program as mandated by federal and state legislation.

Information Resources for Siblings

For further information on sibling networks contact:

The Sibling Information Network
249 Glenbrook Road, Box U-64
Department of Educational Psychology
The University of Connecticut
Storrs, CT 06268

Siblings for Significant Change
105 East 22nd Street
New York, NY 10017
(212) 420-0430

For information on how you can obtain a subscription to *Especially Grandparents*, contact:

Especially Grandparents
King County ARC
2230 Eighth Avenue
Seattle, WA 98121
(206) 622-9292

For further information on the SEFAM Project write:

Don Myer
SEFAM
Experimental Education Unit

WJ-10
Child Development and Mental Retardation Center
University of Washington
Seattle, WA 98195
(206) 543-4011

Source: *News Digest*, November 1985, The National Information Center for Handicapped Children and Youth, Box 1492, Washington, DC 20013.

Intervention and Treatment Approaches

Because your child's developmental difficulties may have multiple components, a comprehensive intervention strategy is probably a multi-disciplinary one. This may include clinical consultations geared toward developmentally appropriate caregiver-child interaction, speech therapy, occupational therapy, mediated play with peers, home-based and educational programs, bio-medical approaches, and possibly other techniques. Getting started as early as possible and pursuing an intensive program of intervention increases the likelihood of success for your child.

YOUR ROLE IN YOUR CHILD'S INTERVENTION

Your role in your child's intervention is critical. Children learn best when they are motivated to learn, when the learning is orchestrated by their emotions and desires. There is no one more qualified than you to tap into your child's emotions and desires, thereby helping him connect to the world.

DEVELOPMENTAL, INDIVIDUAL-DIFFERENCE, RELATIONSHIP-BASED (D.I.R.)

One therapeutic approach, advocated by experts associated with the Interdisciplinary Council, is the Developmental, Individual-Difference, Relationship-Based (D.I.R.) approach. This approach involves meeting your child at his current developmental level and building upon his particular set of strengths to help him develop. The approach suggests following the child's lead: tuning in to his interests and desires in interactions and play to harness the power of his motivation and help him climb the developmental ladder. It also involves tailoring these interactions to the child's individual differences in sensory reactivity, processing, and motor planning.

An important part of this program, in addition to the therapies mentioned earlier, is engaging in developmentally appropriate interactions at every opportunity. This is often referred to as "floor time," which literally involves getting down on the floor to play with your child.

By following your child's interests, joining what he is doing and wooing him with warm but persistent attempts to engage his attention, you can lead him to climb the developmental ladder. Through playful, engaging interactions, you can help him *want* to learn to pay attention, *want* to engage in some sort of dialogue, and *want* to take initiative, even before he speaks in any meaningful conversation.

By entering into your child's world, you can help your child learn to relate in a meaningful, spontaneous, flexible, and warm way. This does not happen overnight; adopting this approach involves making a commitment to spending a considerable period of time on the floor, playing with your child and becoming a part of his world, even if his activities are limited. It involves responding to his every utterance or gesture, in an effort to spark a response—the beginning of two-way communication with your child.

BEHAVIORAL MODIFICATION APPROACHES, INCLUDING ABA (APPLIED BEHAVIORAL ANALYSIS)

Another therapeutic approach is Applied Behavioral Analysis. ABA is an intensive, structured approach to teaching which involves the use of a technique known as *discrete trial training*. Skills, or lessons, are broken down into small, measurable tasks. A behavioral therapist works with a child using repetition, feedback, and rewards to help the child master these tasks.

Many professionals and public institutions recommend this therapeutic approach because it can yield relatively rapid, measurable changes in a child. Such behavioral techniques can be useful at an early stage in an intervention to help jump start the child's ability to pay attention and may be valuable as an *element* in the child's intervention. However, parents should be cautious about using behavioral approaches to *drive* their child's intervention. These approaches do not meet children at the developmental level. They focus on compliance with rote lessons that may not be meaningful, rather than follow children's interests and desires.

THE TEACCH PROGRAM

The TEACCH program, adopted by many special education programs, emphasizes a highly structured environment, in terms of physical classroom layout, schedule, and teaching methods, as well as the support of visual cues, to help the child learn. When appropriate, it can be one part of a multidisciplinary program. Its strategies can be useful for developing life-long skills for even the most challenged children.

As you plan and, over time, refine the intervention program for your child, remember that success should be measured by the growth of your child's ability to relate to his/her surroundings as well as to think for him/herself.

TRADITIONAL THERAPIES

Therapies may include some or all of the following:

- Speech therapy and oral motor therapy
- Occupational therapy (be sure that the therapist is trained in sensory integration techniques)
- Physical therapy
- Services of a special education teacher or inclusion specialist
- Interactive, developmental play therapy (for insurance purposes, this therapy should be referred to as "psychotherapy")
- Peer play: as soon as your child is ready, it is very important for him to have regular play dates so that he can practice his social skills

There are many ways for children to receive such services. They may receive services at home, attend a typical school with the support of an aide and/or other therapists, or attend a special education school where services are integrated into the program and a continuum of inclusion services may be offered.

Include professionals in your child's intervention team who respect your point of view and who see your child's possibilities as well as his or her difficulties.

ALTERNATIVE THERAPIES

There are numerous alternative therapies which can be explored. While many parents view such therapies as optional or complementary to the child's core of traditional therapies, some find alternative therapies to play a more central role because of the profound effect a particular therapy may have on the child's progress.

Because of the lack of definitive studies on alternative therapies, parents need to review their options with their primary physician and therapeutic team, and most importantly, observe carefully to see how a particular treatment affects all aspects of their child.

Some general categories include:

1. Bio-medical interventions. This involves treating any existing biological issues, such as allergies, nutritional deficits, and digestive problems which may be contributing to children's difficulties. It may include dietary restrictions, nutritional supplements, and the use of homeopathic or prescription drugs.

   It is important to note that many prescription medications for child mood and behavior have not been sufficiently studied in young children and therefore their effects must be very closely monitored. These include positive signs, such as improved self-regulation, relating, communicating and thinking, as well as signs of irritability, increased self-absorption, repetitive behavior, and sleeping, eating, or other health problems.
2. Interventions to help the child's sensory processing. Examples include:

   • Technologies to improve auditory perception, such as the Tomatis, Berard, or Samonas methods.

- Technologies to improve auditory processing, including computer-assisted therapies such as FastForword, Earobics, and Away We Go.
- Approaches to improve visual motor and visual spatial processing.

3. Inclusion opportunities. Activities such as music, gym, dance, or drama can build on your child's interests while providing her with opportunities to develop motor planning and social skills.

WHERE CAN YOU GO FOR HELP?

Private practitioners and therapists are available and may be covered by some health insurance plans. Contact a regional children's hospital to get help putting together a team of professionals who can evaluate your child. Networking with other parents with experience in this area is another good way to get information about professionals who can help evaluate and/or treat your child. Many children enter through Child Find.

Federal law mandates that all children may receive evaluation testing. For those identified with developmental delays, services are to be delivered with no cost to the family. Administration of this early intervention program varies by state. In many states, the program is delivered at a county or local level through the Department of Education, the Department of Health, or the Department of Social Services. Contact your local school district to find out who in your area administers the early intervention program for children.

Strongly consider obtaining private evaluations. Some communities offer treatment centers with teams of professionals who perform evaluations. In other communities, individual practitioners may do them. Many regional universities have child study centers with appropriate teams of evaluators.

RECOMMENDED READING—FOR STARTERS

Books

Greenspan, Stanley I., and Serena Wieder. (1998). *The Child with Special Needs: A comprehensive approach to encouraging intellectual and emotional growth in children.* Reading, MA: Addison-Wesley.

Kranowitz, Carol S. (1998). *The Out-of-Sync Child: Recognizing and coping with sensory integration dysfunction*. New York: A Perigree Book.

Web sites

www.icdl.com. (The Interdisciplinary Council on Developmental and Learning Disorders) Publications available through this site include *For Parents, By Parents, A Resource Guide,* an extensive, detailed compilation of resources.

www.eunicorn.com. The Unicorn Children's Foundation provides more in-depth detail of the topics covered in this road map, as well as links to other sites.

www.devdelay.org. The Developmental Delay Registry provides numerous links to relevant sites.

www.autism.com/ari. (Autism Research Institute) See their DAN! Practitioner list to find practitioners who can conduct a health review of your child.

www.nichcy.org. (The National Information Center for Children and Youth with Disabilities) This site provides information about how to obtain therapeutic services by state. NICHCY can also be reached by phone at 800-695-0285.

www.autismNDI.com. This is the Autism Network for Dietary Intervention site.

www.feingold.org. This is the Feingold dietary program site which provides information on the potential role of food and synthetic additives in the treatment of behavioral, learning, and health problems.

Overview of the Individuals with Disabilities Education Act Amendments of 1997 (P.L. 105–17)

Bernadette Knoblauch

On June 4, 1997, President William J. Clinton signed the bill reauthorizing and amending the Individuals with Disabilities Education Act (IDEA). The bill became Public Law 105-17, the Individuals with Disabilities Education Act Amendments of 1997; it was the 17th law passed by the 105th Congress.

IDEA organized in four parts: Part A, General Provisions; Part B, Assistance for the Education of All Children with Disabilities (school age/preschool programs); Part C, Infants and Toddlers with Disabilities, and Part D, National Activities to Improve the Education of Children with Disabilities (support programs). P.L. 105-17 retains the major provisions of earlier federal laws in this area, including the assurance of a free appropriate public education (FAPE) in the least restrictive environment (LRE) and the guarantee of due process procedures. It also includes modifications to the law. Some of the changes that affect special education practice nationwide include:

- Participation of students with disabilities in state and districtwide assessment (testing) programs (including alternative assessment)
- Development and review of the individualized education program (IEP), including increased emphasis on participation of children and youth with disabilities in the general education teachers in developing the IEP
- Enhanced parent participation in eligibility and placement decisions
- Streamlined student evaluation/reevaluation requirements

- Identification of transition service needs within a child's course of study beginning at age fourteen, the age at which transition services should begin
- The availability of mediation services as a means of more easily resolving parent-school differences
- Disciplinary procedures for students with disabilities, including allowances for an appropriate interim alternative educational setting
- Allowing children ages three to nine to be identified as developmentally delayed; previously it was ages three to five.

Following are some of the highlights of the new law:

- Requires that parents be informed about the educational progress of their child at least as often as parents of nondisabled children.
- Specifies that a statement of transition services needs relating to course of study be included in the student's IEP beginning at age fourteen.
- Requires that instruction in and use of Braille be considered for students who are blind or visually impaired.
- Adds "orientation and mobility services" to the definition of related services.

PROCEDURAL SAFEGUARDS

In the area of procedural safeguards, IDEA 97:

- Requires more "user-friendly language" in delivering information to parents about their child's rights.
- Requires that parents be given access to all records relating to their child, not just those "relevant" records on the identification, evaluation, and educational placement of their child.
- Preserves existing procedural safeguards, such as due process and the right of the parents to recover reasonable attorneys' fees and costs if they prevail in administrative or judicial proceedings under IDEA. (In most cases, however, attorneys' fees cannot be reimbursed for IEP meetings.)

- Requires each state to establish a voluntary mediation process, with qualified impartial mediators who are knowledgeable about mediation techniques as well as special education laws and regulations.

DISCIPLINE

In the area of discipline, IDEA 97:

- Ensures that no student with a disability is denied ongoing educational services due to behavior. Schools must continue to provide educational services for students with disabilities whose suspension or expulsion constitutes a change in placement (usually more than ten days in a school year).
- Gives schools the authority to remove students with disabilities to alternative settings for behavior related to drugs or guns and other dangerous weapons for up to forty-five days.
- Allows schools to place a student in an "interim alternative educational setting" (AES), another setting, or suspend a student for up to ten days in a school year, in the same way students without disabilities are disciplined.
- Requires the IEP Team to conduct a "manifest determination" once a school decides to discipline a student with a disability. The IEP Team must determine within ten calendar days after the school decides to discipline a student—whether the student's behavior is related to the disability. If the behavior is not related to the disability, the student maybe disciplined in the same way as a student without a disability, but special education and related services must continue.
- Permits school personnel to report crimes allegedly committed by students with disabilities to law enforcement authorities.

OUTCOMES AND STANDARDS

In the area of outcomes and standards, IDEA 97 requires states to:

- Include students with disabilities in state and districtwide testing programs, with accommodations when necessary.
- Establish performance goals for students with disabilities.

EVALUATIONS AND CURRICULUM

In the area of evaluations and IEPs, IDEA 97:

- Requires an explanation in the IEP, if necessary, of how state and districtwide assessments will be modified so that students with disabilities can participate in these assessments.
- Requires states to ensure that students with disabilities have access to the general education curriculum, and, if a student will not be participating in the general education program and extracurricular activities, an explanation in the student's IEP is required.
- Requires regular education teachers to be included on the IEP team if the student is participating or might be participating in general education classes.
- Expressly requires that the IEP address positive behavioral intervention strategies, if appropriate.
- Requires state and local educational agencies to ensure that parents are members of any group that makes placement decisions.
- Streamlines the reevaluation process, allowing parents and school districts to determine any areas in which reevaluation dates are not needed.
- Requires informed parental consent for all evaluations and reevaluations unless the school district can demonstrate that it has taken reasonable measures to obtain consent and the parent has failed to respond.

EARLY INTERVENTION AND PRESCHOOL SERVICES

In the area of early intervention and preschool services, which is now Part C, IDEA 97:

- Requires that local school districts participate in a transition planning conference for toddlers with disabilities who are about to enter preschool.
- Explicitly calls for delivery of early intervention services in natural environments.

- Clarifies that the early intervention programs is payor of last resort.

TEACHER TRAINING AND PREPARATION

In the area of teacher training and preparation, IDEA 97:
Creates a new system of grants to improve results for students with disabilities through system reform, emphasizing personnel training, and training for regular education teachers of early grades.

REFERENCES

Bazelon Center for Mental Health. *A New Idea: A Parent's Guide to the Changes in Special Education Law for Children with Disabilities*. Washington, D.C.: Bazelon Center for Mental Health, 1998.

The Council for Exceptional Children. *IDEA 97: Let's Make It Work*. Reston, Va.: The Council for Exceptional Children, 1998.

New Jersey Developmental Disabilities Council. *Common Ground. Illinois Assistive Technology Project 1997 Tech Talk*. 1997.

Individuals with Disabilities Education Act Amendments of 1997. (P.L. 105-17). 1997. 20 U.S.C. Chapter 33.

Kupper, L. (Ed.). The IDEA Amendments of 1997. NICHCY New Digest 26 (Rev. ed.). 1998. Washington, D.C.: National Information Center for Children and Youth with Disabilities.

The Individuals with Disabilities Education Act (IDEA) Amendments of 1997

WHAT IS THE INDIVIDUALS WITH DISABILITIES ACT?

The Individuals with Disabilities Education Act, first enacted in 1975, guarantees the right to a free appropriate public education for all children with disabilities ages three through twenty-one, inclusive. The law provides federal funding to assist states and local school systems to pay for special education and related services. In addition, IDEA contains provisions which help fund programs for infants and toddlers with disabilities and their families, and a number of discretionary programs which help support the guarantees under the basic state grant program.

WHY DID THE CONGRESS CHANGE THE LAW?

There were several motivations that resulted in the Congress doing a full review of this vital law. First, the authority for IDEA's so-called discretionary programs and the Early Intervention Program for Infants and Toddlers had expired, and they needed to be reauthorized. Second, the law had never been comprehensively reviewed in its twenty-two-year history. Third, society and schools in general have changed substantially over the past two decades, resulting in new and difficult challenges and pressures to our nation's schools. Discipline and school safety, serious funding crises, the lack of student achievement, and the accountability of schools and their leaders have troubled our country for some time. Special education has not escaped these problems.

Fourth, special education has suffered from an escalating backlash from many parents of children without disabilities, many school authorities, and from the media. Fifth, even some parents of special education students were disgruntled with the implementation of IDEA as it related to their child. For example, many are unhappy with the inability of their child to be educated with their nondisabled peers. Finally, special education has been severely criticized by the very professionals who are responsible for implementing IDEA. Many school boards, administrators, and teachers criticized the law from several perspectives.

WHAT ARE THE KEY ASPECTS OF THE REVISED IDEA?

President Clinton signed the 1997 IDEA amendments into law (P.L. 105-17) on June 4, 1997. The revised law represents a fair and balanced compromise, leaving no party involved in the legislation process completely satisfied. From The Arc's perspective, there are many improvements to the law and several serious concerns.
Key positives in IDEA include:

- Cessation of education services is prohibited.
- Educational improvement is emphasized.
- Parental participation in decision making is improved.
- Individualized educational programs are strengthened.
- Dispute resolution through mediation is encouraged.
- Funding formulas for schools are revised.
- Special purpose programs are revamped.

Potential concerns include:

- Limitations on attorney fee reimbursements for parents.
- Expanded and stricter discipline provisions.
- Potential misinterpretations and misapplications of the new law by school authorities.

HOW WILL THE NEW LAW HELP PARENTS BETTER PARTICIPATE IN THEIR CHILD'S EDUCATION?

First, it is critical for parents to know that the basic guarantee of a free appropriate public education (FAPE) and the due process procedures to protect this guarantee remain in the law.

One major improvement in the law now guarantees that parents will be part of any decision made about where the child will receive his or her education. Allowing parents to participate in the placement decision will help those who seek to see their child included in classes and programs with nondisabled children.

Schools must now provide parents of special education students with regular reports on student progress, at least as often as parents of nondisabled children receive them, usually through report cards.

IDEA also provides funding for parent training centers to help parents be educated and receive training and technical assistance on the new law. School authorities are also now required, where necessary and when feasible, to communicate directly with parents about parents' rights in simple terms and using the native language of the family.

WHAT NEW PROVISIONS IN THE LAW WILL HELP STUDENTS WITH DISABILITIES DO BETTER IN SCHOOL?

Many new parts of IDEA aim to improve results for students with disabilities.
These include:

- emphasis on access to the general education curriculum;
- a statement of transition service needs of the child beginning at age fourteen and beginning at age sixteen and younger, if needed, a statement of transition services included in the child's individualized education program;
- school officials must give an explanation in the child's individualized education program as to the extent that child will not be educated with nondisabled children; including students with disabilities in all state and district-wide assessments;
- providing alternative assessments for those students who cannot reasonably be expected to participate in general assessments;
- eliminating unnecessary testing and evaluations and making reevaluations more instructionally relevant; and
- requiring appropriate behavior interventions to prevent and address disciplinary concerns.

HOW DOES IDEA ADDRESS THOSE CONCERNS EXPRESSED BY SCHOOL AUTHORITIES?

The revised IDEA contains numerous provisions to help school officials meet their special education responsibilities. In regard to funding, the law revises the funding formula. Eventually, the child count system in effect for twenty years will be replaced by a formula that distributes "new" money based 85 percent on the general population and 15 percent on a poverty factor. This formula will be in effect once the IDEA State Grant Program is funded at a level exceeding just over $4.9 billion (currently funded at $3.1 billion).

Local school systems would also get relief when funding exceeds $4.1 billion for the IDEA state grant program. When that appropriation is reached, a school system can use up to 20 percent of its Part B funding that exceeds the amount it received under Part B the previous year for other purposes. The new IDEA also established stronger provisions for interagency agreements with other state agencies to help with the cost of special education.

In addition to fiscal issues, schools will be helped with reductions in paperwork burdens and limitations on parents' access to certain attorneys' fees even though parents prevail in court. Regular education teachers involved with a special education child will now be included in individualized education plan (IEP) decisions, and by stricter discipline measures.

HOW DOES IDEA PROMOTE SAFER, BETTER DISCIPLINED STUDENTS?

IDEA substantially changes the law regarding discipline. School officials will still be able to discipline any student with a disability for up to ten school days when students violate school rules. Very importantly, students will return to their original placements (unless the parents and school officials agree otherwise) in most disciplinary matters.

School officials will now be able to place students with disabilities in an interim alternative educational setting for the same amount of time a child without disability would be subject to discipline, but no more than up to forty-five school days:

- if students bring a weapon to school or to a school function;
- if students knowingly possess, use, or sell illegal drugs in school or at a school function; or
- a hearing officer may order a change in placement for a child with a disability to an interim alternative educational setting for not more than forty-five days if the hearing officer finds that the student is likely to injure him/herself or others.

Before a removal of more than ten school days, a "manifestation determination" must be made to ascertain if the students' actions are related to their disability. If the action is determined to be unrelated to the disability, students with disabilities may be disciplined the same way students without disabilities are disciplined. In making the manifestation determination, the hearing officer must also consider whether the child's disability impaired his or her ability to (1) understand the impact and consequences of the behavior and (2) control the behavior. However, no student with a disability may have his or her education ceased. Free appropriate public education must be provided during any removal beyond ten school days.

WHO DECIDES IF A STUDENT IS "SUBSTANTIALLY LIKELY TO INJURE" AND WHAT STANDARD IS USED TO MAKE THAT DETERMINATION?

A hearing officer makes the decision, using a standard higher than the one previously used by the courts in such cases. Local school authorities must prove substantial likelihood of injury by "substantial evidence." Substantial evidence is further defined as "beyond a preponderance of evidence," using the Honig Supreme Court decision as the basis of decisions. In addition, the hearing officer must consider the appropriateness of the child's current placement and whether school officials made reasonable efforts to minimize the risk of injury.

In the alternative placement, the child must continue to participate in the general curriculum and continue to receive services and modifications, including those in his or her current IEP that will enable the child to meet the IEP goals and to receive services that are designed to address the behavior that led to the placement of the child in that setting.

HOW WILL "DISRUPTIVE" BEHAVIOR BE ADDRESSED IN THE LAW?

Although the issue of "disruptive" students was given serious consideration during the debate over the reauthorization of IDEA, the IDEA amendments of 1997 contain no mention of "disruptive" students. The Arc was adamantly opposed to any such provision.

There are a number of provisions, however, in the IEP process aimed at addressing the behavior of students with disabilities. For example, when a child's behavior impedes his or her learning or that of other students, the IEP team shall consider, when appropriate, strategies, including positive behavioral interventions, strategies, and supports, to address that behavior.

HOW DOES THE LAW HELP PARENTS AND SCHOOL SYSTEMS RESOLVE DISPUTES?

For the first time, IDEA requires each state to put in place and find a mediation system. Mediation is voluntary for both parents and the schools. Each mediator must be qualified and impartial. Mediation cannot be used to deny or delay a parent's right to a due process hearing. Parents who decide not to enter mediation, however, may be counseled about the utility of mediation in resolving disputes and encouraged to use it by a disinterested party. Attorneys' fees need not be awarded for mediation at the discretion of the state for a mediation that is conducted prior to filing a due process complaint by the parent.

CAN PARENTS STILL BE REIMBURSED FOR THE COSTS OF ATTORNEYS' FEES IF THEY PREVAIL IN DUE PROCESS?

Yes, but with certain new limits. For example, attorneys' fees are not reimbursable for the use of an attorney at the IEP meeting, unless the IEP meeting is the result of an "administrative proceeding or judicial action." As stated earlier, attorneys' fees cannot be awarded for mediation prior to filing a due process complaint unless the state allows for such reimbursement.

Courts can reduce fees if the parents' attorney did not provide the school district with appropriate information as required by law. Parents are also required, directly or through their attorney, to notify the school system of their concerns prior to filing a due process action if they later wish to claim fees. Included in the information parents must provide to the school system are the child's name, the child's address, and the school of the student, a description of the nature of the problem with the child's education, and if known, a proposed resolution.

Attorneys' fees can also be reduced if the Court concludes that the parents unreasonably protracted a final resolution of the situation. Conversely, fees cannot be reduced if the Court finds that the school system unreasonably protracted matters.

HOW DOES IDEA NOW DEAL WITH THE TRANSFER OF PARENTAL RIGHTS?

Essentially, the new law allows states to permit the child with a disability to obtain all relevant rights at the age of majority, with two exceptions. First, the child will not obtain such rights if he or she has been found incompetent under state law. Second, if the child has not been deemed incompetent but is unable to provide informed consent in decision making, states may establish a procedure less burdensome than a competency hearing to allow parents to retain the rights.

ARE THERE ANY CHANGES TO PART H, THE EARLY INTERVENTION STATE GRANT FOR INFANTS AND TODDLERS?

Part H will now be known as Part C, beginning on July 1, 1998. Although The Arc and other disability groups sought a permanent authority for Part H, the Congress reauthorized the new Part C for five years. A number of find tuning provisions were added to Part C. They include:

- the addition of a new definition of "at risk infant and toddler" to mean a child under three years of age who would be at risk of experiencing a substantial developmental delay if early intervention services were not provided;

- a number of new provisions altering the statewide system requirements;
- a number of new provisions to the Individualized Family Service Program; including a provision requiring the service agency to justify the extent, if any, that services will not be provided in a natural environment (e.g., the family home); and
- new membership requirements and role revision for the State Interagency Coordination Council.

WHAT HAPPENS TO THE IDEA DISCRETIONARY PROGRAMS?

The new law makes massive changes to the IDEA discretionary programs. First and foremost, the number of programs decreases from fourteen to three. One represents a new federal initiative while the other two merge and consolidate existing programs. These became Part D of the law.

The new program established a competitive grant program, called the State Program Improvement Grants, aimed at reforming special education programs. Seventy-five percent of the funds (fifty percent under certain conditions) will address personnel preparation, particularly in-service training. States that receive grants will receive from half a million to two million dollars annually. The grants emphasize partnerships with local school systems and other state agencies and disability groups, including parents.

The other two programs consolidate existing discretionary programs. The coordinated research and personnel preparation section will deal with issues such as:

- early childhood education
- serious emotional disturbance
- personnel development
- severe disabilities
- innovation and development
- transition services

The coordinated technical assistance, support, and dissemination program will embrace the following activities:

- parent training
- information clearinghouse
- technology
- regional resource centers

Part D programs are authorized for five years, through FT 2002.
The Part I Family Support Program is reauthorized, but only until October 1, 1998. This unfunded program will need to find a home in another law. The Arc intends to seek reauthorization of this as yet unfunded program in legislation related to programs housed within the Department of Health and Human Services.

ARE ALL THE PROVISIONS OF IDEA EFFECTIVE UPON ENACTMENT?

No, there are a number of dates where specific components of IDEA will take effect. Some of the more important implementation dates are:

- October 1, 1997 Part D Discretionary Programs
- July 1, 1998 IEP revisions, Part C Early Intervention
- July 1, 2001 Alternative assessment for those students who cannot participate in regular assessments

Most of the key provisions in the IDEA State Grant Program will be in effect for the school year that starts on or about September 1, 1997.

NOW THAT THE LEGISLATION IS LAW, WHAT ARE THE RELEVANT IMPLEMENTATION ISSUES?

The work of the Congress is not done. Attention now shifts to the FY 1998 appropriations process. Funding for IDEA is contained in the Departments of Labor, Health and Human Services, and Education appropriations bill.

Since the new fiscal year begins on October 1, 1997, the Congress has until then to appropriate funding for the revamped IDEA. Republican leaders in the House and the Senate have pledged to secure major funding increases ($1 billion) for IDEA. The Arc will work to support increased funding for all components of IDEA, the Part B State Grant Program, the Preschool Program, Part C Early Intervention, and Part D Discretionary Programs.

Much attention now shifts to the U.S. Department of Education, which must develop regulations to implement the new law. Preliminary plans call for the department to promulgate proposed rules in the *Federal Register* by the end of September or early October. A ninety-day public comment period follows. Plans also call for six regional hearings to be held on the proposed regulations. Final regulations are scheduled to be published by the end of April 1998. The Arc must be fully prepared to comment on the proposed rules this fall.

The Department of Education will also undertake major training and technical assistance activities to inform all affected parties about the changes to IDEA. It is vital that parents take part in these sessions to learn about the new law.

WHAT CAN LEADERS OF THE ARC DO TO MAKE SURE THAT THE RIGHTS OF STUDENTS WITH MENTAL RETARDATION AND THEIR PARENTS REMAIN GUARANTEED AND THAT EDUCATIONAL OUTCOMES FOR STUDENTS WITH DISABILITIES MEET THE PROMISE OF THE NEW IDEA?

Almost all aspects of the new law fall to state and local educational agencies to implement. It is vital that leaders of The Arc at the state and local levels first learn about new law and then work closely with state and local school authorities as they set policy to implement the law. The Arc at all levels should participate in training and other activities aimed at full and accurate implementation of the law.

The Arc at all levels has monitored special education implementation for more than two decades. Enactment of the IDEA amendments of 1997 requires a redoubling of monitoring efforts since the promise of this law will not be realized in many communities unless strong monitoring takes place.

HOW CAN THE ARC FURTHER ADVOCATE FOR INCLUSION FOR STUDENTS WITH MENTAL RETARDATION UNDER THE NEW LAW?

For decades, The Arc has demonstrated and decried the lack of inclusion of students with mental retardation in regular education settings. New tools are now available to help parents and students achieve this goal. Parents are now part of the placement decision-making process. School systems must now give an explanation in the IEP of the extent to which a child is not included with nondisabled peers. These two provisions can give those parents who seek to have their child in regular classes unprecedented leverage. Parents must be informed and trained about these important provisions and then use them to secure appropriate educational programs for their children.

ARE THERE ISSUES THAT SHOULD CAUSE SERIOUS CONCERN FOR PARENTS?

Yes. The Arc is especially concerned about potential abuse by school officials of the new "substantially likely to injure" provision. This provision could be used inappropriately by those teachers and administrators who don't want students with mental retardation in regular educational settings. Although the Congress set a high standard for school authorities to prove a student would be "substantially likely to injure," this provision will require close monitoring by the federal and state governments, as well as parents and advocates.

Numerous other provisions could be adversely manipulated by school officials to the detriment of students. Again, knowledgeable parents and advocates must step in and be heard when such abuses arise.

WHERE CAN I GET MORE INFORMATION ABOUT THE NEW IDEA?

Many entities, governmental and public, are now developing materials to explain the new law. Check with the Parent Training and Information Center in your state. Their information will be slanted for use by parents.

Contact your state chapter of The Arc for the location of your PTI. The U.S. Office of Special Education Programs is also developing materials. They can be contacted by writing to OSEP, Switzer Building, 330 C Street, Washington, D.C. 20202 or by calling (202) 205-5507.

The Arc's Governmental Affairs Office is always available to assist you. Write to 1730 K Street, NW, Suite 1212, Washington, D.C. 20006, call (202) 785-3388, or send e-mail to arcga@radix.net. The Governmental Affairs Office has also sent a package of preliminary materials developed by several sources about IDEA to all state chapters of The Arc, as well as a copy of the law and a useful video on the new law.

Note: This document was reviewed for consistency with the Individuals with Disabilities Education Act (P.L.. 105-17) by the United States Office of Special Education Programs.

*This Q&A has been prepared to provide an early introduction of the 1997 Amendments to IDEA. It presents aspects of the law's development, describes changes to the law, and discusses implementation issues. It will be most helpful when read in conjunction with *The New IDEA: Knowing your rights* video.

Readings on the IDEA Amendments of 1997

Bock, S. J. et al. Suspension and Expulsion: Effective Management for Students. *Intervention in School and Clinic*, 34, no. 1 (1998): 50–52.

This article provides a brief review of legal procedures that schools have available under the Individuals with Disabilities Education Act (IDEA) Amendments of 1997 and discusses problems with using suspension and expulsion, including recidivism, increased dropout rates, overrepresentation of minorities receiving suspension or expulsion, and indiscriminate suspension and expulsion.

Bureau of Indian Affairs, Dept. of Interior. Educational Rights of Parents under Provisions of the Individuals with Disabilities Education Act Including the Amendments of 1997 (Special Education). ED416661. Washington, D.C.: Bureau of Indian Affairs, 1997.

This pamphlet describes the educational rights of parents provided under provisions of the IDEA, including the amendments of 1997. It discusses rights in the following areas: free appropriate public education, prior notice to parents, parental consent, independent educational evaluations, educational surrogate parents, students records, mediation, discipline, state complaint procedures, impartial due process hearings, and private school placement. The pamphlet ends with a summary of parents' rights.

IDEA 1997: Let's Make It Work. Reston, Va.: Council for Exceptional Children, 1998.

This document explains provisions of the 1997 amendments to IDEA (Public Law 105-17), and is divided into sixteen topics, most of which address specific sections of the law. Topics include parental involvement; developmental delay; cultural diversity; evaluation and reevaluation; the individualized education program (IEP); related services and technology; early childhood; procedural safeguards; mediation; behavior and discipline; state and local fiscal management responsibilities; private school placements; performance goals, indicators, and assessments; and national support programs. Two additional sections provide a summary of IDEA, an index of topics located in the legislation, and a list of general resources for IDEA.

Johns, B. H. What the New Individuals with Disabilities Education Act (IDEA) Means for Students Who Exhibit Aggressive or Violent Behavior. (Theme Issue: Aggression and Violence in the Schools-What Teachers Can Do.) *Preventing School Failure*, 42, no. 3 (1998): 102–05.

This article outlines new provisions in the reauthorized Individuals with Disabilities Education Act that benefit children with behavior or emotional disorders. Provisions that focus on keeping students in school, accurate assessment of student behavior, positive behavioral interventions, and children who bring weapons or drugs to school are discussed.

Landau, J. K. *Statewide Assessment: Policy Issues, Questions, and Strategies*. PEER Policy Paper. 7p. (ED number to be assigned). 1988. Washington, D.C.: ERIC.

This policy paper provides a list of questions and associated strategies that parents and parent organizations can address in an effort to ensure that statewide assessment systems fully and fairly include students with disabilities as required by the 1997 IDEA and other federal laws. Introductory material notes the purposes of these large-scale assessments and the relation of statewide assessment programs to education reform initiatives. Suggested questions address the following issues: type of assessment used, use of "off the shelf" or contracted assessments, the process for developing the assessment, the consequences for students of the statewide assessments, inclusion of all students with disabilities in the assessment, responsibility for determining if a student with disabilities needs accommodations to participate in the assessment, types of accommodations available to students with disabilities, how test results are to be used, and how test scores of students with disabilities will be reported. Among seven strategies recommended to parents are the following: obtain copies of state's education reform and assessment legislation, regulations, and policy documents; identify who makes policy decisions about participation of students with disabilities; and get involved in the decision-making process.

McConnell, M. E. et al. Functional Assessment: A Systematic Process for Assessment and Intervention in General and Special Education Classrooms. *Intervention in School and Clinic*, 34, no. 1 (1998): 10–20.
This article describes a ten-step process that educators can use when conducting functional assessments and developing Behavioral Intervention Plans required under the IDEA 1997 for students with disabilities with behavior problems.

Manasevit, L. M. et al. *Opportunities and Challenges: An Administrator's Guide to the New IDEA*. ED415649. 1997.
This manual is designed to help state and local administrators, school board members, and other education advocates understand the complex requirements of the newly authorized IDEA. This manual provides step-by-step instruction on IDEA's administrative and procedural requirements. It discusses some of the problems with the old act and highlights the nature of and reasons for the changes. The manual identifies new questions arising from the reauthorized IDEA and discusses potential outcomes under the new statute. It offers insight into the interpretations likely to follow in regulations or the courts and provides practical guidance for understanding IDEA. The manual focuses primarily on the requirements of Part B, the state grant program which provides financial assistance for educating children with disabilities. Individual chapters discuss the changes to state and local planning requirements; identification, evaluation, and placement of children with disabilities; the IEP process; discipline; procedural

safeguards; and fiscal obligations. The manual also gives an overview of the program that provides assistance for infants and toddlers with disabilities, known as Part C of the Act.

National Information Center for Children and Youth with Disabilities (NICHCY). *The IDEA Amendments of 1997* (rev. ed.) (ED number to be assigned). Washington, D.C.: National Information Center for Children and Youth with Disabilities, 1998.

This news digest summarizes the reauthorized IDEA with emphasis on changes in the new law. These changes include participation of children and youth with disabilities in state and districtwide assessment programs, the way in which evaluations are conducted, parent participation in eligibility and placement decisions, development and review of the IEP, transition planning, and voluntary mediation as a means of determining if each child continues to be a child with a disability.

O'Leary, E. *Transition: Terms and Concepts*. ED419330. 1998. Washington, D.C.: ERIC.

This paper provides explanations and case examples of some terms and concepts related to transition of students with disabilities under the 1997 amendments to IDEA. Explanations and examples focus on the concepts of "statement of transition service needs" and "statement of needed transition services." The statement of transition service needs focuses on the student's course of study and other educational experiences and is required on an IEP for every student who is fourteen years of age and older. The statement of needed transition services is a long-range two- to four-year plan for adult life and is required for every student with an IEP who is sixteen years of age and older (younger, if appropriate). This statement must include long-range post-school planning in the areas of instruction, employment, community experiences, post-school adult living, and related services. Also addressed is involvement of other agencies in cooperation with the schools. A sample form for meeting transition requirements includes space for specifying desired post-school outcomes, the present level of educational performance, the statement of transition service needs, and the statement of needed transition services (presented in a matrix form showing specific services, activities/strategies, agency/responsibilities, and who will provide and/or pay).

Palmer, S. *Early Intervention Services for Children Birth through Age 2 Enacted by P.L. 105-17 (IDEA 97)*. ED416647. 1997. Washington, D.C.: ERIC.

This fact sheet uses a question-and-answer format to summarize early intervention services for children (birth through age two) provided by Part C of the Individuals with Disabilities Education Act of 1997 (Public Law 105-17). Questions and answers address the following topics: the purpose of Part C (early identification and intervention with infants and toddlers), eligibility for services under Part C (children under age three with developmental delay or diagnosed conditions), services mandated to eligible children and their families, the Individualized Family Service Plan, procedural safeguards under Part C, the role of the state and federal governments in providing services, services that each state must provide (such as a comprehensive child and referral system), and paying for early intervention services.

No Child Left Behind Act

NCLB REGULATIONS & COMPLIANCE

Title I, Sec. 1118, Parental Involvement

A. Local Educational Agency Policy

1. In General—A local educational agency may receive funds under this part only if such agency implements programs, activities, and procedures for the involvement of parents in programs assisted under this part consistent with this section. Such programs, activities, and procedures shall be planned and implemented with meaningful consultation with parents of participating children.

2. Written Policy—Each local educational agency that receives funds under this part shall develop jointly with, agree on with, and distribute to, parents of participating children a written parent involvement policy. The policy shall be incorporated into the local educational agency's plan developed under section 1112, establish the agency's expectations for parent involvement, and describe how the agency will—

   A. involve parents in the joint development of the plan under section 1112, and the process of school review and improvement under section 1116;

   B. provide the coordination, technical assistance, and other support necessary to assist participating schools in planning and implementing effective parent involvement activities to improve student academic achievement and school performance;

C. build the schools' and parents' capacity for strong parental involvement as described in subsection (e);

D. coordinate and integrate parental involvement strategies under this part with parental strategies under other programs, such as the Head Start Program, Reading First Program, Early Reading First Program, Even Start program, Parents as Teachers Program, and Home Instruction Program for Preschool Youngsters, and State-run Preschool Programs.

E. Conduct, with the involvement of parents, an annual evaluation of the content and effectiveness of the parental involvement policy in improving the academic quality of the schools served under this part, including identifying barriers to greater participation by parents in activities authorized by this section (with particular attention to parents who are economically disadvantaged, are disabled, have limited English proficiency, have limited literacy, or are of any racial or ethnic minority background), and use the findings of such evaluation to design strategies for more effective parental involvement, and to revise, if necessary, the parental involvement policies described in this section; and

F. involve parents in the activities of the schools served under this part.

3. Reservation—

A. In General—Each local educational agency shall reserve not less than 1 percent of such agency's allocation under subpart 2 of this part to carry out this section, including promoting family literacy and parenting skills, except that this paragraph shall not apply if 1 percent of such agency's allocation under subpart 2 of this part for the fiscal year for which the determination is made is $5,000 or less.

B. Parental Input—Parents of children receiving services under this part shall be involved in the decisions regarding how funds reserved under subparagraph (A) are allotted for parental involvement activities.

    C. Distribution of Funds—Not less than 95 percent of the funds reserved under subparagraph (A) shall be distributed to schools served under this part.

B. School Parental Involvement Policy—

1. In General—Each school served under this part shall jointly develop with, and distribute to, parents of participating children a written parental involvement policy, agreed on by such parents, that shall describe the means for carrying out the requirements of subsections (c) through (f). Parents shall be notified of the policy in an understandable and uniform format and, to the extent practicable, provided in a language the parents can understand. Such policy shall be made available to the local community and updated periodically to meet the changing needs of parents and the school.

2. Special Rule—If the school has a parental involvement policy that applies to all parents, such school may amend that policy, if necessary, to meet the requirements of this subsection.

3. Amendment—If the local educational agency involved has a school district-level parental involvement policy that applies to all parents, such agency may amend that policy, if necessary, to meet the requirements of this subsection.

4. Parental Comments—If the plan under section 1112 is not satisfactory to the parents of participating children, the local educational agency shall submit any parent comments with such plan when such local educational agency submits the plan to the State.

C. Policy Involvement—Each school served under this pare shall—

1. convene an annual meting, at a convenient time, to which all parents of participating children shall be invited and encouraged to attend, to inform parents of their school's participation under this part and to explain the requirements of this part, and the right of the parents to be involved;

2. offer a flexible number of meetings, such as meetings in the morning or evening, and may provide, with funds provided under this part, transportation, child care, or home visits, as such services relate to parental involvement;

3. involve parents, in an organized, ongoing, and timely way, in the planning, review, and improvement of programs under this part, including the planning, review and improvement of the school parental involvement policy and the joint development of the school-wide program plan under section 1114 (b) (2), except that if a school has in place a process for involving parents in the joint planning and design of the school's programs, the school may use that process, if such process includes an adequate representation of parents of participating children;

4. provide parents of participating children—

   A. timely information about programs under this part;
   B. a description and explanation of the curriculum in use at the school, the forms of academic assessment used to measure student progress, and the proficiency levels students are expected to meet; and
   C. if requested by parents, opportunities for regular meetings to formulate suggestions and to participate, as appropriate, in decisions relating to the education of their children, and respond to any such suggestions as soon as practicably possible.

5. if the school-wide program plan under section 1114 (b) (2) is not satisfactory to the parents of participating children, submit any parent comments on the plan when the school makes the plan available to the local educational agency.

D. Shared Responsibilities For High Student Academic Achievement— As a Component of the school-level parental involvement policy developed under subsection (b), each school served under this part shall jointly develop with parents for all children served under this part a school-parent compact that outlines how parents, the entire school staff, and students will share the responsibility for improved student academic advisement and the means by which the school and parents will build and develop a partnership to help children achieve the State's high standards. Such compact shall—

1. describe the school's responsibility to provide high-quality curriculum and instruction in a supportive and effective learning environment that enables the children served under this part to meet the State's student academic achievement standards, and the ways in which each parent will be responsible for supporting their children's learning, such as monitoring attendance, homework completion, and television watching; volunteering in their child's classroom; and participating, as appropriate, in decisions relating to the education of their children and positive use of extracurricular time; and

2. address the importance of communication between teachers and parents on an ongoing basis through, at a minimum—

    A. parent-teacher conferences in elementary schools, at least annually, during which the compact shall be discussed as the compact relates to the individual child's achievement;

    B. frequent reports to parents on their children's progress; and

    C. reasonable access to staff, opportunities to volunteer and participate in their child's class, and observation of classroom activities.

E. Building Capacity for Involvement—To ensure effective involvement of parents and to support a partnership among the school involved, parents, and the community to improve student academic achievement, each school and local educational agency assisted under this part—

1. shall provide assistance to parents of children served by the school or local educational agency, as appropriate, in understanding such topics as the State's academic content standards and State student academic achievement standards, State and local academic assessments, the requirements of this part, and how to monitor a child's progress and work with educators to improve the achievement of their children;

2. shall provide materials and training to help parents to work with their children to improve their children's achievement, such as literacy training and using technology, as appropriate, to foster parental involvement;
3. shall educate teachers, pupil services personnel, principals, and other staff, with the assistance of parents, in the value and utility of contributions of parents, and in how to reach out to, communicate with, and work with parents as equal partners, implement and coordinate parent programs, and build ties between parents and the school;
4. shall, to the extent feasible and appropriate, coordinate and integrate parent involvement programs and activities with Head Start, Reading First, Early Reading First, Even Start, the Home Instruction Programs for Preschool Youngsters, the Parents as Teachers Program, and public preschool and other programs, and conduct other activities, such as parent resource centers, that encourage and support parents in more fully participating in the education of their children;
5. shall ensure that information related to school and parent programs, meetings, and other activities is sent to the parents of participating children in a format and, to the extent practicable, in a language the parents can understand;
6. may involve parents in the development of training for teachers, principals, and other educators to improve the effectiveness of such training;
7. may provide necessary literacy training from funds received under this part if the local educational agency has exhausted all other reasonably available sources of funding for such training;
8. may pay reasonable and necessary expenses associated with local parental involvement activities, including transportation and child care costs, to enable parents to participate in school-related meetings and training sessions;
9. may train parents to enhance the involvement of other parents;
10. may arrange school meetings at a variety of times, or conduct in-home conferences between teachers or other educators, who work directly with participating children, with parents who are

unable to attend such conferences at school, in order to maximize parental involvement and participation;

11. may adopt and implement model approaches to improving parental involvement;

12. may establish a district-wide parent advisory council to provide advice on all matters related to parental involvement in programs supported under this section;

13. may develop appropriate roles for community-based organizations and businesses in parent involvement activities; and

14. shall provide such other reasonable support for parental involvement activities under this section as parents may request.

F. Accessibility—In carrying out the parental involvement requirements of this part, local educational agencies and schools, to the extent practicable, shall provide full opportunities for the participation of parents with limited English proficiency, parents with disabilities, and parents of migratory children, including providing information and school reports required under section 1111 in a format and, to the extent practicable, in a language such parents understand.

G. Information from Parental Information and Resource Centers—In a State where a parental information and resource center is established to provide training, information, and support to parents and individuals who work with local parents, local educational agencies, and schools receiving assistance under this part, each local educational agency or school that receives assistance under this part and is located in the State shall assist parents and parental organizations by informing such parents and organization of the existence and purpose of such centers.

H. Review—The State educational agency shall review the local educational agency's parental involvement policies and practices to determine if the policies and practices meet the requirements of this section.

Parent Due Process Checklist

- The right to examine all school records concerning your child.
- The right to obtain an independent evaluation.
- The right to determine whether the hearing will be closed or open to the public.
- The right to advice of counsel and representation by counsel at the hearing.
- The right to bring your child to the hearing.
- The right to keep your child in his or her current educational placement until all due process hearing appeals have been completed.
- The right to written notification about the hearing in the primary language or mode of communication of the parent.
- The right to present evidence and testimony.
- The right to prohibit the introduction of any evidence which has not been disclosed to parents at least five days prior to the hearing.
- The right to cross-examine and challenge all testimony presented during the hearing.
- The right to receive a verbatim transcript of the hearing, at reasonable cost.
- The right to appeal the decision of the hearing officer or hearing panel.

The Manifestation Determination Review: Was the Child's Behavior a Manifestation of His or Her Disability?

WHEN IS AN MDR REQUIRED?

(4) (A): If a disciplinary action is contemplated as described in paragraph (1) or paragraph (2) [see page 6] for a behavior of a child with a disability described in either of those paragraphs, or if a disciplinary action involving a change in placement for more than 10 days is contemplated for a child with a disability who has engaged in other behavior that violated any rule of code of conduct of the local educational agency that applies to all children.

(i) no later than the date on which the decision to take action is made, the parents shall be notified of that decision and all procedural safeguards accorded under this section; and (ii) immediately if possible, but in no case later than 10 school days after the date on which the decision to take that action is made, a review shall be conducted of the relationship between the child's disability and the behavioral subject to the disciplinary action. [Section 615 (k) (4) (A)]

Who conducts the MDR?————————————————————V

(4) (B) INDIVIDUALS TO CARRY OUT REVIEW—A review described in subparagraph (A) [see above, under "When."] shall be conducted by the IEP Team and other qualified personnel. [Section 615 (k) (4) (B)]

How is the MDR conducted?————————————————V

(4) (C) CONDUCT OF REVIEW—In carrying out a review described in subparagraph (A), the IEP Team may determine that the behavior of the child was not [emphasis added] a manifestation of such child's disability only if the IEP Team—

(i) first considers, in terms of behavior subject to disciplinary action, all relevant information, including—(I) evaluation and diagnostic results, including such results or other relevant information supplied by the parents of the child; (II) observations of the child, and (III) the child's IEP and placement, and

(ii) then determines that—(I) relationship to the behavior subject to disciplinary action, the child's IEP and placement were appropriate and the special education services, supplementary aids and services, and behavior intervention strategies were provided consistent with the child's IEP and placement; (II) the child's disability did not impair the ability of the child to understand the impact and consequences of the behavior subject to disciplinary action; and (III) the child's disability did not impair the ability of the child to control the behavior subject to disciplinary action. [Section 615 (k) (4) (C)]

And then what happens?————————————————————V

(5) DETERMINATION THAT BEHAVIOR WAS NOT MANIFESTATION OF DISABILITY.—

(A) IN GENERAL—If the results of the review described in paragraph (4) [A, B, & C above] is a determination, consistent with paragraph (4) (C), that the behavior of the child with a disability was not a manifestation of the child's disability, the relevant disciplinary procedures applicable to children without disability may be applied to the child in the same manner in which they may be applied to children without disabilities, except as provided in section 612 (a) (1) [the requirement that schools provide FAPE to children with disabilities who have been suspended or expelled from school].

(B) ADDITIONAL REQUIREMENT—If the public agency initiates disciplinary procedures applicable to all children, the agency shall ensure that the special education and disciplinary records of the child with a disability are transmitted for consideration by the person or persons making the final determination regarding the disciplinary action. [Section 615 (k) (5)]

Parent Appeal——————————————————————————V

(6) (A) IN GENERAL—(i) If the child's parent disagrees with a determination that the child's behavior was not a manifestation of the child's disability or with any decision regarding placement, the parent may request a hearing. (ii) The State or local educational agency shall arrange for an expedited hearing in any case described in this subsection when requested by a parent.

(B) REVIEW OF DECISION—(i) In reviewing a decision with respect to the manifestation determination, the hearing officer shall determine whether the public agency has demonstrated that the child's behavior was not a manifestation of such child's disability consistent with the requirements of paragraph (4) (C) [see (4) (C), Conduct of Review].

(ii) In reviewing a decision under paragraph (1) (A) (ii) [when school personnel change the child's placement for up to 45 days] to place the child in an interim alternative educational setting, the hearing officer shall apply the standards set out in paragraph (2) [when a hearing officer orders a change in placement for not more than forty-five days]. [Section 615 (k) (6)]

Placement During Appeal—————————————————————V

(7) PLACEMENT DURING APPEALS—
(A) IN GENERAL—When a parent requests a hearing regarding a disciplinary action described in paragraph (1) (A) (ii) or paragraph (2) to challenge the interim alternative educational setting or the manifestation determination, the child shall remain in the interim alternative educational setting pending the decision of the hearing officer or until the expiration of the time period in paragraph (1) (A) (ii) or paragraph (2), whichever occurs first, unless the parent and the State of local educational agency agree otherwise.

(B) CURRENT PLACEMENT—If a child is placed in an interim alternative educational setting pursuant to paragraph (1) (A) (ii) or paragraph (2) and school personnel propose to change the child's placement after expiration of the interim alternative placement, during the pendency of any proceeding to challenge the proposed change in placement, the child shall remain in the current placement (the child's placement prior to the interim alternative educational setting), except as provided in subparagraph (C) [below].

(C) EXPEDITED HEARING — (i) If school personnel maintain that it is dangerous for the child to be in the current placement (placement prior to removal to the interim alternative educational setting) during the pendency of the due process proceedings, the local educational agency may request an expedited hearing.

(ii) In determining whether the child may be placed in the alternative educational setting or in another appropriate placement ordered by the hearing officer, the hearing officer shall apply the standards set out in paragraph (2).

Referral to and Action by Law Enforcement and Judicial Authorities ───V

(9) (A) Nothing in this part shall be construed to prohibit an agency from reporting a crime committed by a child with a disability to appropriate authorities or to prevent State law enforcement and judicial authorities from exercising their responsibilities with regard to the application of Federal and State law to crimes committed by a child with a disability.

(B) An agency reporting a crime committed by a child with a disability shall ensure that copies of the special education and disciplinary records of the child are transmitted for consideration by the appropriate authorities to whom it reports the crime." [Section 615 (k) (9) and (B)]

Abstract: A Guide for Spanish Parents Relevant to IDEA

ED 417 536	EC 306 279
AUTHOR	Seltzer, Tammy
TITLE	Una Nueva IDEA: Una Guia para Padres acerca de los Cambios en la Ley de Educacion Especial para Ninos con Incapacidades (A New Idea: A Parent's Guide to the Changes in Social Education Law for Children with Disabilities)
INSTITUTION	Bazelon Center for Mental Health Law, Washington, DC
PUB DATE	1998-00-00
NOTE	25p.; Translated into Spanish from English language version, see EC 306 278. Financial support also provided by the Center on Crime, Communities, and Culture and the Lois and Richard England Foundations.
AVAILABLE FROM	Bazelon Center for Mental Health Law, 1101 15th Street, N.W., Suite 1212, Washington, DC 2005-5002; telephone: (202) 467-5730; TDD: (202) 223-0409; e-mail: HN1660@ handsnet.org; www.bazelon.org.
PUB TYPE	Guides—Non-Classroom (055)—Translations (170)
LANGUAGE	Spanish
EDRS PRICE	MF01/PC01 Plus Postage

DESCRIPTORS   Compliance (Legal); Decision Making; *Disabilities; *Discipline; *Educational Legislation;
Elementary Secondary Education; Federal Legislation; Individualized Education Programs; *Parent Participation; Parental Rights; Parent School
Relationship; Spanish; *Special Education; Student Placement; Student Rights; Suspension

IDENTIFIERS   *Individuals with Disabilities Education Act Amend

ABSTRACT   This guide for parents, in Spanish, explains the
changes in the federal special education law resulting from the 1997 amendments to the Individuals with Disabilities Education Act (IDEA).
Changes related to the parent's role in decisions
about the child's education and how schools can
discipline special education students are highlighted. A question-and-answer format is generally used throughout the guide. After a section
summarizing the importance of parental involvement, the next section considers such topics as eligibility under IDEA, disagreements with the
school regarding testing, and retesting requirements. Following a section on the parent's role in
the placement decision, a section on writing the
Individualized Education Program (IEP) offers
tips for parent participation in IEP meetings,
members of the IEP team, and placement decisions. The section on disciplining students is explained in questions and answers on suspensions
of ten days or fewer, requirements if the child is
suspended for longer than ten days, the requirement that schools conduct a "manifestation determination" (which determines whether the child's
behavior was caused by or related to the disability), misbehavior involving weapons or drugs, and
placement in an Interim Alternative Educational
Setting. The final two sections summarize parental
rights and identify related laws. (Contains a listing
of "words to know" and resources.)

Interest Survey—Parent Workshops

Please check topics that would be of most interest to you.

General Topics for Parents of Special Education Students

_____ 1. The Challenge of Being a Single Parent
_____ 2. Assertive Discipline—Creating a Positive Atmosphere at Home
_____ 3. Divorce and Separation—Effects on Families
_____ 4. Parent Roles in Sex Education
_____ 5. Stepfamilies—How to Live in One Successfully
_____ 6. Parent-Teacher Conferencing—Tips for Parents
_____ 7. Helping Children Build Good Study Habits
_____ 8. Getting the Help You Need When Your Child Has Problems in School
_____ 9. Self-Esteem—Helping Kids Feel Good about Themselves
_____10. Freedom and Control—Setting Limits for Children
_____11. Communicating with Children
_____12. Helping Your Child Develop Language
_____13. Spending Quality Time with Children
_____14. Home Activities for the Young Child
_____15. Living with Your Adolescent
_____16. Drug and Alcohol Use and Abuse
_____17. Helping Your Child Plan His or Her Future
_____18. Stresses of Parenting an Exceptional Child
_____19. Helping Siblings of the Disabled
_____20. Sex Education for the Disabled Individual

_____21. Helping the Learning Disabled Child
_____22. The IEP Process—Legal Issues and Parent Role
_____23. Behavior Management Techniques for Difficult Children
_____24. Dealing with Professionals: Teachers, Therapists, Diagnosticians, Principals
_____25. Your Child Has Been Referred to Special Education—What Does This Mean?

Resources for Parents

Following is a web link that will take you to a list of organizations and web sites (scroll down to the middle of the page) that provide information and support for children with special needs and their families: www.icdl.com/forparentsbyparents/overview/overviewcontent.htm

Another great resource is www.nichcy.org. This web site lists the most current information about a number of organizations. The direct link is www.nichcy.org/pubs/genresc/gr2.htm, or you can click on "Search for Information," and then "Organizations." If you still have trouble locating an organization, e-mail us or give us a call.

SUGGESTED READING FOR PARENTS

General Books

After the Tears: Parents Talk about Raising a Child with a Disability, Robin Simon, New York: Harcourt Brace Jovanovich, 1985.
Asperger's Syndrome: A Guide for Parents and Professionals, Tony Atwood, London: Jessica Kingsley Publishers, 1998.
The Bereaved Parent, Harriet Sarnoff Schiff, New York: Crown, 1977.
Body, Mind and Sport, John Douillard, New York: Crown Trade Paperbacks, 1995.
The Broken Cord, Michael Dorris, New York: Harper Collins, 1990.
Brothers and Sisters: A Special Part of Exceptional Families, Thomas H. Powell and Peggy A. Gallagher, Baltimore: Paul H. Brookes Publishing Co., Inc., 1993.

Brothers and Sisters with Special Needs, D. J. Lobato, Baltimore: Paul H. Brookes Publishing Co., Inc., 1990.

The Challenging Child, Stanley I. Greenspan, M.D. with Jacqueline Salmon, New York: Perseus Press, 1995.

The Child Who Never Grew, Pearl Buck, Rockville, Md.: Woodbine, 1992

The Child with Special Needs, Stanley I. Greenspan, M.D., and Serena Wieder, Ph.D., New York: Perseus Press, 1998.

The Dancing Animal Woman, Anne Hillman, North Bergan, NJ: Bramble Books, 1994.

A Difference in the Family, Helen Featherstone, New York: Basic Books, 1980.

Don't Accept Me as I Am, Reuven Feuerstein, New York: Plenum Publishing Corporation, 1998.

Emergence: Labeled Autistic, Temple Grandin, New York: Warner Books, Inc., 1996.

From Ritual to Repertoire, Arnold Miller and Eileen Eller-Miller, New York: John Wiley & Sons, 1989.

A Gift of Hope: How We Survive Our Tragedies, Robert Veninga, New York: Ballentine, 1985.

God Plays Piano Too: The Spiritual Lives of Disabled Children, Brett Webb-Mitchell, New York: Crossroads, 1993.

Infancy and Early Childhood: The Practice of Assessment and Intervention with Emotional and Developmental Challenges, Stanley I. Greenspan, M.D., Guilford, Conn.: International Universities Press, 1992.

Laughing and Loving with Autism, Wayne Gilpin, Arlington, Tex.: Future Education, 1993.

Living with a Brother or Sister with Special Needs, Donald J. Meyer, Patricia F. Vadasy, and Rebecca R. Fewell, Seattle: University of Washington Press, 1985.

Mixed Blessings, William and Barbara Christopher, Nashville: Abington Press, 1989.

The Neurobiology of Autism, Margaret Bauman, M.D. and Thomas Kemper, M.D., Baltimore: Johns Hopkins University Press, 1997, 800.537.5187.

The New Social Stories, Carol Gray, Arlington, Tex.: Future Horizons, Inc., 1994, 800.489.0727 817.277.2270 edfuture@onramp.net www.onramp.net/autism.

News from the Border, Jane Taylor McDonnell, New York: Ticknor & Fields, 1993.

Nobody's Perfect: Living and Growing with Children Who Have Special Needs, Nancy B. Miller, Ph.D., M.S.W., Baltimore: Paul H. Brookes Publishing Co., Inc., 1994.

Not Me! Not My Child: Dealing with Parental Denial and Anxiety (audio tapes), Kenneth Moses, Chicago: Resource Networks, 1985.

Ordinary Families, Special Children, Milton Seligman and Rosalyn B. Darling, New York and London: Guilford Press, 1997.

The Original Social Story Book, Carol Gray Arlington, Tex.: Future Horizons, Inc., 1993, 800.489.0727 817.277.2270 edfuture@onramp.net www.onramp.net/autism.

The Out-of-Sync Child, Carol Stock Kranowitz, M.A., New York: Aperigee Book, The Berkley Publishing Group, 1998.

Parent Survival Manual, Eric Schopler, New York: Plenum Press, 1995 800.221.9369.

A Parent's Guide to Autism, Charles A. Hart and Claire Zion, New York: Simon & Schuster, 1993.

A Place for Noah, Josh Greenfield, New York: Harcourt Brace, 1989.

Playground Politics: The Emotional Life of the School Age Child, Stanley I. Greenspan, M.D., with J. Salmon, Reading, Mass.: Addison-Wesley, 1993, 800.822.6339.

Ritalin Free Kids, Judyth Reichenberg-Ullman, N.D., and Robert Ullman, N.D., Rocklin, Calif.: Prima Publishing, 1996, 916.632.4400 www.primahealth.com

The Road Less Traveled, M. Scott Peck, New York: Simon & Schuster, 1998.

Siblings of Children with Autism, Sandra L. Harris, Ph.D., and Michael D. Powers, Bethesda, Md.: Woodbine House, 1994, 800.843.7323.

The Siege, Clara Claiborne Park, Boston: Little Brown, 1988.

Since Owen: A Parent to Parent Guide for the Care of the Disabled Child, Charles R. Callahan, Baltimore: Johns-Hopkins University Press, 1990.

A Slant of Sun: One Child's Courage, Beth Kephart, New York: W. W. Norton & Co., 1998

Special Children, Challenged Parents: The Struggles and Rewards of Raising a Child with a Disability, Robert Naseef, Ph.D., Secacus, NJ: Birch Lane Press, 1997.

Strategies for Helping Parents of Exceptional Children, Milton Seligman, New York: Free Press, 1979.

Thinking in Pictures, and Other Reports of My Life with Autism, Temple Grandin and Oliver Sacks, New York: Knopf, 1996.

Toilet Training for Individuals with Autism and Related Disorders, Maria Wheeler, Arlington, Tex.: Future Horizons, Inc., 1998, 800.489.0727 or 817.277.2270.

What about Me? Growing up with a Developmentally Disabled Sibling, Bryna Siegel, New York: Stuart Silverstein Plenum Press, 1994.

When Bad Things Happen to Good People, Harold Kushner, New York: Avon, 1981.

When Listening Comes Alive: A Guide to Effective Learning and Communication, Paul Madaule, 1994 Order from General Distribution at 800.805.1083 or from Hushion House Publishing, Ltd. 416.285.6100.

Without Reason: A Family Copes with Two Generations of Autism, Charles Hart, NY: Harper & Row, 1989 (Out of print).

Books for Children

This section is taken largely from Robert Naseef's book, *Special Children, Challenged Parents*. His extensive list includes brief descriptions of the books.

Russell Is Extra Special, Charles Amenda, New York: Bruner Mazel, 1992.

Eukee, the Jumpy Jumpy Elephant, Clifford Corman and Esther Trevino, Plantation, Fla.: Specialty Press, 1994.

What Do You Mean I Have a Learning Disability?, Kathleen Dwyer, New York: Walker and Company, 1991.

Joey and Sam, Illana Katz and Edward Ritvo, Northridge, Calif.: Real Life Storybooks, 1993.

Kristy and the Secret of Susan, Ann M. Martin, New York: Scholastic, Inc., 1990.

A Team Approach to Diagnosing and Evaluating Children with Disabilities

The goal of the evaluation process is to get a complete picture of your child's strengths and weaknesses as a basis for determining how to intervene. It is very important to evaluate your child's development across a range of areas.

For some parents, the idea that their child may have a delay or difficulty in more than one area can seem overwhelming. However, it is important to think of such delays as different dimensions of one interlocking problem, rather than as distinct problems to deal with. For example, a child with a language difficulty may also have fine and gross motor delays that are not necessarily apparent to the parents. When these motor planning problems are identified and treated, the child's language skills can develop much more readily.

As the parent, you play a vital role in the evaluation process. You are the resident "expert" on your child, and your observations and understanding of your child, along with the evaluations performed by professionals, are essential to getting a complete picture of where your child is developmentally. Work with professionals who value your input, and work with all of them together to reach a consensus.

The evaluation process should not rely exclusively on standardized testing. Many people have difficulty performing upon command for strangers; this is especially true for children with communication, learning, and/or social relating difficulties. Results from such testing are valid only to the degree that your child has the processing capacities to take the test. For example, a test may call for a child to follow verbal instructions in order to demonstrate his or her skills in a particular area. A child with auditory processing problems may not perform because he or she is unable to understand the instruction; the test results, therefore, do not represent the child's true abilities.

THE EVALUATION TEAM

If at all possible, parents should seek independent evaluations.

There is an inherent conflict of interest in having one institution (such as the local school district or county) responsible for identifying difficulties which, by law, it is required to remedy. If you can have an independent evaluation, you are more likely to obtain a higher level of public services for your child.

The evaluation should be conducted by a team of professionals from a variety of disciplines. The "team" may not be in one place; go to the best experts you can find in each discipline, including at least one session each with one of the following professionals: (visit www.icdl.com/ forparentsbyparents/overview/overviewcontent.htm for more information):

- A psychologist or psychiatrist with expertise in early childhood development
- A speech/language pathologist experienced in *receptive and expressive language* issues
- An occupational therapist skilled in *sensory integration*

Depending on your child's needs, the evaluation team may also need to include one or more of the following:

- Doctor or health professional experienced with conducting health reviews of children with developmental difficulties. A child with a communication, learning, or social relating problem may appear to be generally healthy, but may indeed suffer from health problems, such as allergies, nutritional deficits, and digestive problems, not readily apparent to traditional pediatricians.
- Developmental pediatrician
- Pediatric neurologist

- Physical therapist
- Special educator
- Social worker

WHAT IS INCLUDED IN AN EVALUATION?

You should expect to meet with the team, or the team's representative, to review the results of the evaluation, which should be given to you in writing. These reports should include:

- Observations of parent-child interactions (both parents or other significant caregivers). Multiple observations are recommended.
- Description of the issues which led you to have your child evaluated
- Developmental history of your child*, including:

  1. Pregnancy
  2. Labor, delivery, and birth history
  3. Early infancy
  4. Developmental milestones
  5. Medical history
  * For adopted children: any remarkable exposure to deprivation or drugs or alcohol, institutional experiences (orphanages/foster care), details about the pre-placement environment, and the child's age at placement in the adopted home.

- Description of your child's daily living skills, including:

  1. Relationships with significant people (e.g., parents, siblings, grandparents)
  2. Eating
  3. Sleeping
  4. Bathing
  5. Dressing
  6. Toilet training
  7. Other self-help skills

- Descriptions of your child's strengths and weakness
- Assessment of your child's development in all areas of functioning, including:

1. Fine and gross motor skills
2. Receptive and expressive language
3. Sensory reactivity, processing, and motor planning
4. Functional emotional milestones: this assessment, based on at least thirty to forty-five minutes of observation of parent-child, includes:

   a. Regulation and attention
   b. Engaging with the parent
   c. Using gestures to communicate needs
   d. Using gestures to problem solve
   e. Using ideas for pretend play
   f. Using language to carry on conversations
   g. Reasoning and thinking

- Results of the formal evaluations by each member of the team
- Conclusions and recommendations for further evaluations, interventions, or treatments. You can negotiate changes in the evaluation if you are not satisfied with it. Each evaluation should outline detailed prescriptions for treatment which must be strongly supported by the findings of the evaluation. Each functional area should be addressed. Evaluations must be specific as to the frequency and nature of the therapy to help you obtain the services your child needs.
- Plan for follow-up

Be aware that insurance companies often do not cover services or treatment for a diagnosis that refers to a developmental, rather than a physiological, origin. Parents and evaluators can discuss insurance issues before the evaluation is finalized.

Glossary

Amended Raine Decree—Judicial decision which required the state to provide special education to school-age children with disabilities ages five to twenty (preceded P.L. 94-142).

Architectural Barriers—Those structural and physical obstructions which, merely by existing, exclude or discriminate against handicapped people (i.e., elevators, phone booths, etc.).

ARD Committee—Admission, Review, and Dismissal Committee (required by state, not federal law) maintained by the LEA and comprised of individuals familiar with the child's current level of functioning (i.e., direct services deliverers, health department personnel, and a special educator). The ARD Committee refers for placement and reviews the individualized educational program of every child with a disability.

Assessment—Extensive procedure given to all children who have been identified through screening as potentially in need of special education programs. It shall consist of reading, math, spelling, written and oral language, and perceptual motor functioning, as appropriate. Cognitive, emotional, and physical factors shall also be assessed, as appropriate. Each assessment report shall also include a description of the child's behavior which establishes the existence of a disabling condition; a statement which describes, in terms of special education services needed, the child's performance as it deviates from developmental milestones and/or general education objectives; a statement of criteria used to establish the deviation of the child's behaviors; and the signature of the assessor.

Children with Disabilities—Those children who have been determined through appropriate assessment as having temporary and long-term special education needs arising from cognitive, emotional, or physical factors or any combination of factors. Their ability to meet general educational objectives is impaired to such a degree that services in the general education programs are inadequate in preparing them to achieve their educational potential.

Due Process—A right to have any law applied reasonably and with sufficient safeguards, such as hearings and notice to ensure that an individual is dealt with fairly. A due process hearing is held when there is disagreement between the parent and the educational agency (either local or state) as to the identification, evaluation, and/or placement of a child with a disability into a special education program. Parents have the right to present evidence, require the attendance of, and cross-examine witnesses, and obtain independent assessments which must be considered.

Early Identification—Programs provided by LEAs for the preschool-age child who may be in need of special education services.

Evaluation—An additional review of the child's program which occurs at least annually and is conducted to determine: (a) whether the child has achieved the goals set forth in his or her IEP, (b) whether the child has met the criteria which would indicate readiness to enter into a less restrictive/intensive special education program, and (c) whether the program the child is in should be specifically modified so as to make it more suitable.

FAPE—Free Appropriate Public Education—The federal phrase which describes the education to which children with disabilities are entitled.

FERPA—Family Education Rights and Privacy Act—Also known as the Buckley Amendment, permits parents to examine and copy (at reasonable cost) any and all material in the child's permanent record.

IEP—Individualized Education Program—A written comprehensive outline for total special education services which describes the special education needs of the child and the services to be provided to meet those needs. It is developed in a collaborative meeting with LEA representatives, parents, teachers, the student, when appropriate, and all other persons having direct responsibilities for the implementation of the IEP. The IEP must be developed before placement, approved by the ARD Committee, signed by the parent, and implemented within thirty calendar days after development.

IHO — Impartial Hearing Officer — Person who is knowledgeable in the fields and areas significant to the review of the child's education. Three IHOs preside at each state-level hearing. (It can be one person at a local-level hearing.) No person may serve as an IHO who is an employee of a local school system, an employee of an agency involved in the education or care of the child, an employee of the SEA, or a member of the State Board of Education. All IHOs in Maryland's state-level hearings have completed a comprehensive training program.

LEA — Local Education Agency, also known as the LSS (Local School System). There are twenty-four in Maryland (the twenty-three counties and Baltimore City). The LEA is responsible for providing the actual education receives.

LRE — Least Restrictive Environment — The educational setting that is considered educationally appropriate, to the maximum extent possible with nonhandicapped children.

Native Language — The term, when used with reference to an individual of limited English proficiency, means the language normally used by the individual, or in the case of the child, the language normally used by the parents of the child.

SEA — State Education Agency — The SEA is responsible for monitoring the LEAs' educational programs provided to children with disabilities.

Bibliography

Aefsky, F. (1995). *Inclusion confusion: A guide to educating students with exceptional needs*. Thousand Oaks, CA: Corwin Press.

Ainsworth, F. (1969). Parent education on family therapy: Does it matter which comes first? *Child Youth Care Forum, 25*, 101–110.

Allen, R. Petr, C. and Brown, B. (1995). *Family-centered behavior scale and user's manual*. Lawrence, KS: University of Kansas, Beach Center on Families and Disability.

Alper, S. K., Schloss, P. J., Etscheidt, S. K., and MacFarlane, C. A. (1995). *Inclusion: Are we abandoning or helping students?* Thousand Oaks, CA: Crowin Press.

Alper, S. K., Schloss, P. J., and Schloss, C. N. (1994). Families of students with disabilities. Boston, MA: Allyn and Bacon.

Ames, C. (1992). Home and school cooperation in social and motivational development. ERIC Document Reproduction Service No. ED 411 629.

Amlund, J. T. and Kardash, C. M. (1994). In S. K. Alper, P. J. Schloss, and C. N. Schloss (Eds.), *Families of students with disabilities*. Boston, MA: Allyn and Bacon.

Anotonak, R. F. and Larrivee, B. (1995). Psychometric analysis and revisions of the opinions relative to mainstreaming scale. *Exceptional Children, 62*, 139–149.

Armstrong, S. W. and McPherson, A. (1991). Homework as a critical component in social skills instruction. *Teaching Exceptional Children*, 24 (1), 45–47.

Astone, N. M. and Lanahan, S. S. (1998). Family structure, parental practices, and high school completion. American Sociology Review, 56 (3), 309–320.

Atkinson, D. R. and Juntunen, C. L. (1994). School counselors and school psychologists as school-home-community liaisons in ethnically diverse schools. In P. Pederson and J. C. Carey (Eds.), *Multicultural counseling in schools: A practical handbook*. Boston, MA: Allyn and Bacon.

Bailey, D. B., Palsha, S. A., and Simeonsson, R. J. (1991). Professional skills, concerns, and perc*eived importance of work with families in early intervention. Exceptional Children*, 58 (2), 156–165.

Baker, E. T., Wang, M., and Walberg, H. G. (1995). The effects of inclusion on learning. *Educational Leadership*, 59 (4) 33–35.

Baker, J. and Zigmond, N. (1990). *Full-time mainstreaming: Are learning disabled students integrated into the instructional program?* Paper presented at the Annual Meeting of the American Educational Research Association. Boston, MA. ERIC Document Reproduction Service No. ED 320373.

Bandura, A. (1977). Social learning: Child-rearing practices and their effect. In G. David and R. Busey (Eds.), *Social Development* (pp. 79–85). Englewood Cliffs, NJ: Prentice Hall.

Bank, L., Marlowe, J. H., Reid, J. B., Patterson G. R., and Weinrott, M. R. (1991). A comparative evaluation of parent-training interventions for families of chronic delinquents. *Journal of Abnormal Child Psychology*, 19, 15–33.

Bannerji, M. and Dailey, R. (1995). A study of the effects of an inclusion model on students with specific learning disabilities. *Journal of Learning Disabilities*, 28, 511–522.

Barnwell, D. A. and Day, M. (1996). *Providing support to diverse families*. In P. J.

Barth, R. (1990). *Improving schools from within*. San Francisco, CA: Jossey-Bass, Inc.

Batshaw, M. (1997). *Children with disabilities*. Baltimore, MD: Paul H. Brookes Publishing Co., Inc.

Bauer, A. and Shea, T. (2003). *Parents and schools*. Columbus, OH: Merrill Prentice Hall.

Barry, A. L. (1995). Easing into inclusion classrooms. *Educational Leadership*, 52 (4), 4–6.

Bennett, R., Deluca, D., and Burns, D. (1997). Putting inclusion into practice. *Exceptional Children*, 64 (1), 115–131.

Berger, S. (1995). Inclusion: A legal mandate: An educational dream. *Updating School Board Politics*, 26 (4), 104.

Berry, J. O. and Hardman, M. L. (1998). *Lifespan perspectives on the family and disability*. Boston, MA: Allyn and Bacon.

Biklen, D. (1989). Making a difference ordinary. In W. Stainback and M. Forest (Eds.), *Educating all children in the mainstream of regular education*. Baltimore, MD: Paul H. Brookes Publishing Co. Inc.

Blacker, J. (1984). Sequential stages of parental adjustment to the birth of a child with handicaps: Fact or artifact? *Mental Retardation*, 22 (2), 55–68.

Blue-Banning, M., Summers, J. A., Franklin, H. C., Nelson, L.L., and Beegle, G. (2004). Dimensions of family partnerships: Constructive guidelines for collaboration. *Exceptional Children*, 70 (2), 167–184.

Boesel, D., Hudson, L., Deich, S., and Masten, C. (1994). Final report to Congress, National Assessment of Vocational Education, Volume II: *Participation in and quality of vocational education*. Washington, DC: Office of Research, Office of Educational Research and Improvement, U.S. Department of Education.

Booth, A. and Dunne, J. (Eds.). (1996). *Family-school links: How do they affect educational outcomes?* Hillsdale, NJ: Erlbaum.

Borthwick-Duffy, S. A., Palmer, D. S., and Lane, K. L. (1996). One size doesn't fit all: Full inclusion and individual differences. *Journal of Behavioral Education*, 6, 311–329.

Bradley, D. F., King-Sears, M., and Tessier-Switlick, D. M. (1997). *Teaching students in inclusive settings*. Boston, MA: Allyn and Bacon.

Bradley, V. J., Knoll, J., and Agosta, J. M. (1992). *Emerging issues in family support*. Washington, DC: The American Association on Mental Retardation.

Brandt, R. (1998). Listen first. *Educational Leadership*, 55 (8), 25–30.

Bricker, D. (1995). The challenge of inclusion. *Journal of Early Intervention*, 19, 179–194.

Briggs, M. H. (1997). Building early intervention teams: working together for children and families. Gaithersburg, MD. Aspen.

Bristor, M. W. (1984). The birth of a handicapped child: A holistic model for grieving. *Family Relations*, 33, 25–32.

Bronfenbrenner, U. (1979). *The ecology of human development*. Cambridge, MA: Harvard University Press.

Brotherson, M. J., Berdine, W. H., and Sartini, V. (1993). Transition to adult services: Support for ongoing parent participation. *Remedial and Special Education*, 14, 44–51.

Brown, L. P., Schwarz, A., Unvari-Solner, E. F., Kampshroer, F., Johnson, J., Jorgensen, J., and Greenwald, L. (1991). How much time should students with severe disabilities spend in regular classrooms and elsewhere? *Journal of the Association for Persons with Severe Disabilities*, 16, 39–47.

Bruce, E., Schultz, C., Smyrnios, K., and Schultz, N. (1994). Grieving related to development: A preliminary comparison of three age cohorts of parents of children with intellectual disability: *British Journal of Medical Psychology*, 67, 37–52.

Bryan, R. (1990). *Assessment of children with learning disabilities who appear to be socially incompetent*. Paper presented at the Annual Conference of the Council for Exceptional Children. Atlanta, GA.

Cairney, T. H., Ruge, J., Buchanan, J., Lowe, K., and Munsie, L. (1995). *Developing partnerships: The home, school, and community interface*. Canberra: Department of Employment, Education and Training.

Caldwell, L. (1997). Tips to parents from your preschooler. *Child Care Information Exchange*, 113, 89.

Callahan, K., Rademacher, J. A., and Hildreth, B. L. (1998). The effect of parent participation in strategies to improve the homework performance of students who are at risk. *Remediation and Special Education*, 19, 131–141.

Casas, M. and Furlong, M. J. (1994). School counselors as advocates for increased Hispanic parent participation in schools. In P. Pederson and J. C. Carey (Eds.), *Multicultural counseling in schools: A practical handbook*. Boston, MA: Allyn and Bacon.

Cassidy, E. (1988). *Reaching and involving black parents of handicapped children in their child's education program*. ERIC Document Reproduction Service ED 302982

Cavarretta, J. (1998). Parents are a school's best friend. *Educational Leadership*, 55 (8), 12–15.

Chavkin, N. F., (1993). *Families and schools in a pluralist society*. Albany, NY: State University of New York Press.

Cheney, D., Manning, B., and Upham, D. (1997). Project DESTINT. *Teaching Exceptional Children*, 30, 24–29.

Christenson, S.L., Hurley, C.N., Sheriden, S.M., and Fenstermacher, K. (1997). Parents and school psychologists' perspectives on parental involvement activities. *The School Psychology Review*, 26, 111–130.

Christenson, S. L., Rounds, T., and Franklin, M. J. (1992). Home-school collaboration: Effects, issues, and opportunities. In S. L. Christenson and J. C. Conoley (Eds.), *Home-school collaboration: Enhancing children's academic and social competence*. Bethesda, MD: National Association of School Psychologists.

Clark, R. M. (1993). *Family life and school achievement*. Chicago: University of Chicago Press.

Clemens-Brower, T. J. (1997). Recruiting parents and the community. *Educational Leadership*, 54, 58–60.

Cloud, J. (1993). Language, culture, and disability: Implications for instruction and Teacher Preparation. Teacher Education and Special Education, 16, 60–72.

Cohn-Vargas, K. and Grose, K. (1998). A partnership for literacy. *Educational Leadership*, 55 (8), 45–48.

Cole, K., Mills, P., Dale, P., and Jenkins, J. R. (1991). Effects of preschool integration for children with disabilities. *Exceptional Children*, 58, 36–43.

Coleman, M. C. (1986). *Behavior disorders: Theory and practice*. Englewood Cliffs, NJ: The Free Press.

Coots, J. J. (1998). Family resources and parent participation in schooling activities for their children with developmental delays. *The Journal of Special Education*, 31, 498–520.

Cordisco, L. K. and Laus, M. K. (1993). Individualized training in behavioral strategies for parents of preschool children with disabilities. *Teaching Exceptional Children*, 25, 43–46.

Council for Exceptional Children Today. (2003). *Despite opposition: House approves Bill on IDEA, 10 (1) , 1, 5, 13, 15*. Arlington, VA: Council for Exceptional Children Today.

Covey, S. R. (1989). *"The seven habits of highly effective people."* New York: Simon and Schuster. www.state.oh.us/Ohioddc/PUB/ESCParent.htm.

Cross, T. (1988). Services to minority populations: What does it mean to be a culturally competent professional? *Focal Point*, 2 (4), 1–3.

Cullingford, C. (1996). The reality of childhood. *Time Educational Supplement*, 4193, 15.

Cunningham, C. and Davis, H. (1985). *Working with parents: Framework for collaboration*. London: University Press.

Cummings, J. (1984). *Bilingual and special education: Issues in assessment pedagogy*. San Diego, CA: College Hill Press.

Dabkowski, D. M. (2004). Encouraging active parent participation in IEP team meetings. *Teaching Exceptional Children*, 36 (3), 34–39.

Dalli, C. (1991). *Scripts for children's lives: What do parents and early childhood teachers contribute to children's understanding of events in their lives*. ERIC Document Reproduction Service No. ED 344664.

Darling, R. B. (1979). *Families against society: A study of reactions of children with birth defects*. Beverly Hills, CA: Sage.

Davies, D. (1996). Partnership for students success. *New Schools New Communities*, 12 (13), 14–21.

Delgado-Gaitan, C. (1991). Involving parents in the schools: A process of empowerment. *American Journal of Education*, 100, 20–46.

Dettmer, P., Thurston, L. P., and Dyck, N. (1993). *Consultation, collaboration, and teamwork for students with special needs*. Boston, MA: Allyn and Bacon.

Dewitt, P. (1994). The crucial early years. *Time Magazine, 143*, (16), 68.

DiMartino, E. C. (1990). The remarkable social competence of young children. *International Journal of Early Childhood*, 22, 23–31.

Dunst, G. J. (2000). Revisiting "Rethinking early intervention." *Topic in Early Childhood and Special Education*, 20, 95–104.

Dunst, G. J., Trivette, C. M., Hamby, D., and Pollock, B. (1991). Family systems correlate the behavior of young children with handicaps. *Journal of Early Intervention*, 14 (3), 204–218.

Dyson, L. L. (1996). The experiences of families of children with learning disabilities: Parental stress, family functioning, and sibling self-concept. *Journal of Learning Disabilities*, 29, 280–286.

Eccles, J. S. and Harold, R. D. (1993). Parent-school involvement during the early adolescent years. *Teachers College Record*, 94, 568–587.

Education Commission of the States. (1996a). *Listen, discuss, and act*. Denver, CO: Author.

——. (1996b). *Bending without breaking*. Denver, CO: Author.

Edwards, P. A. (1992). Involving parents in building reading instruction for African-American children. *Theory Into Practice*, 31 (4), 350–359.

——. (1995). Combining parents' and teachers' thoughts about storybook reading at home and school. *In family literacy: Connections in schools and communities*, edited by L. M. Morrow. College Park, MD: International Reading Association.

Egan, G. (1998). *The skilled helper* (6th ed.). Pacific Grove, CA: Brooks/Cole.

Egan, I., Frederick, B., Hendrickson, K., Peterson, J., and Moore, W. (1983*). Manual on associated work skills for the severely handicapped*. Monmouth, OR: Teaching Research Publications.

Eisner, E. (1991). What really counts in school? *Educational Leadership*, 10, 17.

Epstein, J. L. (1991). Effects on student achievement of teachers' practices of parent involvement. In S. B. Silver (Ed.), *Advances in reading/language research*, Vol. 6. Literacy through family, community, and school interaction (pp. 261–276). Greenwich, CT: JAI Press.

——. (1989). Family structures and student motivation: A development perspective. In C. Ames and R. Ames (Eds.). *Research on motivation in education*, Vol. 3. *Goals and cognitions* (pp. 259–295). New York: Academic Press.

——. (1995). School, family, community, partnerships: Caring for the children we share. *Phi Delta Kappan*, 77 (9), 701–712.

——. (1996). Perspectives and previews on research and policy for school, family, and community partnerships. In A. Booth and J. F. Dunn (Eds.), *Family-*

school links: How do they affect educational outcomes (pp. 209–246). Mahway, NJ: Lawrence Erlbaum Associates.

Epstein, J. L. and Hollifield, J. H. (1996). Title I and school-family-centered community partnerships: Using research to realize the potential. *Journal of Education for Students Placed at Risk, 1*, 263–278.

Erikson, E. H. (1995). Identity and life cycle. *Psychological Issues Monograph, 1*. New York, NY: International Universities Press.

Federal Register. (1997, August 23). Washington, DC: U.S. Government Printing Office.

Fiedler, C. R. (1986). Enhancing parent-school personnel partnerships. *Focus on Autistic Behavior, 1*, 1–8.

Filbin, J., Connolly, T., and Brewer, R. (1996). *Individualized learner outcomes: Infusing student needs into the regular education curriculum.* ERIC Document Reproduction Service No. ED 400641.

Finders, M. and Lewis, C. (1994). Why some parents don't come to school. *Educational Leadership, 51*, 50–53.

Fine, M. J. and Carson, C. (1992). *The handbook of family-school intervention: A system perspective.* Needham Heights, MA: Allyn and Bacon.

Finn, J. D. (1993). *School engagement and students at risk.* Washington, DC: National Center for Educational Statistics.

———. (1998). Parental engagement that makes a difference. *Educational Leadership, 55* (8), 20–24.

Fitton, L. and Gredler, G. R. (1996). Parental involvement in reading remediation with young children. *Psychology in the Schools, 33*, 325–332.

Floyd, L. (1998). Joining hands: A parental involvement program. *Urban Education, 33*, 123–125.

Friend, M. and Bursuck, W. D. (1996). *Including students with special needs.* Boston, MA: Allyn and Bacon.

Fuchs, D. and Fuchs, L. (1994). Inclusive schools movement and the radicalization of special education reform. *Exceptional Children, 60*, 294–309.

———. (1995). Sometimes separate is better. *Educational Leadership, 50* (4), 22–26.

Fuchs, D., Fuchs, L., and Bishop, N. (1992). Teacher planning for students with learning disabilities: Differences between general and special education. *Learning Disabilities Research and Practice, 7*, 120–128.

Gallagher, J. J. (1989). The impact of policies for handicapped children on future early education policy. *Phi Delta Kappan, 121*–124.

Gartner, A., Lipsky, D. K., and Turnbull, A. P. (1991). *Supporting families with a child with disabilities.* Baltimore, MD: Paul H. Brookes Publishing Co., Inc.

Gavidia-Payne, S. and Stoneman, Z. (1997). Family predictors of maternal and parental involvement in programs for young children with disabilities. *Child Development*, 68, 701–717.

Giangreco, M., Dennis, R., Cloninger, C., Edelman, S., and Schattman, R. (1993). I've counted JON: Transformation experiences of teachers educating students with disabilities. *Exceptional Children*, 59, 359–371.

Giannetti, C. C. and Sagarese, M. M. (1997). *The roller-coaster years: Raising your child through the maddening yet magical middle school years.* New York, NY: Broadway Books.

———. (1992). *The roller-coaster years: Raising your child through the maddening yet magical middle school years.* New York, NY: Broadway Books.

———. (1998). Turning parents from critics to allies. *Educational Leadership*, 55 *(8)*, 40–42.

Gibbs, E. D. and Teti, D. M. (1990*). Interdisciplinary assessment of infants: A guide for early intervention professionals.* Baltimore, MD: Paul H. Brookes Publishing Co., Inc.

Goldring, E. B. and Hausman, C. (1997). Empower parents for productive partnership. *Education Digest*, 62, 25–29.

Gorman, J. C. and Balter, L. (1997). Culturally sensitive parent education: A critical review of quantitative research. *Review of Educational Research*, 67, 339–369.

Gough, P. B. (1991). *Tapping parent power. Phi Delta Kappan*, 72 (95), 339.

Graft, O. L. and Henderson, B. (1997). Twenty-five ways to increase parental participation. *High School Magazine, 4*, 36–41.

Graves, D. H. (1996). Parent meetings: Are you ready? How you prepare matters most in talking about a child's writing. *Instructor*, 105, *42–43*.

Green, R. (1998). A parent's perspective. *Exceptional Parent*, 28 (8), 32–33.

Green, S. K. and Shinn, M. R. (1995). Parent attitudes about special education and reintegration: What is the role of student results. *Exceptional Children*, 6 (3), 269–281.

Greenbaum. F. K. (1994). Disability really isn't that romantic. *Exceptional Parent*, 24 (7), 46–47.

Greer, M. H. (1996). The challenge of family involvement. *Exceptional Parent*, 26, 72.

Griffith, J. (1998). The relationship of school structure and social environment to parental involvement in elementary schools. *Elementary School Journal*, 99, 53–80.

Guralnick, M. J. (2001). A framework for change in early childhood inclusion. In M. J. Guralnick (Ed.), *Early childhood inclusion: Focus on change.* Baltimore, MD: Paul H. Brookes Publishing Co. Inc.

Hamlett, H. E. (1997). Effective parent-professional communication. *Exceptional Parent*, 27, 51.

Hanline, M. F. and Halvorsen, A. (1989). Parent perceptions of the integration transition process: Overcoming artificial barriers. *Exceptional Children*, 55, 487–492.

Hardman, M. L., Drew, C. S., Eagan, W. M., and Wolf, B. (1996). *Human exceptionality: Social, school, and family*. Boston, MA: Allyn and Bacon.

Harry, B. (1992). *Cultural diversity, families, and the special education system*. New York: Teachers College Press.

Harry, B., Allen, N., and McLaughlin, M. (1995). Communication versus compliance: African-American parents involvement in special education. *Exceptional Children*, 61 (4), 364–377.

Harshman, K. (1996). Providing resources for parents. *Scholastic Early Childhood*. Today, 11, 11.

Hatch, T. (1998). How community action contributes to achievement? *Educational Leadership*, 55 (8), 16–19.

HEALTH Resource Center. (1985). *Opportunities after high school for persons who are severely handicapped*. Washington, DC: HEALTH Resource Center.

Heddell, F. (1988). *Children with mental handicaps*. Ramsbury, Marlborough, England: Crewood Press.

Henderson, A. T. (1987). *The evidence continues to grow: Parent involvement improves achievement*. Columbia, MD: National Committee for Citizens in Education.

Henderson, A. T. (1988). Parents are a school's best friend. Bloomington, IN: *Phi Delta Kappan*, 135.

Herman, J. L. and Yeh, J.P. (1981). Some Effects of Parent Involvement in Schools, 1980. ERIC Document Reproduction Service No. ED 206 963.

Hermanson, E. (1984). *Securing the future of a disabled child*. Rosslyn, VA: The National Information Center for Handicapped Children and Youth.

Herr, S. S. (1983). *Rights and advocacy for retarded people*. Lexington, MA: D. C. Health Department.

Hess, R. D. and Halloway, S. D. (1984). Family and school as educational institutions. In. R. D. Parke (Ed.), *Review of children development research*, Vol. 7, The family (pp. 179–222). Chicago, IL: University of Chicago Press.

Hindle, J. S. (1998). Parenting in different cultures: Time to focus. *Developmental Psychology*, 34 (4), 698–700.

Ho, E. S. and Williams, J. D. (1996). Effects of parental involvement on eighth-grade achievement. *Sociology and Education*, 69 (2), 126–141.

Hobbs, N., Dokecki, P. R., Hoover-Dempsey, K. V., Moroney, R. M., Shayne, M. W., and Weeks, K. A. (1984). *Strengthening families: Strategies for child care and parent education*. San Francisco, CA: Jossey-Bass, Inc.

Hobbs, T. and Westling, D. L. (1998). Promoting successful inclusion. *Teaching Exceptional Children*, 31 (1), 12–19.

Hock, M. and Boltax, R. (1995). *Improved collaboration, less paperwork: Vermont's new family-centered IEP process*. ERIC Document Reproduction Service No. ED 387 877.

Holohan, A. and Costenbader, V. (2000). A comparison of developmental gains for preschool children with disabilities in inclusive and self-contained classrooms. *Topics in Early Childhood Special Education*, 20, 224–235.

Hoover-Dempsey, K. V. and Sandler, H. M. (1995). Parental involvement in children's education: Why does it make a difference? *Teachers College Record*, 95, 310–331.

———. (1997). Why do parents become involved in their children's education? *Review of Education Research*, 67, 3–42.

Horn, S. (1992). *Focilitative leadership: The imperative for change*. Austin, TX: Southwest Educational Development Laboratory.

Houston, W. R. and Houston, E. (1992). Needed: A new knowledge base in teacher education. In L. Kaplan (Ed.), *Education and the family*. Boston, MA: Allyn and Bacon.

Hundert, J., Mahoney, B., Mundy, F., and Vernon, M. L. (1998). A descriptive analysis of development and social gains of children with severe disabilities in segregated and inclusive preschool in Southern Ontario. *Early Childhood Research Quarterly*, 13, 49–65.

Hynan, M. T. (1996). Coping with crisis: Confronting the emotions of your fear. *Exceptional Parent*, 26, 64.

Hyun, J. K. and Fowler, A. (1995). Respect cultural sensitivity and communication. *Teaching Exceptional Children*, 28 (1), 25–28.

James, A. B. (1996). Helping the parents of a special needs child. *Lutheran Education*, 32, 78–87.

Janko, S., Schwartz, I., Sandall, S., Anderson, K., and Cottam, C. (1997). Beyond microsystems: Unanticipated lessons about the meaning of inclusion. *Topics in Early Childhood Education*, 17, 286–306.

Jenkins, J. R., Odom, S. L., and Speltz, M. L. (1985). Integrating normal and handicapped preschoolers: Effects on child development and social interaction. *Exceptional Children*, 52, 7–17.

———. (1989). Effects of social integration on preschool children with handicaps. *Exceptional Children*, 55, 420–428.

Johnson, N. (1990). Evolving attitudes about family support. *Family Support Bulletin*, 12–13.

Johnston, D., Proctor, W., and Carey, S. (1995). Not a way out: A way in. *Educational Leadership*, 50 (4), 46–49.

Kalyanpur, M. and Rao, S. (1991). Empowering low-income black families of Handicapped children. *American Journal of Orthopsychiatry*, 61, 523–532.

Kaplan, L. (1992). *Education and the family*. Boston, MA: Allyn and Bacon.

Katsiyannis, A., Conderman, G., and Franks, D. L. (1995). State practices on inclusion: A national review. *Remedial and Special Education*, 16, 279–287.

Kazdin, A. (1988). *Child psychotherapy: Developing and identifying effective treatments*. Elmsford, NY: Pergamon Press.

Kelly, G. (1955). *The psychology of personal constructs*. New York: Norton Publishing Company.

Kelly, P. A., Brown, S., Bulter, A., Gittens, P., Taylor, C., and Zeller, P. (1998). A place to hand our hats. *Educational Leadership*, 56 (1), 62–64.

Kines, B. (1999). The parent connection. *Teaching K-8*, 6 (4), 33.

Koerner, B. (1999, Jan.). *Parental power*. U.S. News and World Report. Washington, DC.

Kubler-Ross, E. (1977). On death and dying. New York: Collier.

Lamorey, S. (2002). The effects of culture on special education services: Evil eyes, prayer meetings, and IEPs. *Teaching Exceptional Children*, 34 (5), 67–71.

Langdon, H. W. and Novak, J. M. (1998). Home and school connections: A Hispanic perspective. *Educational Horizons*, 1, 15–17.

Lareau, A. P. (1987). Social class differences in family-school relationships: The importance of cultural capital. *Sociology of Education*, 60, 73–85.

Lareau, A. P. (1989). Home advantage: Social class and parental intervention in elementary education. New York: The Falmer Press.

Larrivee, B. (1992). Factors underlying regularly classroom teachers attitudes toward mainstreaming. *Psychology in the Schools*, 19, 374–379.

Leung, K. (1998). Parenting styles and academic achievement: A cross-cultural study. *Merrill-Palmer Quaterly*, 44 (2), 157–172.

Lewis, R. and Morris, J. (1998). Communities for children. *Educational Leadership*, 55 (8), 34–36.

Lian, M. J., and Aolia, G. (1994). Parental responses, roles, and responsibilities. In S. K. Alper, P. J. Schloss, and C. N. Schloss (Eds.), *Families of students with disabilities*. Boston, MA: Allyn and Bacon.

Liewellyn, G., Dunn, P., Fante, M., Turnbull, L., and Grace, R. (1996). *Families with young children with disabilities and high support needs:* Report to aging and disability department. Family Support Services Project. University of Sydney.

Lin, S. (2000). Coping and adaptations in families of children with cerebral palsy. *Exceptional Children,* 66, 201–218.

Lunenburg, F. C. and Ornstein, A. C. (1991). *Educational administration.* Belmont, CA: Wadsworth.

Lynch, E. W. and Hanson, M. H. (1998). *Developing cross-cultural competencies: A guide for working with children and their families* (2nd ed.) Baltimore, MD: Paul H. Brookes Publishing Co., Inc.

Lynch, E. W., and Stein, R. (1982). Perspectives on parent participation in special education. *Exceptional Education Quarterly,* 3, 56–63.

———. (1987). Parent participation by ethnicity: A comparison of Hispanic, Black, and Anglo families. *Exceptional Children,* 54, 105–111.

Mallory, B. L. (1996). The role of social policy in the life cycle transitions. *Exceptional Children,* 62 (3), 213–223.

Mansbach, S. C. (1993). We must put family literacy on the national agenda. *Reading Today,* 37.

Marion, R. (1981*). Educators, parents, and exceptional children.* Rockville, MD: Aspen.

Markowitz, J. (1984). "Participation of Fathers in Early Childhood Special Education Programs: An Exploratory Study." *Journal of the Division of Early Childhood,* 8, No. 2.

Marsh, D. (1999). *Yearbook: Preparing our schools for the 21st century.* Alexandria, VA: Association for Supervision and Curriculum Development.

Masten, A. C. (1994). Resilience in individual development: Successful adaptations despite risk and adversity. In *Educational Resilence in Inner City America,* edited by M. C. Wang and E. W. Gordon. Hillsdale, NJ: Erlbaum.

May, J. (1991). Commentary: What about fathers? *Family Support Bulletin,* 19.

McBride, S. L., Brotherson, M. J., Joanning, H., Whiddon, D., and Demmitt, A. (1993). Implementation of family-centered services: Perceptions of families and Professionals. *Journal of Early Intervention,* 17 (4), 414–430.

McDonnell, J. (1987). The integration of students with severe handicaps into regular public schools: An analysis of parents' perceptions of potential outcomes. *Education and Training in Mental Retardation,* 22, 98–111.

McGinnis, E. and Goldstein, A. (1984). *Skill streaming the elementary child.* Chicago, IL: Research Press Company.

McGoldrick, M. and Giordano, J. (1996). Overview: Ethnicity and family therapy. In McGoldrick, J., Giordano, J. and J. K. Pearce (Eds*.), Ethnicity and Family Therapy* (2nd ed.). New York: Guilford Press.

McKinney, J. D. and Hocutt, A. M. (1982). Public school involvement of parents of learning-disabled children and average achievers. *Exceptional Education Quarterly,* 3, 64–73.

McLaughlin, C. S. (1987). *Parent-teacher conferencing*. Springfield, IL: Research Press.

McLoughlin, J. A. and Senn, C. (1994). Parental responses, roles, and responsibilities. In S. K. Alper, P. J. Schloss, and C. N. Schloss (Eds.), *Families of students with disabilities*. Boston, MA: Allyn and Bacon.

McNeil, C. D., Eyberg, S., Eisenstadt, T. H., Newcomb, K., and Funderburk, B. (1991). Parent-child interaction therapy with behavior problem children: Generalization of treatment effects to the school setting. *Journal of Clinical Child Psychology*, 20, 140–151.

McWilliam, R. A., Tocci, L., and Harbin, G. L. (1998). Family-centered services: Service providers' discourse and behavior. *Topics in Early Childhood Special Education*, 18, 206–221.

Miller, J. M. (1998). When parents meet: Teacher teams. *The Education Digest*, 64 (4), 65–66.

Mills, D. and Bulach, S. (1996). *Behavior disordered students in collaborative/ cooperative class: Does behavior improve?* Tampa, FL: ERIC Document Reproduction Service No. ED 394224.

Mills, P. E., Cole, K. N., Jenkins, J. R., and Dale, P. S. (1998). Effects of differing levels of inclusion on preschoolers with disabilities. *Exceptional Children*, 65, 79–90.

Mink, I. T. and Nihira, K. (1986). Family life styles and child behaviors: A study of direction of efforts. *Developmental Psychology*, 22, 610–616.

Minuchin, S. C. (1974). *Psychosomatic families*. Cambridge, MA: Harvard University Press.

Moon, M. S. and Beale, A. V. (1984). Vocational training and employment: Guidelines for parents. *The Exceptional Parent*, 14 (8), 35–38.

Morningstar, M. E., Turnbull, A., and Turnbull, N. R. (1996). What do students with disabilities tell us about the importance of family involvement in the transition from school to adult life? *Exceptional Children*, 62, 249–260.

Muir-Hutchinson, L. (1987). Working with professionals. *Exceptional Parent*, 17 (5), 8–10.

Mullin, E., Oulton, K., and James, T. (1995). Skills and training with parents of physically disabled persons. *International Journal of Rehabilitation Research*, 18, 142–145.

Mundschenk, N. A. and Foley, R. M. (1994). Collaborative parental involvement. [usdoe.htm].

Murphy, A. (1990). *Communicating assessment findings to parents*. Chapter 19 in Gibbs, E. D. and Teti, D. M. (1990). Interdisciplinary assessment of infants: A guide for early intervention professionals. Baltimore, MD: Paul H. Brookes Publishing Co., Inc.

Murphy, B. C. and Dillion, C. (1998). *Interviewing in action: Process and practice.* Pacific Grove, CA: Brooks/Cole.

Murnane, R. and Levy, F. (1996*). Teaching the new basic skills: Principles for educating children to thrive in a changing economy.* New York: The Free Press.

Naeef, R. A. (1997). Special children-challenged parents: The struggles and rewards of raising a child with a disability. *Exceptional Parents, 27, 21.*

National Center for Education Statistics. (1998). *Students do better when their families are involved in school.* [On-line]. Available: nces.ed.gov/pubs98/ 98121.html.

National Center for Handicapped Children and Youth National Parent and Teachers Association (PTA). (1997). *National standards for parent/family involvement programs.* Chicago, IL: Author.

National Council on Disability. (1995). Improving the implementation of the individuals with Disabilities Education Act: Making schools work for all America's children. Washington, DC: Author.

National Information Center for Children and Youths with Disabilities (NICHCY). (1997). Parenting a child with special needs: A guide to readings and resources. News Digest. Published by the National Information Center for Children and Youth with Disabilities at www.nichcy.org.

National Information Center for Handicapped Children and Youth. (1984). Work and the severely handicapped: The transition for youth. Washington, DC

Nicholas, K. B. and Bieber, S. L. (1996). Parental abuse versus supportive behaviors and their relation to hostility and aggression in young adults. *Child Abuse and Neglect, 20,* 195–211.

Nicholos, M. P. (1995). *The lost art of listening.* New York: Guilford Press.

Norton, P. and Drew, C. J. (1994). Autism and potential family stressors. *American Journal of Family Therapy, 22,* 68–77.

Odom, S. L. (2000). Preschool inclusion: What we know and where we go from here. *Topics in Early Childhood Special Education, 20* (1), 20–27.

Odom, S. L. and Diamond, K. A. (1998). Inclusion of young children with special needs in early childhood education: The research base. *Early Childhood Research Quarterly, 13,* 3–25.

Ohlrich, K. B. (1996). Parent volunteers: An asset to your technology plan. *Learning and Leading with Technology, 24,* 51–52.

Okagaki, L. and French, P. A. (1998). Parenting and children's school achievement: A multiethnic perspective. *American Educational Research Journal, 25,* 123–144.

O'Shea, D., O'Shea, L., Algozzine, R., and Hammitte, D. (2001). Families and teachers of individuals with disabilities. Boston, MA: Allyn and Bacon.

Osher, T. W. and Osher, D. M. (2002). The paradigm shift to true collaboration with families. *Journal of Child and Family Studies*, 11 (1), 47–60.

Oswald, D. P. and Sinah-Nirbay, N. (1992). Current research on social behavior. *Behavior Modification*, 16, 443–447.

Parette, H. P., Brotherson, M. J., and Huer, M. B. (2000). Giving families a voice in augmentative and alternative communication decision making. *Education and Training in Mental Retardation and Development Disabilities*, 35, 177–190.

Park, J. and Turnbull, A. P. (2003). Service integration in early intervention: Determining Interpersonal and structural factors for success. *Infant and Young Children*, 16, 48–58.

Peck, C. A., Odom, S. L., and Bricker, D. (1993). *Integrating young children with disabilities into community programs: Ecological perspectives on research and implementation*. Baltimore, MD: Paul H. Brookes Publishing Co., Inc.

Penn, S. S. and Lee, R. M. (1992). *Home variables, parent-child activities, and academic achievement: A study of 1988 eighth graders*. Paper presented at the Annual Meeting of the American Education Research Association, San Francisco.

Perl, J. (1995). Improving relationship skills for parent conferences. *Teaching Exceptional Children*, 28 (1), 29–31.

Plank, S. (2001). Career and technical education in the balance: An analysis of high school persistence, academic achievement, and postsecondary destination. St. Paul, MN: National Research Center for Career and Technical Education.

Plunge, M. M. and Kratochwill, T. R. (1995). Parental knowledge, involvement, and satisfaction with their child's special services. *Special Services in the Schools*, 10, 113–138.

Podemski, R. S., Marsh, G. E., Smith, D., Tom, E. C., and Price, J. B. (1995). *Comprehensive administration of special education*. Englewood Cliffs, NJ: Prentice Hall.

Podemski, R. S. and Steele, R. (1981). Avoid the pitfalls of citizen committees. *American School Board Journal*, 16 (4), 440–442.

Podemski, R. S., Marsh, G. E., Smith, T. E., and Price, B. J. (1995*). Comprehensive administration of special education*. Englewood Cliffs, NJ: Prentice Hall.

Potter, L. (1996). Making school parent friendly. *Education Digest*, 62, 28–30.

———. (1998). Making parent involvement meaningful. *Schools in the Middle*, 6, 9–10.

Powell, D. R. (1998). Re-weaving parents into early childhood education programs. *Education Digest*, 64 (3), 22–25.

Powell, D.R. and Diamond, K. E. (1995). Approaches to parent-teacher relationships used in early childhood programs during the twentieth century. *Journal of Education,* 77 (3), 71–94.

Powell, T. H. and Ogle, T. F. (1985). *Brothers and sisters: A special part of exceptional families.* Baltimore, MD: Paul H. Brookes Publishing Co. Inc.

Putnam, M. L. (1992). Characteristics of questions on test administered by mainstream secondary classroom teachers. *Learning Disabilities Research and Practice,* 7 (3), 24–36.

Rich, D. (1998). What parents want from teachers. *Educational Leadership,* 55 (8), 32–39.

Roach, V. (1995). Beyond the rhetoric. *Phi Delta Kappan,* 77, 295–299.

Robbins, F. R. and Dunlap, G. (1992). Effects of task difficulty on parent teaching skills and behavior problems of young children with autism. *American Journal of Mental Retardation,* 96, 631–643.

Roberts, R. and Mather, N. (1995). The return of students with learning disabilities to regular classrooms: A sellout? *Learning Disabilities Research and Practice,* 10 (16), 46–58.

Rogers, J. (1993). The inclusion revolution. *Research Bulletin,* 1 (11), 106.

Ryckman, D. B. and Henderson, R. A. (1965). The meaning of a retarded child to his parents: A focus for counselors. *Mental Retardation,* 3, 3.

Salembier, G. and Furney, K. S. (1997). Facilitating participation: Parents' perception of their involvement in the IEP transition planning process. *Career Development for Exceptional Individuals,* 20, 29–41.

Salisbury, C. and Evans, I. M. (1988). Comparison of parental involvement in regular and special education. *Journal of the Association for Persons with Severe Handicaps,* 13, 268–272.

Salli, C. (1991). *Scripts for children's lives: What do parents and early childhood teachers contribute to children's understanding of events in their lives.* ERIC. Document Reproduction Service No. ED 344664.

Sawyer, R., McLaughlin, M., and Winglee, M. (1994). Is integration of students with disabilities happening? An analysis of national data trends overtime. *Remedial and Special Education,* 15, 204–215.

Schaef, A. W. (1992). *Women's reality.* San Francisco, CA: Harper Collins.

Schaffer, H. (1984). *The child's entry into a social world.* London: Academic Press.

Schmelkin, L. P. (1981). Teachers' and non-teachers' attitudes toward mainstreaming. *Exceptional Children,* 48, 42–27.

Scruggs, T. E. and Mostropieri, M. A. (1996). Teachers perceptions' of mainstreaming/inclusion: A research synthesis. *Exceptional Children,* 63 (1), 59–74.

Selby, D. and Murphy, S. (1992). Graded of degraded: Perception of letter grading form mainstreamed and learning disabled students. *BC Journal of Special Education,* 16, (1), 92–104.

Seligman, M. (1991a). *The family with a handicapped child* (2nd ed.). Boston, MA: Allyn and Bacon.

———. (1991b) Siblings of disabled brothers and sisters. In M. Seligman (Ed.), *The family with a handicapped child* (2nd ed.). Boston, MA: Allyn and Bacon.

———. (2000). *Conducting effective conferences with parents of children with disabilities.* New York: The Guilford Press.

Seligman, M. E. P. (1995). The effectiveness of psychotherapy. *American Psychologist,* 50, 965–974.

Semmel, M. I., Abernathy, T. V., Butera, G., and Lesar, S. (1991). Teachers' perceptions of the regular education initiative. *Exceptional Children,* 57, 9–23.

Senge, P. (1990). *The 5th dimension: The art and practice of the learning organization.* New York: Doubleday.

Sergiovanni, T. J. (1996). Leadership for the schoolhouse. San Francisco, CA: Jossey-Bass, Inc.

Shanker, A. (1995). Full inclusion is neither force nor appropriate. *Educational Leadership,* 50 (4), 18–21.

Sharpe, M. N., York, J. L., and Knight, J. C. (1994). Effects of inclusion on the academic performance of classmates without disabilities. *Remedial and Special Education,* 15, 281–287.

Shea, T. and Bauer, A. M. (1991). *Parents and teachers of children with exceptionalities: A handbook for collaboration.* Boston, MA: Allyn and Bacon.

Shirley, D. (1997). *Laboratories of democracy: Community organizing for school perform.* Austin, TX: University of Texas Press.

Sileo, T. W. and Prater, M. A. (1998). Preparing professionals for partnerships with parents of students with disabilities: Textbook considerations regarding cultural diversity. *Exceptional Children,* 64, 513–528.

Simpson, R. L. (1996). *Working with parents of exceptional children.* Austin, TX: Pro Ed.

Slavin, R. E., Karweit, N. L., and Wasik, B. A. (1993). Preventing early school failure: What works? *Educational Leadership,* 50, 10–18.

Smith-Davis, J. (1983). *When handicapped children grow up.* Rosslyn, VA: Information on Center for Handicapped Children and Youth.

Solo, L. (1997). School success begins at home. *Principal,* 77 (2), 29–30.

Sommers-Flanagan, J. and Sommers-Flanagan, R. (1993). *Foundations of therapeutic interviewing.* Needham Heights, MA: Allyn and Bacon.

Sontag, J. C. and Schacht, R. (1994). An ethnic comparison of parent participation and information needs in early intervention. *Exceptional Children,* 60, 422–433.

Staub, D. and Hunt, P. (1993). The effects of social interaction training on high school peer tutors of schoolmates with severe disabilities. *Exceptional Children,* 60, 41–57.

Staub, D. and Peck, C. (1995). What are the outcomes for non-disabled students? *Educational Leadership,* 50, (4), 36–39.

Stevenson, H. W. and Baker, D. P. (1987). The family-school relation and the child's school performance. *Child Development,* 58, 1348–1357.

Stewart, C. (1996). The coach-parent meeting: The initial contact. *Strategies,* 10, 13–15.

Stoneman, Z. and Berman, P. W. (1993). *The effects of mental retardation, disability, and illness on sibling relationships.* Baltimore, MD: Paul H. Brookes Publishing Co., Inc.

Strickland, B. and Turnbull, A. P. (1993). *Developing and implementing program* (3rd ed.). New Jersey: Prentice-Hall, Inc.

Sullivan, P. (1998). The PTA'S national standards. *Educational Leadership,* 55 (8), 43–44.

Summers, J. A., Steeples, T., Peterson, C., Naig, L., McBride, S., Wall, S., Liebow, H., Swanson, M., and Stowitschek, J. (2001). Policy and management support for effective service integration in Early Head Start and Part C Programs. *Topics in Early Childhood Special Education,* 21, 16–30.

Swick, K. L and Broadway, F. (1997). Parental efficacy and successful parent involvement. *Journal of Instructional Psychology,* 24, 69–75.

Swideret, B. (1997). Parent conferences. *Journal of Adolescent and Adult Literacy,* 40, 580–581.

Switzer, L. S. (1990). Family factors associated with academic progress for children with learning disabilities. *Elementary School Guidance and Counseling,* 24, 200–206.

Taylor, G. R. (1997). *Curriculum strategies: Social skills intervention for young African-American males.* Westport, CT: Praeger Publishers.

———. (1998). *Curriculum strategies for teaching social skills to the disabled: Dealing with inappropriate behaviors.* Springfield, IL: Charles C. Thomas.

———. (1999). *Curriculum models and strategies for educating disabled children in inclusive settings.* Springfield, IL: Charles C. Thomas.

———. (2000). *Parental involvement.* Springfield, IL: Charles C. Thomas.

———. (2001). *Educational intervention and services for children with exceptionalities* (2nd. Ed.). Springfield, IL: Charles C. Thomas.

———. (2003). *Educating the disabled: Enabling learners in inclusive settings.* Lanham, MD: The Scarecrow Press.

Taylor, G. R. and Harrington, F. T. (2003). *Educating the disabled: Enabling learners in inclusive settings.* Lanham, MD: Scarecrow Press.

Taylor, R. D. (1996). Adolescents' perceptions of kinship support and family management practices: Association with adolescent adjustment in African-American families. *Child Development,* 32 (4), 687–695.

Thompson, S. (1998). Moving from publicity to engagement. *Educational Leadership,* 55 (8), 54–57.

Thorp, E. K. (1997). Increasing opportunities for partnership with culturally and linguistically diverse families. *Intervention in School and Clinic,* 32, 261–269.

Trivette, C. M., Dunst, C. J., Boyd, K., and Hamby, D. W. (1995). Family-oriented program models help give practices and parental control appraisal. *Exceptional Children,* 62, 237.

Turnbull, A. P. (1983). Parental participation in the IEP process. In J.A. Mulick and S. M. Pueschel (Eds.), *Parent-professional participation in developmental disabilities services: Foundations and prospects* (pp. 107–123). Cambridge, MA: The Ware Press.

Turnbull, A. P. and Turnbull, H. R. (1990). *Families, professionals, and exceptionality: A special partnership* (2nd ed.). Columbus, OH: Merrill.

———. (1993). *Participating research on cognitive coping: From concepts to research planning.* In A. P. Turnbull , J. M. Patterson, S. K. Behr, D. L. Murphy, D. L. Marquis, and M. J. Blue-Banning (Eds.), *Cognitive coping, families, and disabilities.* Baltimore, MD: Paul H. Brookes Publishing Co., Inc.

———. (1996). *Families, professionals, and exceptionality.* Upper Saddle River, NJ: Merrill.

———. (2001). *Families, professionals, and exceptionality: A special partnership* (4th ed.). Upper Saddle River, NJ: Merrill Prentice Hall.

Turnbull, A. P., Turnbull, H. R., and Shankon, L. D. (1995). *Exceptional lives: Special education in today's schools.* Englewood Cliffs, NJ: Merrill.

Ulrich, M. E. and Bauer, A. M. (2003). Levels of awareness: A closer look at communicating between parents and professionals. *Teaching Exceptional Children,* 35 (6), 20–24.

Upshur, C. C. (1991). Families and the community service MAZE. In M. Seligman (Ed.), *The family with a handicapped child* (pp. 91–114). Boston, MA: Allyn and Bacon.

U.S. Department of Education. (1994). *Strong families, strong school: Building community partnerships for learning.* Washington, DC: U.S. Department of Education.

———. (1995). *Individuals with Disabilities Education Act Amendments of 1995.* Washington, DC: U.S. Department of Education.

———. (1997). *Individuals with disabilities education act amendments of 1997.* Washington, DC: U.S. Department of Education.

——. (1998a). *FY 1999 annual plan,* Volume 2. Washington, DC: U.S. Department of Education.

——. (1998b). *Goals 2000: Reforming education and improve student achievement.* Washington, DC: U.S. Department of Education.

——. (1998c). *Profiles of successful school-wide programs.* Washington, DC: U.S. Department of Education.

U.S. Department of Education Office of Special Programs. (1998d). *OSEP Memorandum 98–4: Guidance related to state program improvement grants to improve education for children with disabilities.* Washington, DC: U.S. Department of Education.

Vadasy, P. F. (1982, May-June). Extending the scope of family involvement. *Counter Point,* 18.

Vander Klift, E. and Kunc, N. (1996). Beyond benevolence: Friendship and the politics of help. In J. S. Thousand, R. A. Villa, and A. I. Nevin (Eds.), *Creativity and collaborative learning: A practical guide t empowering students and teachers* (pp. 391–401). Baltimore, MD: Paul H. Brookes Publishing Co. Inc. Reprinted in Lovett, H. (1996). *Learning to listen: Positive approaches and people with difficult behavior* (pp. 35–36). Baltimore, MD: Paul H. Brookes Publishing Co., Inc.

Vann Hasselt, V. B., Strain, P. S., and Hersen, M. (1988). Handbook of development and physical disabilities. New York: Pergammon.

Vargas, B. C. and Grose, K. (1998). A partnership for literacy. *Educational Leadership,* 55 (8), 45–48.

Voor, R. (1997). Connecting kinds and parents to school. *Education Digest,* 62, 20–21.

Waldron, N. L. and McLeskey, J. (1998). The effects of an inclusive school program on students with mild and severe learning disabilities. *Exceptional Children,* 64 (3), 395–405.

Waler, J. A. (1998). Promoting parent/community involvement in school. *Education Digest,* 63 (8), 45–47.

Walker, B. and Singer, G. H. S. (1993). Improving collaborative communication between professionals and parents. In G. H. S. Singer and L. E. Powers (Eds.). *Families, disabilities, and empowers: Active coping skills and strategies for family intervention.* Baltimore, MD: Paul H. Brookes Publishing Co., Inc.

Walther-Thomas, C., Hazel, J. S., Schumaker, J. B., Vernon, S., and Deschler, D. D. (1991). In M. Fine (Ed.), *Collaboration with parents of exceptional children.* Brandon, VT: CPPC.

Wang, J. and Wilderman, L. (1996). The relationship between parental influence and student achievement in seventh grade mathematics. *School Science and Mathematics,* 96, 395–399.

Wang, M. C., Haertel, G. D., and Walberg, H. J. (1993). Toward a knowledge base for school learning. *Review of Educational Research,* 63 (3), 249–294.

Wang, M. C., Reynold, M. C., and Walberg, H. J. (1995). Serving students at the margins. *Educational Leadership,* 50 (4), 12–17.

Watkins, Thomas J. (1997). "Teacher Communications, Child Achievement, and Parent Traits in Parent Involvement Models," *The Journal of Educational Research* (91) 1, 3–14.

Wayman, K. L., Lynch, E. W., and Hanson, M. J. (1990). Home-based early childhood services: Cultural sensitivity in a family systems approach. *Topics in Early Childhood Special Education,* 10, 56–75.

Webster-Stratton, C., Hollinsworth, T., and Kolpacoff, M. (1989). Self-administered videotape therapy for families with problem children: Comparison of two cost-effective treatments and a control group. *Journal of Consulting and Clinical Psychology,* 56, 550–566.

Wells, K. L. (1997). Professional development for parents. *American School Board,* 184, 38–39.

Westling, D. C. (1996). What do parents with moderate and severe mental disabilities want? *Education and Training in Mental Retardation and Development Disabilities,* 21, 86–114.

White, A. E. and White, L. L. (1992). A collaborative model for students with mild disabilities in middle schools. *Focus on Exceptional Children,* 24 (9), 1–10.

Whitechurch, G. G. and Constantine, L. L. (1993). Systems theory. In P. G. Boss, W. J. Doherty, R. LaRossa, W. R. Schumm, and S. K. Steinmetz (Eds.), *Sourcebook of family theory and methods: A contextual approach* (pp. 325–352). New York, NY: Plenum.

Whiteford, T. (1998). Math for moms and dads. *Educational Leadership,* 55 (8), 64–66.

Wikler, L. (1981). Chronic stresses of families of mentally retarded children. *Families Relations,* 30, 281–288.

Wilczenski, F. L. (1992). Measuring attitudes toward inclusive education. *Psychology in the Schools,* 29, 306–312.

Wilson, J. H. (1997). Communication, collaboration, caring family-center care. *Exceptional Parent,* 28, 61.

Winter, S. (1999). *The early childhood inclusion model: A program for all children.* Olney, MD: Association for Childhood Education International.

Winton, P. J. (1994). Families of children with disabilities. In H. G. Haring, L. McCormick, and T. G. Haring (Eds.), *Exceptional children and youth* (6th ed.). New York, NY: Merrill.

———. (2000). Early childhood intervention personal preparation: Backward mapping for Future planning. *Topics in Early Childhood Special Education,* 20, 7–94.

Woeppel, P. (1990). *Facilitating social skills development in learning disabled and/or attention deficit disorder second to fifth grade children and parents.* Ed.D Practicum. Ohio: Nova University.

Wolf, J. M. (1998). Just read. *Educational Leadership,* 55 (8), 61–63.

Yanok, J. and Derubertis, D. (1989). Comparative study of parental participation in regular and special education programs. *Exceptional Children,* 56, 195–199.

Ypsilanti Public Schools. (1998). *National African-American parent involvement day.* [On-line] Available: scnc.yps.k12.mi.us.

Ysseldyke, J. E., Algozzine, B., and Thurlow, M. L. (1992). *Critical issues in special education* (2nd ed.). Boston, MA: Houghton Mifflin.

Zigmond, N., Jenkins, J., Fuchs, L., Deno, S., Fuchs, D., Baker, J., Jenkins, L., and Couthino, M. (1995). Special education in restructured schools: Findings from three multi-year studies. *Phi Delta Kappan,* 76, 531–540.

Author Index

Subject Index

About the Author

George R. Taylor, Ph.D., is professor of special education and former chairperson of the Department of Special Education at Coppin State College, Baltimore, Maryland, and CORE faculty, The Union Institute and University, Cincinnati, Ohio. Dr. Taylor has made significant contributions to the professional literature in the area of Special Education through research and publication. Additionally, he has served as a consultant, on the local level, to parental groups involved with disabled individuals.